Transitional Justice in Nepal

The civil conflict in Nepal (1996–2006) resulted in an estimated 15,000 deaths, 1,300 disappearances, along with other serious human rights and humanitarian law violations. Demands for peace, democracy, accountability and development have abounded in the post-conflict context. Although the conflict catalysed major changes in the social and political landscape in Nepal, the transitional justice (TJ) process has remained deeply contentious and fragmented.

This book provides an in-depth analysis of the TJ process in Nepal. Drawing on interviews with a diverse range of stakeholders, including victims, ex-combatants, community members, human rights advocates, journalists and representatives from diplomatic missions, international organisations and the donor community, it reveals the differing viewpoints, knowledge, attitudes and preferences about TJ and other post-conflict issues in Nepal. The author develops an actor typology and an action spectrum, which can be used in Nepal and other post-conflict contexts. The actor typology identifies four main groups of TJ actors – experts, brokers, implementers and victims – and highlights who is making claims and on behalf of whom. The action spectrum, based on contentious politics literature and resistance literature, demonstrates the strategies actors use to shape the TJ process. This book argues that the potential of TJ lies in these dynamics of contention. It is by letting these dynamics play out that different conceptualisations of TJ can arise. While doing so may lead to practical challenges and produce situations that are normatively undesirable for some actors, particularly when certain political parties and national actors seem to 'hijack' TJ, remaining steadfast to the dominant TJ paradigm is also undesirable.

As the first book to provide a single case study on TJ in Nepal, it makes theoretical and empirical contributions to: TJ research in Nepal and the Asia-Pacific more broadly, the politics versus justice binary and the concept of victimhood, among others. It will be of interest to a wide range of scholars in the study of transitional justice, peace and conflict studies, human rights, sociology, political science, criminology, law, anthropology and South Asian Studies, as well as policy-makers and NGOs.

Yvette Selim is a Senior Research Associate and Lecturer at the Institute for Public Policy and Governance, University of Technology Sydney, Australia. Her research interests include transitional justice, conflict resolution, peacebuilding, human rights, health and development.

Routledge/Asian Studies Association of Australia (ASAA) South Asian Series

Edited by Duncan McDuie-Ra, The University of New South Wales, Australia

Published in Association with the Australian Studies Association of Australia (ASAA), represented by Ernest Koh, chair of the ASAA Publications Committee, Monash University, Australia.

Founded in 1986 to publish outstanding work in the social sciences and humanities, the SAPS entered a new phase in 2010 when it joined with Routledge to continue a notable tradition of Australian-based research about South Asia. Works in the series are published in both UK and Indian editions.

SAPS publishes outstanding research on the countries and peoples of South Asia across a wide range of disciplines including history, politics and political economy, anthropology, geography, literature, sociology and the fields of cultural studies, communication studies and gender studies. Interdisciplinary and comparative research is encouraged.

Suicide and Society in India
Peter Mayer

Women and Domestic Violence in Bangladesh
Seeking A Way Out of the Cage
Laila Ashrafun

Transitional Justice in Nepal
Interests, Victims and Agency
Yvette Selim

Transitional Justice in Nepal

Interests, Victims and Agency

Yvette Selim

Routledge
Taylor & Francis Group
LONDON AND NEW YORK

First published 2018
by Routledge

2 Park Square, Milton Park, Abingdon, Oxfordshire OX14 4RN

52 Vanderbilt Avenue, New York, NY 10017

Routledge is an imprint of the Taylor & Francis Group, an informa business

First issued in paperback 2020

British Library Cataloguing in Publication Data
A catalogue record for this book is available from the British Library

Library of Congress Cataloging in Publication Data
Names: Selim, Yvette, author.
Title: Transitional justice in Nepal : interests, victims and agency / Yvette Selim.
Description: New York, NY : Routledge, 2018. | Series: Routledge/Asian Studies Association of Australia (ASAA) South Asian series ; 3 | Includes bibliographical references and index.
Identifiers: LCCN 2018003998| ISBN 9781138047921 (hardback) | ISBN 9781315170534 (ebook)
Subjects: LCSH: Transitional justice–Nepal. | Reparation (Criminal justice)–Nepal.
Classification: LCC KPK97.74 .S45 2018 | DDC 954.96–dc23
LC record available at https://lccn.loc.gov/2018003998

ISBN: 978-1-138-04792-1 (hbk)
ISBN: 978-0-367-58937-0 (pbk)

Typeset in Times New Roman
by Taylor & Francis Books

Contents

Illustrations

Figures

Tables

Acknowledgements

As I put pen to paper there are many people whose presence, support and encouragement made this research possible. First and foremost, I am indebted to the people in Nepal who entrusted me with their stories. I still consider the complexities of this interaction and I hope that my research will in some way illuminate the ways you seek to deal with the conflict. I am also humbled by the kindness, generosity and support of many people I met in Nepal. Thank you Prateek for your advice, company and assistance. Thank you also to Dipendra, Surya, Deepak and Ram who catalysed some of my most profound insights into this topic and to James, Surendra, Kishor, Padma and each my research assistants. I am profoundly grateful for the friendships I formed in Nepal.

In the academic arena, this research would not have been possible without the support of Professor Duncan McDuie-Ra. Thank you for our stimulating, challenging and sometimes random conversations. Your advice has been invaluable in shaping me into the pracacademic I am today. Thank you also to Professor Tim Murithi, Professor Hilary Charlesworth, Professor John Braithwaite, Dr Dominic Fitzsimmons, Professor Marc Williams, Associate Professor Adam Czarnota, Dr Robert Shelley, Dr Srinjoy Bose, the students and academics at the Centre for International Governance and Justice at the Australian National University and the members of the Oxford Transitional Justice Research network at the University of Oxford. Thank you Professor Harvey Weinstein for your support, determination and tireless efforts. I would also like to thank Professor Roberta Ryan and my colleagues at the Institute for Public Policy and Governance at the University of Technology Sydney.

Without my experiences as a Rotary Peace Fellow at the University of Bradford I may not have encountered this topic called ‘transitional justice’. I am deeply thankful to Professor Tom Woodhouse, Rotary Peace Fellows Class VII, the Bradford Rotary Peace Fellows Committee, particularly Dick Hazlehurst, Caringbah Rotary Club and the Rotary Foundation. The gestation for this research began during my conversations with Professor Jim Whitman. I am indebted to you for spurring me to commence my research sooner rather than later and for your ongoing support. Thank you also to Ian and Jean Slim for opening their home to me and for spotting my ‘Yvettisms’.

To my dear friends from the Department of Peace Studies and Cecil Ave thank you for the thought-provoking and playful conversations we shared over cups of tea and glasses of wine.

I am grateful to Dorothea Schaefter and Lily Brown at Routledge for their diligent efforts seeing this book through to publication. Sections of this book have previously been presented in various articles. These publications were: Selim, Yvette (2017), 'Contestation and resistance: the politics of and around transitional justice in Nepal', *Conflict, Security & Development* 18(1): 39–60; Selim, Yvette (2017), 'Examining victims and perpetrators in post-conflict Nepal', *International Review of Victimology*, 23(3): 275–301; Selim, Yvette (2014), 'The opportunities and challenges of participation in transitional justice: examples from Nepal', *Journal of International Development*, 1–26; Selim, Yvette, and Tim Murithi (2011) 'Transitional justice and development: Partners for sustainable peace in Africa?' *Journal of Peacebuilding and Development* 6(2): 58–72; and, Selim, Yvette (2012) 'Transitions: Creating space to address injustice after conflict or political turmoil', openDemocracy (www.opendemocracy.net/opensecurity/yvette-selim/transitions-creating-space-to-address-injustice-after-conflict-or-politica).

To my dear friends from Sydney, Bradford, Berkeley, Kathmandu and beyond, whose laughs and encouragement during some of the hardest moments of this journey helped sustain me, thank you. A big thank you to Jamie, my writing guru, and to Jeremy, for your patience and hard work.

To my family, without your support, none of this would have been possible. Uncle Neil, you have been the greatest mentor I could have asked for. To my second family, the Mikhails, you have always been there for me. To my parents, Emile and Faten, and my brother, Andrew, your love has inspired and sustained me. You instilled in me a curiosity about justice and a deep sense of compassion. I struggle to thank you for your countless sacrifices. Lachlan, thank you for being my rock. Here's to many more adventures to come. I dedicate this book to my family.

List of abbreviations

Advocacy Forum	Advocacy Forum-Nepal
AMMAA	Agreement on Monitoring of the Management of Arms and Armies
APWLD	Asia Pacific Forum on Women, Law and Development
CDO	Chief District Officer
CHHE	Caste Hill Hindu Elite
CIEDP	Commission of inquiry into enforced Disappearances
CPA	Comprehensive Peace Agreement (2006)
CPN-M	Communist Party of Nepal (Maoist)
CPN-UML	Communist Party of Nepal (Unified Marxist–Leninist)
CVC	Conflict Victims' Committee
CVCP	Conflict Victims Common Platform
CVSJ	Conflict Victim Society for Justice
CVSJ	Conflict Victim Society for Justice - Nepal
EU	European Union
HRW	Human Rights Watch
ICRC	International Committee of the Red Cross
ICG	International Crisis Group
ICTJ	International Center for Transitional Justice
IDP	Internally Displaced Persons
IFAD	International Fund for Agricultural Development
INGO	International non-governmental organisation
ILO	International Labour Organization
INSEC	Informal Service Sector Center
IOM	International Organization for Migration
IRP	Interim Relief Program
LPCs	Local Peace Committees
MoPR	Ministry of Peace and Reconstruction
NAWHRD	National Alliance of Women Human Rights Defenders
NEFAD	National Network of Families of Disappeared and Missing Nepal
NGO	Non-governmental organisation
NHRC	National Human Rights Commission

NPR	Nepalese Rupee
NPTF	Nepal Peace Trust Fund
NTTP	Nepal Transitions to Peace
OHCHR	Office of the High Commissioner for Human Rights
PLA	People's Liberation Army
TADO	Terrorist and Disruptive Activities (Control and Punishment) Ordinance
TJ	transitional justice
TJ Act	*Commission on Investigation of Disappeared Persons, Truth and Reconciliation Act* (2014)
TJRC	Transitional Justice Resource Centre
TRC	Truth and Reconciliation Commission
TRIAL	Track Impunity Always
UCPN-M	Unified Communist Party of Nepal (Maoist)
UK	United Kingdom
UN	United Nations
UNDP	United Nations Development Programme
UNIRP	UN Inter-Agency Rehabilitation Programme
UNMIN	United Nations Mission in Nepal
US	United States
USAID	United States Agency for International Development
USD	United States Dollar
USIP	United States Institute of Peace
WHR	Women for Human Rights
WOREC	Women's Rehabilitation Center

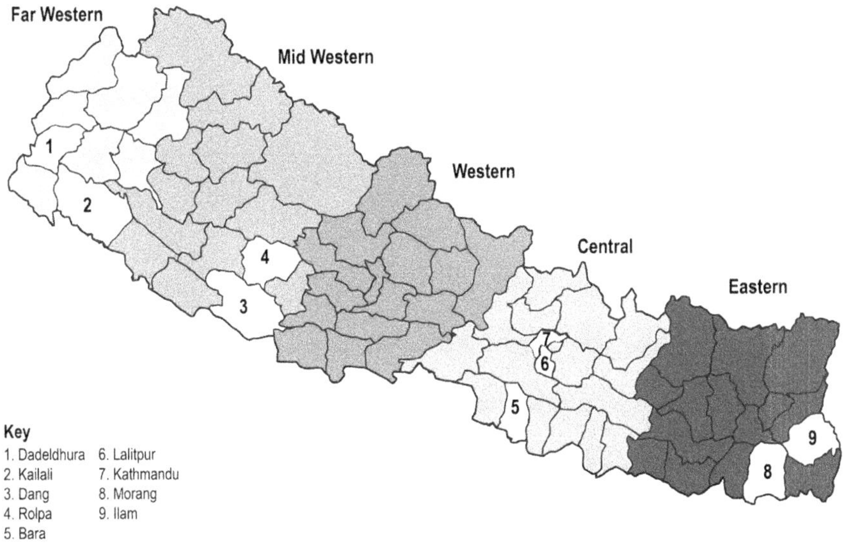

Map of Nepal and districts where research was conducted

Part I

1 Introduction

> Post-conflict societies are often confusing, complex, contested and changeable sites in which it is a challenge both to see what is going on and to chart appropriate strategies.
>
> (McEvoy 2012, 312)

On 4 February 1996 the Maoists launched a People's War in Nepal. Based on the ideology of Marxism–Leninism–Maoism, the Maoists adopted a guerrilla strategy initially concentrated in a few Maoist strongholds in western Nepal: Rolpa and Rukum (Mid-Western region), Sindhuli (Central region) and Gorkha (Western region). For approximately five years of the conflict the government of Nepal deemed the insurgency to be a security problem in the ambit of the police. However by 2001, as the Maoists increasingly gained more ground, the government elevated the insurgency to a military problem. Throughout the course of the conflict there were serious human rights violations committed by both sides of the conflict, including rape, torture, kidnapping, killings and enforced disappearances. There were an estimated 15,000 people killed, over 1300 people disappeared and numerous other incidents of human rights violations. On 21 November 2006, some ten years after the insurgency was launched, the Comprehensive Peace Agreement was signed, ushering major changes in the social and political landscape in Nepal. These included the official abolition of the monarchy, the declaration of Nepal as a federal democratic republic and the first Constituent Assembly elections in which the Maoists won the largest number of votes. It was during the peace negotiations that discussions commenced about transitional justice (TJ) in Nepal (Farasat and Hayner 2009; Tyynela 2014, 84).

Almost six years after the end of the conflict, I met with victims, ex-combatants, human rights activists, NGO workers, political representatives and donors, among others in Nepal. In the Maoist heartland in Rolpa I met a female ex-combatant from the People's Liberation Army (the Maoist rebels' army).[1] She explained to me that before the conflict she was active in student politics. Initially, she did not know much about Marxism and Leninism but, as she saw 'educated people' leaving their jobs to join the Maoists, she came to believe the party was 'the greatest party with greatest slogans'. She and her friends became 'diehard supporters' and she told me: 'We and the leaders had so many dreams for the people. Now we realise where have those dreams gone?' This ex-combatant and other Maoist supporters I spoke with explained to me that they felt frustrated with the way the Maoist leaders had joined mainstream politics and become like the politicians and political parties against which they had waged the insurgency. An analogy offered by a Maoist guerrilla was that the resulting/post-war political situation was like a 'farmer who worked the whole day every day and then reaped nothing'.[2]

In another interview I had the opportunity to hear the thoughts of two Nepali human rights workers involved in the TJ process.[3] One moment particularly stands out: when I asked about the impact of politics on TJ in Nepal. They explained to me that two of the major political parties in Nepal, the Maoists and Nepali Congress, were evading calls for justice to ensure the protection of party leaders and their cadres. For one of the human rights workers, the interests of the political parties 'finally met' as they 'realised that they both did terrible things' during the conflict. The other respondent added, '[t]here is a Nepali proverb "kale kale milera kham bhale" which means "You are black, I am also; so let's celebrate together." This is self-protection.' For both of these respondents this approach to TJ will not deliver justice. I came to realise that their observations encapsulated and highlighted the ways (elite) politicians made claims and bargained using the process, institutions and language and process of TJ.

It was also in Rolpa where I spoke with a widow in her tailoring shop. We sat on a wooden bench at the entrance of her shop and, with the hum of sewing machines in the background, we spoke about how her life had changed after the passing of her husband during the conflict.[4] People occasionally passed her shop as she told me that she began her tailoring business after receiving livelihood training, offered to a small number of 'conflict-affected women'. She now led a women's group in her community for widows and wives of the disappeared. In the same district I spoke with a widower who was a Maoist Commissar. He relayed the details of his wife's murder, which occurred while he was on combat duty in another district.[5] He considered himself 'emotionally' to be a victim but because he was involved in the People's Liberation Army he felt that he had worked and suffered for a larger cause. He had remarried and his family members wandered in and out of the rooms in his home while we spoke. It occurred to me that his story and other widowers' stories about the impact of the conflict on their lives seemed to stand in juxtaposition with the day-to-day challenges and experiences I heard the widows and wives of the disappeared endured.

Conversations such as these provided me with a glimpse of the ways the conflict impacted people's everyday lives, including their identities. They also provided insights into the ways key notions (such as politics, truth and justice) intersected in post-conflict Nepal and assisted to complicate simplistic assumptions and practices about TJ.

I cut short my trip to Nepal due to the instability that arose in the lead up to the Constitution deadline and the subsequent dissolution of the

Constituent Assembly[6] in May 2012. When I returned home I realised I had not uncovered 'the answers' I had hoped for. But this (research) conundrum reveals a great deal about TJ. It is a deeply messy, complicated affair. In the wake of conflict there are multiple and usually competing demands by the international community, politicians, human rights advocates, victims and community members, among others. Calls for peace, stability, accountability, democracy, development and economic growth abound, but are viewed differently by different stakeholders. TJ operates in this dynamic space seeking to deliver a gamut of objectives including peace, accountability, truth, reconciliation and justice. Determining what these notions mean to victims, affected communities, politicians and external actors – and indeed how to achieve these notions – is the source of much contention. However, what I came to realise is that much of the potential of TJ in fact lies in the contentions of and around it. While a limited number of TJ practitioners recognise this potential, often the way in which TJ is designed and operated belies the complexity of the politics on the ground.

This is what makes examining TJ so fascinating. As Orentlicher (2007, 10–11) asserts:

> few issues have proved as vexing as the set of challenges bound up in the notion of transitional justice. Should – must? – societies attempt to bring to justice those who bear key responsibility for past atrocities? Does justice inevitably entail prosecutions or does its meaning instead turn upon each society's historically and culturally specific experience? Besides trials, what roles can truth commissions, reparations programmes and other measures of transitional justice play in transforming a society that has been shattered by unspeakable crimes? Should – does? – international law constrain or shape States' responses to crimes of the past? How do the answers to these questions turn upon the political constraints that define a nation's transition? These questions only begin a long, and ever-lengthening, catalogue of quandaries that vex societies confronting the challenges bound up in political transition and the professionals who seek to assist them.

Turning to Nepal, when civil conflicts result in one of the warring sides becoming part of the government, can we really expect that this political party will pursue justice, particularly when this pursuit has the potential to incriminate the party's leaders and cadres? How do we expect the current global TJ toolkit, which prioritises institutions, to be relevant to victims the majority of whom have historically been removed from the workings of the state? How do we understand what justice, peace and reconciliation mean in the context of Nepal?

It is against this backdrop that this book examines TJ in Nepal. There are three primary reasons why I contend Nepal provides an interesting and significant case study. First, rather than study (apparently) unequivocally successful TJ interventions or abject TJ failures, Nepal is compelling as a case because it sits somewhere in between. Initially, there was little knowledge or national support for pursuing TJ, however over time it is apparent that various actors, including politicians, NGO workers and victims' groups and their members, have gradually come to see the ways the process of TJ can be utilised to advance particular, although at times deeply conflicting, interests. Second, large amounts of resources have been invested in TJ in Nepal. In some cases these resources may have been diverted from other post-conflict priorities, and more recently post-disaster priorities, yet there is a great deal of debate as to whether TJ lives up to even the most modest of goals or expectations. Third, there has been limited scholarly work about TJ in Nepal and indeed the Asia-Pacific more broadly. There have been two books that compare aspects of the TJ process in Nepal with another Asian case study: Timor-Leste (Robins 2013) and Afghanistan (Sajjad 2013).[7] Robins' participatory action research in Nepal and Timor-Leste explored the needs of families of the disappeared and the effectiveness of TJ mechanisms in meeting those needs. Sajjad undertook a comparative cross-national analysis in Nepal and Afghanistan. Her research focused on how local understandings are addressed in TJ processes. While my research has elements in common with the approaches adopted in these projects, it differs from and extends upon them. The majority of the research on TJ in Nepal has been produced by national and international NGOs. The remainder of the research has been dominated by anthropological and ethnographic research[8] on Nepal that touches upon the conflict to varying extents but does not provide an in-depth analysis of TJ (see for example Shneiderman et al. 2016; Marsden 2011; Thapa 2003; Manandhar and Seddon 2010; Pettigrew 2012; Pettigrew and Adhikari 2009). This book seeks to fill this gap.

I argue that TJ in Nepal is a complex, multifaceted process, which eschews absolute characterisations of success or failure (e.g. being 'still-born'[9]). While the Truth and Reconciliation Commission and the Commission of Investigation on Enforced Disappeared Persons were only established in 2015, some eight years since the end of the conflict, *much* transpired before this time with various politicians, victims, donors and human rights advocates using the process and language of TJ to promote their interests. It is through an in-depth examination of these actors, interests, interactions and their post-conflict priorities that the limits and potential of TJ in Nepal become evident. Given that TJ efforts are continuing in Nepal, I argue that TJ actors need to be cognisant of the ways they engage with each other and seek to advance their interests. This constantly shifting and uncertain ground does not fit well with best practices, toolboxes and 'cut and paste' projects that are ubiquitous in peacebuilding and development, but it is in these margins and intersections where richer, more context-specific – and indeed victim-centric – approaches can be found. The next section outlines the evolution of TJ to contextualise how TJ discussions arose in Nepal.

Situating transitional justice

The evolution of transitional justice

It was not until the early 1990s that the term 'transitional justice' was coined; however, most literature traces the beginnings of TJ to the aftermath of the Second World War with the Nuremberg and Tokyo military tribunals. From the late 1980s the term gained traction following the regime changes in Latin America and Eastern Europe, often referred to as the third wave of democratisation (see Kora 2010; Teitel 2014; Anders and Zenker 2014; Lawther, Moffett, and Jacobs 2016). During this period TJ developed through the 'set of interactions' between lawyers, human rights advocates, legal and comparative politics scholars and others dealing with transitional contexts (Arthur 2009). In this context of political change, justice 'was generally conceived in terms of the establishment of trials and truth commissions to address past human rights violations' (Jeffery and Kim 2013, 4).

The mid-1990s saw a period of increased civil and ethnic conflicts (e.g. Rwanda, the Balkans and Timor-Leste). During this time the nature of 'transition' in TJ began to expand into areas of peacebuilding and conflict resolution (Jeffery and Kim 2013, 4). Jeffery and Kim (2013, 5) explain:

> what followed was not simply the encroachment of transitional justice into conflict resolution and peace building, but the simultaneous redefinition of peace building to include the pursuit of justice as a key priority. The result was the establishment of this second type of transition from conflict to peace as a key concern of transitional justice along with justice associated with transitions from authoritarian rule.

It was also by the mid-1990s that an identifiable toolkit of TJ mechanisms – truth-seeking, prosecutions, memorialisation initiatives, vetting and lustration and reparations – had merged.

As TJ came to be applied to post-authoritarian and to post-conflict settings, it rapidly evolved from a study within human rights law to a 'field' of study and practice driven by practitioners and scholars from a diverse range of disciplines (Bell 2009). This shift to a 'field' of interdisciplinary practice and scholarship has been influenced by a range of disciplines including anthropology, development studies, cultural studies, education, history, ethics, philosophy, theology, psychology and sociology (Bell 2009, 9). For example, efforts to clarify the meaning of reconciliation in TJ discussions has resulted in a range of definitions, typologies and categories being offered by political scientists, peace studies scholars, theologians, philosophers and peacebuilders and many more (Weinstein 2011, 7). However, not all scholars and practitioners are in agreement about TJ's 'fieldhood'. Prominent among them is Bell who argues that TJ does not, in fact, constitute a coherent field and is a label that aims to 'rationalise a set of diverse bargains in relation to the past as an integrated endeavour, so as to obscure the quite different normative, moral and political implications of the bargains' (2009, 6).[10]

Given the range of disciplinary influences over time the spectrum of definitions of TJ provided by scholars and practitioners has expanded. For instance Teitel's narrow definition states that TJ is 'the view of justice associated with periods of political change, as reflected in the phenomenology of primarily legal responses that deal with the wrongdoing of repressive predecessor regimes' (2003b, 893). Roht-Arriaza contends that TJ is a 'set of practices, mechanisms and concerns that arise following a period of conflict, civil strife or repression, and that are aimed at directly confronting and dealing with past violations of human rights and humanitarian law' (2006, 2). Mani's definition encompasses 'restoring justice within the parameters of peacebuilding' (2002, 17). For Hoogenboom and Vieille, TJ goes further as it 'seeks to identify and address the root causes of violence and mass atrocities in an attempt to facilitate the transition to peace at the state as well as at the community level' (2009, 4). The multiplicity of definitions is further compounded at an operational level where TJ overlaps with related concepts, such as judicial reform, security sector reform and governance reform.

Other definitions have been provided by international organisations and NGOs. The United Nations (UN) defines TJ as:

> the full range of processes and mechanisms associated with a society's attempts to come to terms with a legacy of large-scale past abuses, in order to ensure accountability, serve justice and achieve reconciliation. These may include both judicial and non-judicial mechanisms, with differing levels of international involvement (or none at all) and individual prosecutions, reparations, truth-seeking, institutional reform, vetting and dismissals, or a combination thereof.
>
> (UN Security Council 2004, 4)

Actors working in the field of TJ often adopt the definition articulated by the International Center of Transitional Justice (a specialist TJ INGO) (Olsen, Payne, and Reiter 2010, 10–11). According to this definition TJ is:

> a response to systematic or widespread violations of human rights. It seeks recognition for victims and promotion of possibilities for peace, reconciliation and democracy. Transitional justice is not a special form of justice but justice adapted to societies transforming themselves after a period of pervasive human rights abuse.
>
> (ICTJ 2009, 1)

The latter definitions reveal TJ's broad goals and the tendency for TJ to be connected to democratic measures. What is more, the adoption of these definitions indicates the leading role that organisations such as the UN and ICTJ play in TJ. While I am in favour of a broader understanding of TJ (see Jeffery and Kim 2013, 4), for the purposes of this book I will adopt the UN definition of TJ as it provides a useful starting point for analysis.

In a relatively short timeframe TJ has become normalised, institutionalised and mainstreamed in post-conflict settings (Teitel 2003a, 89; McEvoy 2007, 412; Miller 2008, 270). Today TJ comprises part of most internationally supported peace processes (Thoms, Ron, and Paris 2008, 15; Nagy 2008, 276). A glance at the International Centre for Transitional Justice's World Reports reveals the extent to which TJ practice 'is global in its reach' (Jeffery and Kim 2013, 2). What is more the immense popularity of truth commissions[11] and prosecutions and the strong support from international, human rights and donor communities has created an *implicit obligation* for post-conflict countries to adopt one or both of these TJ mechanisms in order to gain resources and legitimacy (see Mani 2008, 89; Freeman 2006, 26).

While there has been much debate about the definition and scope of TJ, these debates have had little bearing on the practice of TJ in different contexts. Despite debates about the appropriateness of various mechanisms and institutions to achieve the aims of TJ, the same standard mechanisms remain routinely employed. Today talk of a 'holistic approach' now resounds through policy documents, NGO projects and research reports (see, for example, UN 2004, 2008; ICTJ 2009; Fletcher and Weinstein 2002; Sooka 2006). Underpinning this approach is the notion that a *combination* of TJ mechanisms, rather than a single mechanism, is the most effective way to achieve TJ goals (Olsen, Payne, and Reiter 2010, 16, 24–25).

Critiques of transitional justice

Numerous critiques have arisen regarding TJ.[12] A major critique is that within the TJ literature there is a tendency to assume that the process occurs in the context of a complete, or at least intended, transition from non-democratic rule to democracy (Grodsky 2008, 286). This assumption, some critics argue, is derived from the liberal peacebuilding agenda, which presents the transition from conflict to peace with the *endpoint* of a 'liberal democratic peace' (Mac Ginty, 2006 cited in Heathershaw 2008, 600).[13] According to critics the liberal peacebuilding agenda goes far from establishing a non-violent political authority that can legitimately guide a country's post-conflict reconstruction on its own terms; it goes beyond 'peacebuilding' to intervention, beyond assisting a country emerging from war to promoting an explicit or implicit normative agenda (Tschirgi 2004, 5). This critique is particularly problematic as there is growing evidence that the liberal peacebuilding 'template' might be fundamentally ill-suited for post-conflict contexts (see Tschirgi 2004; Snyder 2000; Mac Ginty and Richmond 2009). Cobian and Reátegui (2009, 155) warn that this agenda will not change anytime soon, so it is therefore 'important to clarify that TJ points to issues deeper than those found in the "democratizing" paradigm that remains at the surface of political processes'.

Critics also question the intentions of governments pursuing TJ measures. Despite liberalism being 'the dominant normative lens through which political change was viewed' during the 1980s and 1990s, today TJ has come to encompass liberal *and non-liberal* states' efforts to deal with mass human rights violations and violence (e.g. Bahrain, Rwanda and Sri Lanka). This raises questions about the scope, intention and utility of undertaking TJ. Indeed, as Grodsky writes, '[w]hy should yesterday's oppressors open a broad public investigation into their own past?' (2008, 282). Regardless of the intentions of many TJ proponents to reveal the truth and open space for voices that were previously silenced, TJ may be employed as a means to silence contentious voices (Miller 2008, 267). As Miller asserts:

> Ultimately, transitional justice is a definitional project, explaining who has been silenced by delineating who may now speak, describing past violence by deciding what and who will be punished and radically differentiating a new regime in relation to what actions were taken by its predecessor. Despite its claims to exposure, revelation and memorialization, the project of transitional justice may simultaneously perpetuate invisibility and silence. (2008, 267)

Some critics hold that TJ is overly state-centric, at a time when the state where TJ is implemented usually has limited capacity and legitimacy. While others question whether TJ mechanisms may undermine the transition *and* justice by cloaking impunity and 'replacing justice with mechanisms of unaccountability' (Olsen, Payne, and Reiter 2010, 10).

TJ is also critiqued for lacking theoretical and practical cohesiveness and clarity. More than 70 years since the idea of TJ first emerged, there is as yet no clear understanding of what TJ seeks to achieve, its theoretical content and its intended beneficiaries (Ramji-Nogales 2010, 3; Duggan 2010, see also McEvoy 2007; Clarke 2009). Also TJ's broad normative aims remain relatively unclear. Over the last two decades TJ's aims have expanded from liberal norms (including the rule of law and strengthening of democratic institutions) to include the 'elusive ideas' of healing, closure and reconciliation (see Weinstein 2011, 2; Miller 2008, 266; Thoms, Ron, and Paris 2008, 4). Probingly Weinstein (2011, 3–4) asks:

> what exactly are we striving to achieve? Is it peace, the end of violence; is it contented individuals and families; is it communities where it is safe to walk the streets, to shop, to go to the mosque or church or synagogue, where women do not fear rape and where men and women feel no pressure to take up arms; is it economic opportunity, education for the children and dignity in old age? All of these utopian aspirations are laudable and meaningful, but which of these mean reconciliation and how achievable are these goals within a reasonable time span? Of course, safety and security are critical outcomes, but do they constitute reconciliation and does the terminology matter to those whose lives have been shattered?

Further the commonly adopted definitions of key TJ concepts and ideas – punishment, truth, reconciliation and healing – do not necessarily reflect what affected communities seek in the wake of conflict (see, for example, Selim and Murithi 2011; Wilson 2001; Stanley 2004, 2009).

Another issue is that there is limited evidence to support the contention that confronting human rights violations through TJ mechanisms has beneficial effects on individuals, communities and countries (Wiebelhaus-Brahm 2010, 6). In a critical and expansive examination of the current literature and studies of TJ, Thoms, Ron and Paris conclude that:

> existing empirical knowledge about the impacts of TJ is still limited. Systematic research is nascent, and many early findings are questionable or contradictory … Most studies find that TJ has either a moderately beneficial impact on transitional societies or no measurable impact at all. Only a small minority find that TJ techniques are damaging to peace, human rights or democracy. Nevertheless, all findings should be interpreted with great caution, since there are still only a few rigorous cross-national analyses of TJ.
>
> (2008, 11, emphasis removed)

Even though reflections on TJ are growing, many assess the *institutions* of TJ rather than focusing on the people for whom these institutions are established (see Ramji-Nogales 2010, 2). For instance Kim and Sikkink (2010) point to the positive impacts of prosecutions during and after transitions due to their deterrence and normative socialisation impact (see also Payne and Sikkink 2013). Payne and Sikkink (2013, 60) assert that despite the uncertainty of the effects of employing truth commissions on their own, there is an expectation that if truth commissions are used in conjunction with amnesties and prosecutions they are likely to be more effective. However Snyder and Vinjamuri (2003) highlight the inflated success of truth commissions and the risks TJ presents during peace processes. A more recent study covering 161 countries from 1970–2007 revealed TJ is most successful when a holistic approach is adopted; evidence suggests that using *multiple* TJ mechanisms in *sequence* is the best way to achieve democracy and human rights, the study's two stated goals of TJ (Olsen, Payne, and Reiter 2010, 6–7). Significantly truth commissions by themselves were held to have a negative effect on democracy and human rights.[14] However this stands in contrast to Cohen and Lipscomb's findings from Timor Leste, where 12 TJ mechanisms were employed (2012). The authors explain that:

> more may actually mean less if scarce resources are dispersed rather than concentrated; if a new, equally flawed program is implemented to make up for the shortcomings of another; and if the expectations of the victimized population are unrealistically raised and then disappointed.
>
> (2012, 257)

They add: 'In theory, a holistic approach is desirable; in practice, combining multiple institutions may produce very unsatisfactory results' (2012, 260). Clearly there is no agreement on the best TJ approach(es) or whether it produces the kinds of change desired by its proponents. Also little is known about what conditions encourage or impede the adoption of TJ and its success (Olsen, Payne, and Reiter 2010, 1).

Despite these serious questions about TJ, TJ advocates and practitioners continue to operate with assumptions that are based on faith rather than facts (Ignatieff 1996; Weinstein 2011, 2–3). For the former co-editor of the leading TJ journal, the *International Journal of Transitional Justice*, it is staggering that the field is still grappling with a range of assumptions and anecdotes about TJ given that over a billion dollars has been spent on TJ mechanisms (Weinstein 2011, 1). In many ways the TJ enterprise remains an experiment which encourages the question: has the rhetoric overtaken the evidence (Weinstein et al. 2010, 37)? Key TJ debates and areas of inquiry will be further explored in Chapter 3.

Research questions and arguments

From the discussion above it is apparent that there are ambiguities, assumptions and major problems with the concept and practice of TJ. Yet despite this TJ is mobilised in most post-conflict settings, including in Nepal. I am deeply interested in the relationships and detailed workings within and between individuals and organisations in relation to TJ in Nepal. I refer to this as the politics of TJ. Using a constructivist grounded theory I seek to construct a 'picture that draws from, reassembles, and renders subjects' lives' (Charmaz 2003, 270). As such, I ask the following broad questions in this book: which actors are involved in TJ in Nepal? What are their aims and interests? How does TJ unfold in Nepal nationally and locally? and What can this tell us about TJ in other contexts?

These questions help us to understand how the following dilemmas play out in Nepal. First, TJ operates in politically charged contexts often with dysfunctional or partially functioning institutions. Thus, TJ is not confined to a single realm of politics but draws people into the political sphere and pervades other seemingly non-political arenas. How do people in Nepal contend with this? In what ways do they engage and disengage with TJ? In what ways does TJ provide opportunities for justice and for other ends? Second, TJ actors are frequently homogenised. Yet the identification of both the differences *within and between* actors has the potential to contribute to a more accurate picture of TJ on the ground. How does this work in a complex and unstable post-conflict (and now post-disaster) context? Third, growing recognition of the agency of organisations and individuals has tended to frame agency as either compliance or resistance to TJ prescriptions. How do we account for the *range* of actions undertaken by actors at different levels to provide a more nuanced understanding of agency and its absence in post-conflict settings?

Fourth, TJ functions in a state that is fragmented and characterised by poverty and inequality. What are the relationships between justice and TJ? In Nepal everyday life has been characterised by deprivation and insecurity before, during, and after the conflict, how does the idea of justice exist prior to and beyond TJ discourse and associated interventions? Fifth, in the post-conflict and now post-disaster context there are a range of peacebuilding, development, security, governance and other actors. How do TJ proponents take into account the continuum of activities and different actors in Nepal? How do the activities across a range of fields relate to and shape justice?

To examine these research questions and dilemmas I chose a constructivist grounded theory approach. This means that the research is 'grounded' in the data as it examines the empirical in its real life context, shaped by people's words and everyday lives (Charmaz 2004, 497). This methodology enabled me to develop *context-specific* theoretical explanations of actors' interests and experiences in relation to TJ in Nepal. Also, adopting a single case study approach provided me with specificity and deep insights into Nepal (see Denscombe 2004, 30). This approach 'has the potential to deal with the subtleties and intricacies of complex social situations' (Denscombe 2004, 35); it allowed me to focus on the multiple relationships and detailed workings, within and between individuals and organisations in relation to TJ (see Part III). While these findings are particular to Nepal they also have broader applicability for the theory and practice of TJ as 'studies in one situation can be used to speak or to help form a judgement about other situations' (Schofield 1993, 207, see also Denscombe 2004, 36). Rather than making claims for generalisability from the single case study approach I follow Alasuutari's lead that extrapolation rather than generalisation should be the desired outcome of qualitative research (1995, 156–157). Further details about the research design for this study are provided in Chapter 2.

This book makes four arguments. First, TJ is both a producer and a product of politics,[15] however too often TJ is employed with little appreciation of the politics in the post-conflict landscape. Second, the voices of victims rarely impact the TJ agenda despite various participatory activities (see Selim 2014). This exclusion occurs because the practice of TJ is influenced and circumscribed by experts, implementers and brokers. Third, by privileging the civil conflict period and certain human rights violations, TJ neglects other violence, human rights abuses and other forms of deprivation. It often does not deliver what conflict-affected people need and often demand, because it overlooks their everyday lives (see Selim and Murithi 2011). Fourth, there is little scope to make TJ context-specific when TJ experts and brokers generally pursue the dominant TJ paradigm. Their adherence to norms and the belief that there is only a limited range of institutions worth engaging with makes compromise difficult and neglects the context specificities as well as the *continuum* of post-conflict areas and activities (e.g. development and governance) which are interrelated.

As the first book to provide a single case study on TJ in Nepal this book makes theoretical and empirical contributions to: TJ research in Nepal and the Asia-Pacific more broadly; the politics versus justice binary; the concept of victimhood; and, the literature on participatory approaches in development. By focusing on politics, participation and the everyday realities of people at the local and national level in post-conflict Nepal, this book advocates for deeper critical analysis of the processes, voices, interests and agendas of TJ. I advocate for a measured approach and tempered expectations of what TJ can deliver and for whom, particularly victims. TJ remains a valuable enterprise but a renewed understanding of the inherent limitations of TJ is required. I advocate for a grounded approach that moves beyond the limited recognition of politics to an approach that allows these politics to play out. Finding a way to address the consequences of conflict is not a simple or neat affair. I argue that at the heart of TJ is the need to compromise, something that is often ignored or naively dismissed by various actors. These compromises could include pursuing TJ processes that do not include certain institutions, thinking about *TJ processes* rather than *the TJ process* – which is largely state-centric and remote from the affected communities – and recognising that for communities the material dimensions of life can be the priority of their post-conflict realities rather than revisiting the violence they have lived through. This also requires a broader sense of the stakeholders in TJ. I contend that being willing to conceive of and act upon these compromises will provide greater scope for TJ to achieve some of its goals.

Chapter overview

This book is composed of eight chapters over three parts. Part I (Chapters 1 and 2), introduces the contextual backdrop of the book and my research approach. Part II (Chapters 3, 4 and 5), provides a summary of key TJ debates then shifts the focus to Nepal providing the historical framework of the conflict and the peace process. Part III (Chapters 6, 7 and 8), comprising the analytical chapters and conclusion, situates the ways actors engage with the TJ process in Nepal, wraps up my main arguments and provides my final remarks.

In Chapter 2, *Researching transitional justice in Nepal*, I discuss my methodological and conceptual approaches for this study. I develop an action spectrum using contentious politics literature and resistance literature to outline the actors engaged with TJ in Nepal and the various ways they engage with it. I argue that contentious politics offers a useful way of understanding claim making and repertoires within TJ, particularly at the national level, while resistance literature offers insight in to the everyday, which might fall beyond the purview of politics which is focused at the national level. This spectrum is utilised throughout the remainder of the book, particularly in Chapters 6 and 7.

Part II begins with Chapter 3, *Debating transitional justice*, where I analyse several key TJ debates. These relate to: definitions and understandings of justice; politics versus justice; the timing of TJ interventions; agency; the role of victims in TJ processes and, the victim/perpetrator binary. The debates demonstrate that TJ has undergone a degree of critical scrutiny and that its parameters are far from settled. However, there is an identifiable orthodoxy that has emerged and that informs practice on the ground. Thus, these debates provide the opening for exploring TJ in Nepal, and inform Part III of this book.

Chapter 4, *The civil conflict*, provides the history and context of the conflict in Nepal. The chapter provides an overview of the evolution of state (1768–1996) and national identity in Nepal, with a particular focus on the role of the monarchy and Hinduism. It then examines the conflict (1996–2006) including its causes and impacts followed by providing an outline of the peace process, including the Comprehensive Peace Agreement and the Interim Constitution and the Disarmament, Demobilisation and Reintegration process.

Chapter 5, *The transitional justice process in Nepal*, outlines the TJ process. This chapter also provides my actor typology that maps the key actors involved in TJ in Nepal. I identify four main groups of actors: TJ experts, TJ brokers, TJ implementers and victims. This typology assists with understanding the various actors involved and identifying which actors are making claims and on whose behalf. It also provides a useful means of examining the ways these actors interact with each other and engage with transitional justice. Details are also provided about various TJ programs and participatory activities.

Part III begins with Chapter 6, *The politics of transitional justice in Nepal*, which examines the different ways actors engage with and mould TJ. I argue that actors frequently seek to advance their interests and make claims utilising the process, institutions and language of TJ. I also argue that there is considerable political activity taking place that challenges TJ on multiple levels both *within* organisations (e.g. the UN) and *between* actors (victims' groups, the government of Nepal, human rights agencies and foreign governments). Accordingly, it is more useful to consider actors' actions in relation to TJ on a continuum where there is adoption/compliance, contentious action and resistance with a wide range of variation within each. This chapter also critically analyses the opportunities and challenges of participation in TJ in Nepal. I argue that participation can provide avenues for the voices of victims and other stakeholders to be heard, albeit not without significant challenges.

Chapter 7, *Victims in Nepal*, examines the ways victims have articulated their needs in Nepal highlighting the differing conceptions of justice between and within various TJ actors. I argue that there are disconnections between the ways TJ actors perceive and operationalise justice that fail to adequately embrace victims' everyday lives. This impacts the ability of TJ interventions to be victim-centric and context-specific. I argue the approach adopted by TJ experts and TJ implementers often perpetuates the victim/perpetrator binary, which does not reflect lived realities on the ground. I also argue that TJ experts, brokers and implementers in Nepal and elsewhere tend to have a limited understanding of people's everyday lives. This impacts the ability of TJ interventions to be victim-centric and context-specific.

In the final chapter, *Rethinking Transitional Justice*, I summarise and expound upon the book's main arguments, drawing in particular on the analysis in Chapters 6 and 7. I also outline the book's contributions to: TJ research in Nepal[16] and the Asia-Pacific[17] more broadly; the politics versus justice binary; the concept of victimhood; and, the literature on participatory approaches in development, and highlight points that may be significant for other post-conflict contexts.

Limitations, terminology and definitions

My field research was conducted in 2012 (see Chapter 2) and, despite consulting secondary material and conducting informal interviews after this date, represents the views of various actors at a certain point in time. A major challenge various TJ actors encounter is determining and then translating various actors', and in particular victims', changing positions and perceptions into TJ processes. I too faced this challenge researching TJ. Many of the points raised in this book will apply to other contexts; however, in order to provide a detailed contextual study in Nepal, the implications of other contexts are not discussed at length.

During my fieldwork I realised the words that respondents used and the nature of their responses required greater consideration. For example I was unsure of the meaning respondents attributed to the victim label. Does it only encompass individuals who suffered harm/human rights violations? Does it include their immediate family? What about perpetrators or ex-combatants who identify as victims? The term victim-survivor (or victim/survivor) has emerged as an alternative to the term victim (see, for example, van de Merwe, Baxter, and Chapman 2009; Gready 2011). There are four reasons why I did not employ this term in this book. First, the victim label is part of the existing vocabulary in TJ that I seek to critically assess (see Charlesworth and Chinkin 2000, 2). Second, many individuals label themselves as victims, which indicates that the label may well have personal significance, so removing it from TJ vocabulary may disempower these people. A third reason is that this term has material, institutional, symbolic and pragmatic implications. The fourth and perhaps most important reason is that, while I agree that the term victim–survivor provides a more nuanced view of victims and the spectrum that they occupy, throughout my research it was not used by victims themselves (nor by other actors), so for this reason, and indeed for the sake of clarity, I will continue to utilise the term victim (at times I do so interchangeably with conflict-affected person) while acknowledging the negative connotations and problems associated with the term. I examine the victim/perpetrator binary in Chapter 3.

Another issue that arose in my interviews was that when I asked about the conflict I was unaware that for some people the violence that occurred in the wake of the Comprehensive Peace Agreement in 2006 in the Terai[18] region was viewed as a second conflict. Madheshi activists objected to the 2006 interim constitution because it failed to mention federalism, 'a long-standing demand of both Madheshi and indigenous activists' (Shneiderman et al. 2016, 2053). In protest, Madheshi activists in Kathmandu burnt copies of the interim constitution and were subsequently arrested. Their arrests led to bandhs in the Terai, which escalated into a three-week long movement, which became known as the Madhesh Uprising (Shneiderman et al. 2016, 2053). In 2007 protests and violence erupted regarding the lack of progress in the implementation of the peace process and included demands for a separate *Madhes* state.[19] In the Terai region that year there were bashings and attacks on police; 551 people were killed (Lawoti 2009, 73). TJ examines events during a defined period and this has implications because violations before or after this period are not addressed or included in TJ discussions (see Huyse 2003, 58). For the purposes of this book, however, conflict refers to the civil conflict from 13 February 1996 (when the Maoists launched their first attacks) to 21 November 2006 (when the Comprehensive Peace Agreement was signed) while not discounting the issues posed by referring to Nepal as 'post-conflict' (see Sharrock 2013; Shneiderman and Snellinger 2014). The book examines the TJ process in Nepal until February 2017 when the TJ commissions' mandates were extended for one year.

I often refer to the administrative classification of development regions and districts in which respondents reside or work (see Figure 0.1). I acknowledge that the regions and districts are large; however, I opted to do so as a way to ensure the confidentiality of my respondents given that if I identified the exact location many respondents would be easily identifiable. Occasionally, I identify respondents as male or female to assist with differentiating between various respondents; however, I do not discount the impact that other aspects of identity – such as caste, class, ethnicity, race and religion – may have on people in Nepal.

I also adopt the term 'Maoist' that is commonly used as shorthand for the Communist Party of Nepal-Maoist political party (CPN-M) which in 2009 became the Unified Communist Party of Nepal-Maoist (UCPN-M). Over the last 50 years the Communist political parties in Nepal have undergone a number of divisions and mergers. It is beyond the scope of this book to delve into these changes (for further information see, for example, Accord 2017). In addition, Maoist terms (e.g. 'People's War' and 'People's Liberation Army') are used without quotation marks for the sake of clarity but this does not imply endorsement (see ICG 2005). State security forces include the Nepal Police, the Armed Police Force and the Royal Nepalese Army (which became the Nepalese Army) while combatants are members of the People's Liberation Army (see Chapter 4). The commission of inquiry regarding the disappeared has been referred to by a number of names over the course of the last 11 years; I refer to it as the Commission of Investigation on Enforced Disappeared Persons (CIEDP), although at times in quotes it is referred to as the Commission on Disappearances. Finally, I employ the term Nepali instead of Nepalese to refer to the official language in Nepal, the culture[20] and people from Nepal or with Nepali descent (see Hutt 1997). Also, when contextually relevant, I have sought to include terms in Nepali, predominately in Chapter 7. Although some respondents referred to dates based on the Bikram Sambat Nepali calendar, for ease of comprehension I refer to dates using the Gregorian calendar. I have minimised my use of abbreviations and acronyms for the sake of clarity and use the abbreviation/acronym or the full name interchangeably.[21] The interview quotations included in this book have had minor editing for grammatical purposes. A summary of the key actors and their acronyms is provided in *List of abbreviations* at the start of the book.

Notes

1 Personal interview, 8 September 2012, Rolpa.
2 Personal interview, 9 September 2012, Rolpa.
3 Personal interview, 11 October 2012, Kathmandu.
4 Personal interview, 8 September 2012, Rolpa.
5 Personal interview, 9 September 2012, Rolpa.
6 The Constituent Assembly is the national legislative and executive body in Nepal.
7 Robins conducted semi-structured interviews with families of the disappeared (in ten districts), focus group discussions and elite interviews with government, civil society and political party members in Kathmandu. Sajjad conducted semi-structured interviews with policy-makers, journalists, workers from international and national organisations, government officials, experts and victims' groups in Kathmandu, New York and Washington DC.
8 I thank an anonymous journal reviewer for emphasising this point.
9 See Robins (2011).
10 Bell (2009, 15) contends TJ is 'non-field' whereby '[t]he coexistence of the three stories – transitional justice as human rights, transitional justice as conflict resolution and transitional justice as international intervention – as equally credible accounts of the development of transitional justice, points to an understanding of the term as ambiguous almost from its inception'.
11 The most widely used definition is by TJ expert Priscilla Hayner, which asserts that truth commissions are 'bodies set up to investigate a past history of violations of human rights in a particular country – which can include violations by the military or other government forces or armed opposition forces' (Hayner 1994, 558; see also Hayner 2011; Brahm 2009).
12 Key TJ debates will be further explored in Chapter 3.
13 While there are multiple criticisms of the liberal peacebuilding agenda, the main basis for these criticisms is that liberal peace is pursued by liberal peacebuilding actors based on an unproven link between liberal democracy and peace (Peterson 2009, see Paris 2004, 33).
14 These findings call into question Kim and Sikkink's normative socialisation hypothesis (Payne and Sikkink 2013, 50).
15 This resonates with Slater's view on contentious politics. He argues that contentious politics receives more attention as a product, rather than as a producer, of political phenomena and that greater attention should be given to the 'politics that contentious politics produces' (2010, 275).
16 As discussed, to date there have been two major academic comparative studies by Simon Robins and Tazreena Sajjad, which focus on certain aspects of TJ in Nepal.
17 Until recently research on TJ in this region has been limited (see Jeffery and Kim 2013, 2–3). A recent collection of essays, *Transitional Justice in the Asia-Pacific*,

provides a representative sample of cases in the Asia-Pacific region (Jeffery and Kim 2013, 26–27). These cases were Sri Lanka, Indonesia, Cambodia, East Timor, Solomon Islands and South Korea. While this publication provides an in-depth account of TJ in the region, it does not include Nepal.

18 The flat plains along Nepal's southern border with India are called the Terai.

19 Madhesi people are ethnically Tharu and Maithali and inhabit the Terai.

20 I acknowledge the dangers of referring to a national and unified culture however for the sake of clarity I use the term Nepali culture.

21 While I realise this is not convention, hopefully this aids in clarity.

References

Accord. 2017. *Two steps forward, one step back: The Nepal peace process.* Edited by Thapa Deepak and Alexander Ramsbotham, London: Conciliation Resources.

Alasuutari, Pertti. 1995. *Researching culture: Qualitative method and cultural studies.* London: Sage.

Anders, Gerhard, and Olaf Zenker. 2014. 'Transition and justice: An introduction.' *Development and Change* 45(3):395–414.

Arthur, Paige. 2009. 'How "transitions" reshaped human rights: A conceptual history of transitional justice.' *Human Rights Quarterly* 31:321–367.

Bell, Christine. 2009. 'Transitional justice, interdisciplinarity and the state of the "field" or "non-field"'. *International Journal of Transitional Justice* 3(1):5–27.

Brahm, Eric. 2009. 'What is a truth commission and why does it matter?' *Peace and Conflict Review* 3(2):1–14.

Charlesworth, Hilary, and Christine Chinkin. 2000. *The boundaries of international law.* Manchester: Manchester University Press.

Charmaz, Kathy. 2003. 'Grounded theory: Objectivist and constructionist methods.' In *Strategies of qualitative inquiry*, edited by N.K. Denzin and Y.S. Lincoln, 249–291. London: Sage.

Charmaz, Kathy. 2004. 'Grounded theory.' In *Approaches to qualitative research*, edited by Sharlene N. Hesse-Biber and Patricia Leavy, 496–521. Oxford: Oxford University Press.

Clarke, Kamari Maxine. 2009. *Fictions of justice: The international criminal court and the challenges of legal pluralism in sub-Saharan Africa.* Cambridge: Cambridge University Press.

Cobián, Rolando Ames, and Félix Reátegui. 2009. *Toward systemic social transformation: Truth commissions and development.* International Center for Transitional Justice.

Cohen, David, and Leigh-Ashley Lipscomb. 2012. 'When more may be less: Transitional justice in East Timor.' In *Transitional Justice*, edited by Melissa S. Williams, Rosemary Nagy and Jon Elster, 257–315. New York: New York University Press.

Denscombe, Martyn. 2004. *The Good Research Guide: For small-scale social research projects.* Berkshire: Open University Press.

Duggan, Colleen. 2010. 'Editorial note.' *The International Journal of Transitional Justice* 4:315–318.

Farasat, Warisha, and Priscilla Hayner. 2009. Negotiating peace in Nepal: Implications for Justice. In *IFP MEDIATION Cluster.* Institute for Peacebuilding / International Centre for Transitional Justice.

Fletcher, Laurel E., and Harvey M. Weinstein. 2002. 'Violence and social repair: Rethinking the contribution of justice to reconciliation.' *Human Rights Quarterly* 24 (3):573–639.

Freeman, Mark. 2006. *Truth commissions and procedural fairness.* Cambridge: Cambridge University Press.

Gready, Paul. 2011. *The era of transitional justice: The aftermath of the Truth and Reconciliation Commission in South Africa and beyond.* Abingdon: Routledge.

Grodsky, Brian. 2008. 'Justice without transition: Truth commissions in the context of repressive rule.' *Human Rights Review* 9:281–297.

Hayner, Priscilla. 1994. 'Fifteen truth commissions – 1974 to 1994: A comparative study.' *Human Rights Quarterly* 16(4):597–655.

Hayner, Priscilla. 2011. *Unspeakable truths: Transitional justice and the challenges of truth commissions.* New York: Routledge.

Heathershaw, John. 2008. 'Unpacking the liberal peace: The dividing and merging of peacebuilding discourses millennium.' *Journal of International Studies* 36:597–621.

Hoogenboom, David, and Stephanie Vielle. 2009. 'A preliminary examination of the relationship between transitional justice and the neoliberal discourse.' Annual meeting of the Canadian Political Science Association, Ottawa, 29 May 2009.

Hutt, Michael. 1997. 'Being Nepali without Nepal: Reflections on a South Asian diaspora.' In *Nationalism and ethnicity in Hindu Kingdom: The politics and culture of contemporary Nepal*, edited by D. Gellner, J. Pfaff-Czarnecka and J. Whelpton, 101–143. London: Routledge.

Huyse, Luc. 2003. 'Victims.' In *Reconciliation after violent conflict: A handbook*, edited by David Bloomfield, Teresa Barnes and Luc Huyse, 54–66. Stockholm: International Institute for Democracy and Electoral Assistance.

ICG. 2005. Nepal's Maoists: Their arms structure and strategy. http://nepalconflictreport.ohchr.org/files/docs/2005-10-27_report_icg_eng.pdf.

ICTJ. 2009. What is transitional justice? www.ictj.org/about/transitional-justice.

Ignatieff, Michael. 1996. 'Articles of faith.' *Index on Censorship* 25(5):110–122.

Jeffery, Renee, and Hun Joon Kim. 2013. 'New horizons: Transitional justice in the Asia-Pacific.' In *Transitional justice in the Asia-Pacific*, edited by Renee Jeffery and Hun Joon Kim, 1–31. New York: Cambridge University Press.

Kim, Hunjoon, and Kathryn Sikkink. 2010. 'Explaining the deterrence effect of human rights prosecutions for transitional countries.' *International Studies Quarterly* 54(4):939–963.

Kora, Andrieu. 2010. Transitional justice: A new discipline in human rights. In *Online Encyclopedia of Mass Violence.* www.sciencespo.fr/mass-violence-war-massacre-resistance/en/document/transitional-justice-new-discipline-human-rights.

Lawther, Cheryl, Luke Moffett, and Dov Jacobs, eds. 2016. *Research Handbook on Transitional Justice.* Cheltenham: Edward Elgar Publishing.

Mac Ginty, Roger. 2006. *No war, no peace: The rejuvenation of stalled peace processes and peace accords.* London: Palgrave Macmillan.

Mac Ginty, Roger, and Oliver Richmond, eds. 2009. *The liberal peace and post-war reconstruction: Myth or reality?* London: Routledge.

Manandhar, Prabin, and David Seddon, eds. 2010. *In hope and in fear: Living through the people's war in Nepal.* New Delhi: Adroit Publishers.

Mani, Rama. 2002. *Beyond retribution: Seeking justice in the shadows of war.* Cambridge: Polity.

Mani, Rama. 2008. 'Editorial: Dilemmas of expanding transitional justice, or forging the nexus between transitional justice and development.' *International Journal of Transitional Justice* 2:253–265.

Marsden, R. 2011. 'The politics of loss in the people's war and its aftermath: The disappeared as kin, citizens and warriors.' *Studies in Nepali History and Society* 16 (2):271–295.

McEvoy, Kieran. 2007. 'Beyond legalism: Towards a thicker understanding of transitional justice.' *Journal of Law and Society* 34(4):411–440.

McEvoy, Kieran. 2012. 'Commentary on locality and legitimacy.' In *Critical perspectives in transitional justice*, edited by N. Palmer, C. Clarke and D. Granville, 311–318. Portland, OR: Intersentia.

Miller, Zinaida. 2008. 'Effects of invisibility: In search of the "economic" in transitional justice.' *International Journal of Transitional Justice* 2:266–291.

Nagy, Rosemary. 2008. 'Transitional justice as global project: Critical reflections.' *Third World Quarterly* 29(2):275–289.

Olsen, Tricia D., Leigh A. Payne, and Andrew G. Reiter. 2010. *Transitional justice in balance: Comparing processes, weighing efficacy.* Washington, DC: United States Institute of Peace Press.

Orentlicher, Diane F. 2007. "Settling accounts' revisited: Reconciling global norms with local agency.' *International Journal of Transitional Justice* 1(1):10–22.

Paris, Roland. 2004. *At war's end: Building peace after civil conflict.* New York: Cambridge University Press.

Payne, Leigh A., and Kathryn Sikkink. 2013. 'Transitional justice in the Asia Pacific: Comparative and theoretical perspectives.' In *Transitional Justice in the Asia-Pacific*, edited by Renee Jeffery and Hun Joon Kim, 33–60. New York: Cambridge University Press.

Peterson, Jenny H. 2009. *'Rule of law' initiatives and the liberal peace: The impact of politicised reform in post-conflict states.* Edited by Overseas Development Institute. Oxford: Blackwell Publishing.

Pettigrew, Judith. 2012. 'Unexpected consequences of everyday life during the Maoist insurgency in Nepal.' *Journal of International Women's Studies* 13(4):100–112.

Pettigrew, Judith, and Kamal Adhikari. 2009. 'Fear and everyday life in rural Nepal.' *Dialectical Anthropology* 33:403–422.

Ramji-Nogales, Jaya. 2010. 'Designing bespoke transitional justice: A pluralist process approach.' *Michigan Journal of International Law* 32(1):1–58.

Robins, Simon. 2011. 'Towards victim-centred transitional justice: Understanding the needs of families of the disappeared in postconflict Nepal.' *International Journal of Transitional Justice* 5(1):75–98.

Robins, Simon. 2013. *Families of the missing: A test for contemporary approaches to transitional justice.* New York: Routledge.

Roht-Arriaza, Naomi. 2006. 'The new landscape in transitional justice.' In *Transitional justice in the twenty-first century: Beyond truth versus justice*, edited by Naomi Roht-Arriaza and Javier Mariezcurrena, 1–16. Cambridge: Cambridge University Press.

Sajjad, Tazreena. 2013. *Transitional justice in south Asia: A study of Afghanistan and Nepal.* New York: Routledge.

Schofield, Janet. 1993. 'Increasing the generalizability of qualitative research.' In *Social research: Philosophy, politics and practice*, edited by Martyn Hammersley, 200–225. London: Sage.

Selim, Yvette. 2014. 'The opportunities and challenges of participation in transitional justice: Examples from Nepal.' *Journal of International Development* 29(8):1123–1149
Selim, Yvette, and Tim Murithi. 2011. 'Transitional justice and development: Partners for sustainable peace in Africa?' *Journal of Peacebuilding and Development* 6(2):58–72.
Sharrock, James. 2013. 'Stability in transition: Development perspectives and local politics in Nepal.' *European Bulletin of Himalayan Research* 42:9–38.
Shaw, Rosalind, and Lars Waldorf. 2010. 'Introduction: Localizing transitional justice.' In *Localizing Transitional Justice Interventions and Priorities After Mass Violence*, edited by Rosalind Shaw, Lars Waldorf and Pierre Hazan, 3–26. Stanford, CA: Stanford University Press.
Shneiderman, S., L. Wagner, J. Rinck, A. L. Johnson, and A. Lord. 2016. 'Nepal's ongoing political transformation: A review of post-2006 literature on conflict, the state, identities, and environments.' *Modern Asian Studies* 50(6):74.
Shneiderman, Sara, and Amanda Snellinger. 2014. 'Framing the issues: The politics of "post-conflict".' Last modified 24 March 2014. www.culanth.org/fieldsights/500-framing-the-issues-the-politics-of-post-conflict.
Slater, Dan. 2010. *Ordering power: Contentious politics and authoritarian leviathans in Southeast Asia*. Cambridge: Cambridge University Press.
Snyder, Jack. 2000. *From voting to violence: Democratization and nationalist conflict*. New York: W. W. Norton & Company..
Sooka, Yasmin. 2006. 'Dealing with the past and transitional justice: Building peace through accountability.' *International Review of the Red Cross* 88(862):311–325.
Stanley, Elizabeth. 2004. 'Torture, silence and recognition.' *Current Issues in Criminal Justice* 1(5–25):5–25.
Stanley, Elizabeth. 2009. *Torture, truth and justice: The case of Timor Leste*. London: Routledge.
Synder, Jack and Leslie Vinjamuri. 2003. 'Trials and errors: Principals and pragmatism in strategies of international justice.' *International Security* 28(3):5–44.
Teitel, Ruti. 2003a. 'Transitional justice genealogy.' *Harvary Human Rights Journal* 16 (Spring):69–93.
Teitel, Ruti. 2003b. 'Transitional justice in a new era.' *Fordham International Law Journal* 26 (April):893–906.
Teitel, Ruti. 2014. *Globalizing transitional justice: Contemporary essays*. Oxford: Oxford University Press.
Thapa, Deepak. 2003. *Understanding the Maoist movement of Nepal*. Kathmandu: Centre for Social Research and Development.
Thoms, Oskar N.T., James Ron, and Roland Paris. 2008. The effects of transitional justice mechanisms: A summary of empirical research findings and implications for analysts and practitioners. http://aix1.uottawa.ca/~rparis/CIPS_Transitional_Justice_April2008.pdf
Tschirgi, Neclâ. 2004. 'Post-conflict peacebuilding revisited: Achievements, limitations, challenges.' The WSP International/IPA Peacebuilding Forum Conference, New York, 7 October 2004.
Tyynela, John. 2014. Can truth commissions strengthen peace processes? www.kofiannanfoundation.org/app/uploads/2013/11/ictj-report-kaf-truthcommpeace-2014.pdf.
UN. 2004. *The rule of law and transitional justice in conflict and post-conflict societies. Report of the Secretary-General*. New York: United Nations.
UN. 2008. *Guidance note of the Secretary-General: UN approach to rule of law assistance*. New York: United Nations.

UN Security Council. 2004. *The rule of law and transitional justice in conflicts and post-conflict societies: Report to the Secretary-General.* www.un.org/ruleoflaw/files/2004%20report.pdf.

van de Merwe, Hugo, Victoria Baxter, and Audrey R. Chapman, eds. 2009. *Assessing the impact of transitional justice: Challenges for empirical research.* Washington, DC: United States Institute of Peace.

Weinstein, Harvey M. 2011. 'Editorial note: The myth of closure, the illusion of reconciliation: Final thoughts on five years as co-Editor-in-Chief.' *International Journal of Transitional Justice* 5:1–10.

Weinstein, Harvey M., Laurel E. Fletcher, Patrick Winck, and Phuong N. Pham. 2010. 'Stay the hand of Justice: Whose priorities take priority?' In *Localizing transitional justice interventions and priorities after mass violence*, edited by Rosalind Shaw, Lars Waldorf and Pierre Hazan, 27–48. Stanford, CA: Stanford University Press.

Lawoti, Mahendra 2009. In *Encyclopedia of Human Rights*, edited by David P. Forsythe, 65–75. Oxford: Oxford University Press.

Wiebelhaus-Brahm, Eric. 2010. *Truth commissions and transitional societies: The impact on human rights and democracy.* London: Routledge.

Wilson, Richard A. 2001. *The politics of truth and reconciliation in South Africa: Legitimizing the post-Apartheid state.* New York: Cambridge University Press.

2 Researching transitional justice in Nepal

> Before it was we who used to study other conflicts from around the world, now people come to study the conflict in my country.
>
> (Widower who was kidnapped and tortured, Rolpa, September 2012)

In this chapter I discuss the approach taken in the book and the rationale for the methods chosen. I pay particular attention to the 'action spectrum' that I developed to guide my research on TJ. Derived from the literature on contentious politics and resistance, the action spectrum helps us to identify the range of actions actors employ to engage with, mould and impact the trajectory of TJ and in turn helps to make visible the different understandings of justice.

Conducting research in Nepal

Through the constructivist grounded theory approach I was able to study individuals' experiences and perceptions about TJ in context and interpret the meanings people attribute to TJ and other post-conflict issues in Nepal (see Denzin and Lincoln 2005, 3). The constructivist grounded theory approach holds that the meanings given to the real world are socially constructed and value-laden and that it is through our individual interpretation that we construct our (different) viewpoints of the world. The research is 'grounded' in the data as it examines the empirical in its real life context, shaped by people's words and everyday lives (Charmaz 2004, 497). As Charmaz explains, constructivist grounded theory aims:

> to capture the worlds of people by describing their situations, thoughts, feelings and actions and by relying on portraying the research participants' lives and voices. Their concerns shape the direction and form of the research. The researcher seeks to learn how they construct their experience through their actions, intentions, beliefs, and feelings.
>
> (2004, 499)

Pertinently, the constructivist grounded theory approach of the collection and analysis of data *leads to* a theoretical approach (discussed below).[1]

In 2012 I conducted 125 semi-structured interviews with a range of respondents in Nepal.[2] My interviews provided a means of obtaining information about stakeholders' viewpoints, knowledge, attitudes and preferences about post-conflict issues and TJ in Nepal (see Charmaz 2004; Cohen, Manion, and Morrison 2011, 602). Respondents included victims,[3] ex-combatants, community members, political representatives, human rights advocates, journalists, representatives from diplomatic missions, international organisations and the donor community. In total, I interviewed 35 conflict-affected persons; I group victims and ex-combatants together as conflict-affected persons because, frequently, ex-combatants spoke of their feelings of victimisation and betrayal (see Chapter 7). While this label is not the norm in TJ practice it relocates the conflict-related crimes in a political space (see Finnström 2010; Shaw and Waldorf 2010, 9); it also speaks to how the victim/perpetrator dichotomy neglects the lived realities in Nepal. Other methods I employed included document analysis, informal conversations, observation during meetings and conferences in Nepal and field notes. Since 2012 I have had a number of informal conversations, attended conferences and continued to conduct document analysis.

I conducted my interviews in nine districts (Bara, Dang, Dadeldura, Kailali, Kathmandu, Ilam, Lalitpur, Morang and Rolpa) comprising all five 'development regions' in Nepal (see Figure 0.1). Ultimately these multiple sites allowed me to encounter a number of different perspectives within the context of post-conflict Nepal (see Millar 2010, 486). My first site for fieldwork was Kathmandu. I thought it would be a good starting point as to date TJ – as indeed, most other aspects of life in Nepal – has predominately been viewed with a Kathmandu-centred lens (see Chapter 3). Subsequent sites for interviews during my fieldwork were selected for strategic reasons. Rolpa in the Mid-Western region was chosen because it was the district where the conflict originated and where the Maoists' base was located. Bara and Dang were chosen as districts in the Terai that could shed light on the civil conflict but also the post-conflict ethnic violence, which has been excluded from discussions of TJ in Nepal. Dadeldura and Kailali are districts in the Far-Western region that was the least affected region by the conflict. Morang is in the southern Terai in the Eastern region of the Nepal and was chosen because its headquarters, Biratnagar, is the second largest city after Kathmandu such that many NGO and other actor offices are located there. Ilam, also in the Eastern region but considered Hill terrain, was chosen because it was the district from which originated multiple Maoist attacks. Figure 2.1 reveals the extent of the conflict in each district in relation to the number of conflict-related deaths.

Most victims of the conflict do not reside in district headquarters, so when possible I visited smaller villages and towns to ensure that victims' voices adequately informed my research. The time I spent in each location varied. This was because my research was affected by the frequent and at times rolling local and nationwide *bandhs* (strikes) and several religious holiday festivals.

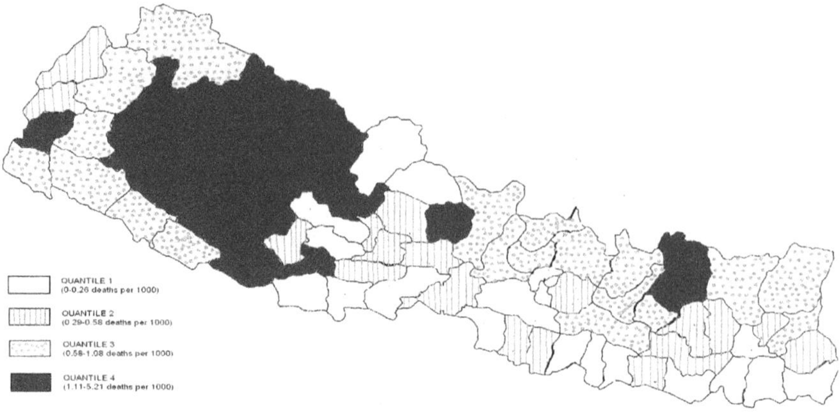

Figure 2.1 Map of the conflict-related deaths
Source: https://creativecommons.org/licenses/by/3.0/igo/.

Disruptions and challenges

My initial field research trip was disrupted by the turmoil surrounding the 27 May 2012 constitution deadline.[4] Missing this deadline, the Constituent Assembly was dissolved, contributing to the ongoing political instability (see Chapter 4). I opted to return to Nepal later in the year to complete my field research to avoid being caught up in ongoing *bandhs* and potential ethnic clashes.[5] I also anticipated that respondents would not be as concerned with questions of TJ when issues of ethno-federalism and the constitution were high on the agenda. This says much about the context in which TJ processes and actors operate.

On a more day-to-day level, the threat or imposition of *bandhs* resulted in a range of issues including being unable to travel within or between cities/towns on vehicles, having to walk to the airport and anticipating and managing the inaccessibility of respondents whose movements were restricted by the *bandhs.* This meant that often I had to assess the developments on each day to decide if and where I would travel/conduct interviews. One instance when there was a *bandh* after a child had been killed in a road accident particularly stands out in my mind. I was travelling by car with three Nepali NGO workers:

> On the journey from Bara to Dang we encountered a traffic jam, one in which we ended up waiting stationary for over five hours. A bystander said there was a road accident ahead and someone had been killed … After some time we joined the steady stream of passengers and villagers walking towards the accident scene (around 200m away). I hesitated to join the current … Close to where the body lay was a line of small boulders which had been meticulously placed in a line, from one end of the road to the other … The body was covered on the road with quilt blankets; a red stain protruded. To my left, on the side of the road, were women and children. Women and children dressed in a clamorous

> combination of colours unified with red as the common thread. They encircled the mother of victim who sat with one or two other women in centre chanting and wailing 'I want to see my son … I want to see my son …' A woman breastfed her child, elderly women sat and squatted close by. Some children played on the steps of the neighbouring property … On the road was a cocktail of police, the armed police force, men and male youth … The gendered groups on the road and around the grieving mother ebbed and flowed, but unanimously ensured that the two currents did not mix. One travel companion told me that road traffic deaths were very common in Nepal in response to my whispering 'It's so sad.' Slowly details emerged … As we stood there I noticed that few people had signs of emotion on their faces … Ebb and flow. Behind me stood a middle aged Nepali man who silently wiped away tears from his eyes …
>
> (Author's field notes, 20 March 2012)

In some ways this experience helped to colour my understanding of how people dealt with some traumatic events in Nepal (see Chapter 7).

Despite my efforts to work with local research assistants I had to resort to employing four different research assistants (three based in Kathmandu and another in the Terai), one of whom was female.[6] Although grounded theory acknowledges that the researcher and the researched co-produce knowledge, I had underestimated the extent to which my research assistants would play a role in knowledge production (see Jones and Ficklin 2012, 106). I encountered numerous challenges, particularly with one of my research assistants who was a young, female journalist from the *Madhesi* ethnic group. I realised that along with my identity, her gender, ethnic identity and her dominating character frequently altered dynamics even before an interview had been granted. This was encapsulated when a contact in Kathmandu told me that many of his colleagues in one district had said that they were too busy to meet with me because of the manner in which she requested an interview. Also my research assistant's dismissive attitude coloured the nature of my interviews and my and the respondent's ability to converse.

Two points are illustrated by my experiences with this research assistant. First, they reveal that researchers (particularly those who are not local) may experience 'reverse power relations', which include the refusal of interviews, guarded responses or patronising attitudes towards the researcher and her work (see Sultana 2007, 379). Second, they demonstrate that my research assistant's background and her actions had a significant impact on my research. This is particularly because '[t]he interpreter may in fact come from another ethnic, religious, cultural or political group that may hold views opposite to the respondents' (Chester 2001, 165). Interestingly Jones and Ficklin (2012, 110) contend that the research assistant's positionality can actually challenge what is sometimes regarded to be the researcher's exclusive hold on agency and power; this was not only cultural power but linguistic and other types of knowledge.

The perceptions of a male, educated, upper caste, research assistant also encouraged me to consider the influence he brought to various interactions. When we were discussing my interview schedule he was adamant that victims (whom he deemed to be poor, simple people) would not understand questions like 'What does justice mean to you?' He did not think they would have the understanding or the vocabulary to engage these types of questions; a position I did not share. For me, any response or lack of a response was rich data, and I believed that people, whether they were illiterate, educated or otherwise, would have opinions on these matters, all of which were valuable and valid. So I retained the questions but I was wary of how he interpreted the question to various people with different education and social statuses. I can recall very few instances when a respondent was unable to answer these types of questions or even paused before responding.

Reflexivity and ethics

Positionality and power

As a researcher, my background, assumptions and interests sensitised me to look for issues and processes in the data. As Charmaz (2001, 6379) explains 'what observers see and hear depends upon their prior interpretative frames, biographies, and interests as well as the research context, their relationships with research participants, and modes of generating and recording data'. I was wary that in the process of the interview I was in some ways taking information from someone so that the 'donor of the information loses control over how the information is used' (Crow 2000, 69). Frequently, I found that just as I, the interviewer, developed an impression of the respondent even before they opened their mouth (see Oppenheim 1992, 95) the same was also true in reverse.[7] At times, I found that being a female researcher assisted in eliciting comments about gender discrimination and personal concerns that may not have been shared with a male researcher. For example, one female respondent who was the coordinator of a Local Peace Committee and political party member told me as a woman I was brave to have travelled all the way to Nepal and that as a woman I needed to speak up and to return to Nepal to share my information, advice and suggestions.

I was fortunate to have friendships and close engagements with Nepalis while I was living in Kathmandu. Also, I travelled with Nepali NGO workers from Kathmandu to various districts and met their colleagues who resided in those areas. I often gained insights into how civil society operated while sharing an evening meal or chai and particularly during the long bus and car journeys. Also, I stayed with one research assistant's relatives (my research assistant's aunt, cousin and his wife and their child) prior to commencing my research in the eastern region. Eating with them on the floor and sharing one of the two bedrooms they occupied in a large building gave me a glimpse of how some families live together in Nepal. This helped to provide context to the difficulties some widows and wives of the disappeared faced when they remained in their in-laws' homes (see Chapter 7). I also witnessed the husband and wife setting off to the temple to worship a Hindu god of water which, along with other religious celebrations I attended, shed light on how religion features in people's everyday lives (discussed further in Chapter 7). It was these short but significant experiences that helped shed light on everyday experiences in Nepal.

Empathy and emotions

I frequently reflected about the inequalities, power relations and injustices between those I researched and myself (see Madge 1993, 297). Even before I had arrived in Nepal I had 'developed an emotional response to what I thought I would find there' (see Jones and Ficklin 2012, 106). For example before commencing my research in Nepal I was concerned that I would display emotion in my interviews with victims. Upon my return I came across Theidon's explanation that:

> The ways in which men and women express the impact of research and writing on violence also have gendered contours … [W]omen, in general, are more likely to acknowledge their emotional responses and are given more "social space" to do so, in part because of gender norms. Indeed, those same gender norms probably influence how we engage with our "informants."
>
> (2014, 5)

Also, I had anticipated that victims themselves would display emotions when relaying their stories (see Jones and Ficklin 2012, 110). I was very aware that in speaking with victims I was asking them to share personal events and experiences, which often I did not feel entitled to hear. Although I was very clear about my role as a researcher (without connections to donors or funders), it was disarming to know that my very presence in the community could have raised expectations and hopes. In one instance, a male respondent whose sister had been murdered allowed another respondent present to speak more extensively with me but he was adamant that I record his name.

Very few victims showed outward signs of emotion. In one situation a male respondent told me he was tortured, widowed and his daughter had gone missing after saying she was going to find work in India (a problem that frequently arises in human trafficking cases). Towards the end of the interview he began to get emotional. My male research assistant later informed me that he thought that the respondent was trying to fool me. It seemed like my research assistant believed that this respondent was playing on my emotions, probably in an effort to garner financial or other support. At the end of the interview the respondent was unable to leave, as there was very heavy rainfall, so I offered the respondent a meal and a drink in the hotel's restaurant. This was to the displeasure of my research assistant and another research assistant staying at the hotel. This example raises the issue of how gender impacts notions of victimhood and the ways people's claims of victimhood can be discounted by other community members (see Chapter 7). It also reveals the difficulties research assistants and researchers have distancing their presumptions from their work. The class divide between the research assistants and the respondent was beyond my control but witnessing it helped shape my understanding of what transpired between research assistants and those interviewed. This encounter assisted me to better contextualise some of the difficulties victims encountered when they spoke through research assistants (e.g. at TJ consultations) (discussed in Chapter 5).

Other respondents spoke about revenge building below the surface while others spoke about conflict-related abuses and events with starkness and what seemed to be fatalistic acceptance (*bahunbad*). At times there seemed to be a mixture of these positions. As I discuss in Chapter 7, I felt ill equipped to unravel this issue. In most situations I tried to balance being empathic with being 'professional'. However, in a few instances I decided to be open about my emotional response. At the end of an interview with a widow who was part of a single women's group and another widow who had been twice evicted from her home (once by her in-laws and then by her parents) I told the women that their determination had greatly moved me. Rather than discount my empathy Jones and Ficklin explain, it 'can be seen as data and analysed in order to illuminate the workings of power relationships, identities, and structures which operate in the fieldwork context' (2012, 110). In fact, '"calculating in" empathy' into the methodological design may 'help the researcher to plan productive and ethical encounters' (Jones and Ficklin 2012, 109).

Deriving an action spectrum

It was important that my research produce theory that is practical and meaningful to those on the ground and that has the ability to transform practice. This is a central tenet of constructivist grounded theory (Denscombe 2004, 111–112; Charmaz 2006). As Locke explains:

> Grounded theory acknowledges its pragmatist philosophical heritage in insisting that a good theory is one that will be practically useful in the course of daily events, not only to social scientists, but also to laymen. In a sense, a test of a good theory is whether or not it works on the ground.
> (2001, 59)

Moreover to develop theory 'there is a need to make meaning that is abstract in nature as well as cognizant of the wider context that has influenced participants in the telling of their stories' (Mills, Bonner, and Francis 2006) (see Chapters 6 and 7).

During my data analysis it became apparent that the ways different actors engaged with and shaped TJ required me to try to pin down the dynamics I was learning about through my grounded theory approach. In some cases it appeared as though actors adopted or resisted TJ; in other cases they negotiated TJ and at other times it appeared as though there were elements of contestation and overtime it appeared as though various actors employed a combination of these actions. To locate and examine how actors engaged with TJ in Nepal I developed a spectrum of actions, adapting contentious politics literature and resistance literature. Contentious politics offers a useful way of understanding claim making and repertoires within TJ, particularly at the national level, while resistance literature offers insight into everyday gestures, which might fall beyond the purview of politics which is focused at the national level. Accordingly I argue it is more useful to consider actors' actions on a continuum where there is adoption/compliance, negotiation, contestation and resistance with a wide range of variation within each. I note that it is not exhaustive.

In conjunction with the actor typology (see Chapter 5), the spectrum (Figure 2.2) illuminates the forms of action exhibited in relation to TJ in Nepal. The spectrum and typology assist with answering the key questions of this book: Which actors are involved in TJ in Nepal? What are their aims and interests? How does TJ unfold in Nepal nationally and locally? and What can this tell us about TJ in other contexts? This spectrum will enable TJ actors and other actors working in the post-conflict space in Nepal to more adequately understand TJ, particularly the range of actors and the various ways they engage with TJ. I discuss contentious politics literature and resistance literature below.

Contentious politics

Contentious politics offers a useful starting point because at the core of contentious politics are 'factions striving and struggling for political power, advantage, and survival' (Slater 2010, 276). According to McAdam, Tarrow and Tilly (2001, 5) contentious politics are:

> episodic, public, collective interaction among makers of claims and their objects when (a) at least one government is a claimant, an object of claims, or a party to the claims and (b) the claims would, if realized, affect the interests of at least one of the claimants.

There are three key components. First, are the actors: who makes claims and why? Second, are (the actual or potential) identities: who do these actors and others say they are and why? Third, are the actions: what forms do these

Adoption/Compliance ------- Negotiation ------- Contestation ------- Resistance

Figure 2.2 Action spectrum
Source: Designed by author.

actors claim making take and why (McAdam, Tarrow and Tilly 2001, 56, 126)? These components interact in that:

> [o]ver the course of contentious politics, actors take action in the names of identities. Identities define their relations to specific others. Their actions actually consist of *inter*actions with those others, interactions that center on claim making. They put on a performance of mutual, public claim making by paired identities.
>
> (McAdam, Tarrow, and Tilly 2001, 137)

Other aspects of contentious politics are extensive. They include the framing process, opportunity, the mobilisation process and structure, repertoires of contention, the interactions between different collective political struggles, the claims made by different groups and the responses of the state and other groups (Lawoti 2007a, 19). I engage with a number of these aspects below and in Part III of the book.

Contentious activities are constrained and incentivised by political opportunities, particularly at the national and local level. Political opportunities comprise formal and informal features of regimes and institutions; they include the following dimensions: the degree of openness of the institutionalised political system; presence of elites, allies or support groups; the degree of stability of elite alignments; and, the state's capacity for repression (McAdam 1996, 26–27). Political opportunities impact 'which political identities people bring into contention,' what claims are possible and the strategies employed (Campbell 2005, 44–48; Tilly and Tarrow 2007, 10, 22, 83). Importantly, these activities 'are shaped by the broader set of political constraints and opportunities unique to the national context in which they are embedded' (McAdam 1996, 3); this highlights the need to understand the political context in which TJ is operating, as discussed in Chapters 4 and 5.[8]

Within the contentious politics literature claim making and political identities have collective dimensions. Tilly and Tarrow assert that '[w]hen contention, politics, and collective action get together, something distinctive happens: power, shared interests, and government policy come into play' (2007, 9). When a group makes claims they become 'political actors' and the collective names that these actors prescribe to others or themselves (e.g. workers) relates to their 'political identities.' Thus, it is useful to consider TJ actors as political actors with political identities. This is of particular importance with regard to TJ brokers and victims' groups which state that they represent victims' voices (see Chapters 5 and 6).

Lawoti's work on contentious politics in Nepal is particularly instructive (2007a, c, b). His research analyses how the neglect, inequality, exclusion and centralisation of the Nepali state and changing political and social conditions have contributed to contentious politics (particularly identity and gender movements) after the 1990 Constitution (Lawoti 2007a, 17, 30, 34). During this period individuals and actors increasingly began to organise, to utilise the opening democratic space and to demand their aspirations and needs (Lawoti 2007a, 34). Pertinently, while some of these contentious activities were conducted by marginalised and disadvantaged groups (e.g. religious minorities and indigenous groups), it was mostly the traditional, elite, and privileged groups who were accommodated by this opening polity and who carried out contentious activities to serve and protect their interests (Lawoti 2007b, 50). This is discussed further in Chapters 4 and 5.

Contentious politics is a useful way to consider how certain actors engage with TJ. Despite its usefulness, however, a major shortcoming is that contentious politics requires public, collective and manifestly political action. This aspect of contentious politics is too narrow, as many activities are not visible in the public sphere nor do they engage directly with the government (Snow 2004, 6). Frequently, governments enter into the process late or reluctantly; the government may even be neutral or a bystander (Goldstone 1998, 126). Although McAdam, Tarrow and Tilly (2001, 243) do acknowledge that contention is not something that is particular to the national political arena, to date the thrust of research on contentious politics has led to what has been coined an emerging hegemonic conception of social movements that constrains how academics think about such phenomena (Snow 2004, 5). Indeed, this focus on the state discounts that many actors direct their grievances to entities and authority structures other than the state (van Dyke, Soule, and Taylor 2004, 28). An example of this would be TJ brokers who have taken victims' claims directly to the UN Human Rights Court and lobbied the UN Special Rapporteur. Ultimately, the '[f]ailure to recognize the multiple targets of collective claims-making paints a biased view of what modern social movements are and what they do' (van Dyke, Soule, and Taylor 2004, 29). In the realm of TJ the emphasis on public and collective acts also fails to account for subtle, hidden and/or individual acts. It is in relation to these acts that resistance literature has much to offer.

Resistance

Resistance literature offers insights into how various actors engage with TJ, particularly at the local level. Resistance has been framed in opposition to power, frequently pitting the powerless, oppressed or subordinate against the powerful, elite, privileged and dominant. Resistance encompasses open, public, direct and organised acts (e.g. protests, demonstrations and declarations). The key is understanding the positions of people and the contexts in which resistance occurs, including the real and imagined boundaries of history, culture and geography (Mohanty 1987, 31, 74).

In resistance literature 'politics' is synonymous with the actions of state or sovereign individuals, however, this is removed from the messy practices of everyday life (Amoore 2005, 7). It is within people's everyday lives that politics are also played out. Everyday life encompasses resistance and it 'is also the site where power is often experienced in its most negative forms' (Richmond 2010, 677). It is:

> a lively yet elusive space in which emotions, interactions, tensions, power struggles, tactics of domination and resistance and small, big, ceremonial or routine events occur … [T]he everyday conjures images of that which falls outside formal institutions, it involves day-to-day practices that are formalized in both private life (as in intimate processes of mourning or family rituals) and public life (as in the legal processes of a trial).
>
> (Riaño-Alcalá and Baines 2012, 387)

By employing an approach that includes everyday life the researcher 'seeks to move past the disjunction of events/moments and the everyday to allow for an appreciation of the everyday itself as *eventful*' (Al-Mohammad and Peluso 2012, 49; see also Das 2007, 6–9).

James Scott has been instrumental in developing the notion of 'everyday peasant resistance.' He coined the term 'infrapolitics' asserting that:

> Infrapolitics is, to be sure, real politics … Real ground is lost and gained … It is the building block for the more elaborate institutionalised political action that could not exist without it.
>
> (Scott 1990, 200–201)

Looking beyond the direct, public and organised acts of resistance, everyday resistance offers insights into individual or collective acts, practices and gestures of resistance which are subtle, marginal and localised (e.g. footdragging, evasion and false deference). Compliance can flow from active ideological support or from grudging resignation but for Scott we should not infer ideological support from the 'most apparently faithful compliance' (1985, 325). Everyday resistance literature contends that in complex societies, as most post-conflict societies are, the absence of explicit contestations 'should not be mistaken for acquiescence' (Mittelman and Chin 2000, 172). In public, people can fake consent to adhere to the 'public transcripts' but in less open arenas they may employ 'hidden transcripts' (e.g. mocking, jokes, parables, songs), which subvert and contradict these dominant scripts.[9] According to Scott (1990, 184), these 'hidden transcripts' are the 'offstage discourse of the powerless' and the weapons of the weak. Everyday resistance can have a diverse range of targets, which include local cultural or elite practices; economic, political or social inconsistencies; deficiencies in needs or rights; dominant state narratives; and, international blueprints (Richmond 2010, 682). The difficulty is ascertaining if and when these acts of resistance occur (see below).

Accordingly, everyday resistance is one appropriate lens through which to consider various actions in relation to TJ. For example, everyday resistance literature assists in the understanding of silences – individuals' and communities' silences in the wake of conflict and in particular in relation to TJ initiatives (see, for example, Ferme 2001; Shaw 2007; Shaw, Waldorf, and Hazan 2010; Eastmond and Selimović 2012; Obradovic´-Wochnik 2013). For example, Thomson reveals that some peasants in Rwanda adopt three types of resistance *vis-à-vis* the state policy on national unity and reconciliation: 'staying on the sidelines, irreverent compliance and withdrawn muteness' (2011, 440). She reveals that in some cases their perceived compliance 'is tactical rather than sincere' (Thomson 2011, 440).

In recent years, resistance literature has been incorporated into TJ research. For example swisspeace, as part of a three-year multi-country project, adopts the following definition of resistance:

> [Resistance is] a *purposeful* act intended by the actor to work against, *prevent* or *disrupt* the intended or implemented formal transitional justice process. It can be organised or unorganised, an act of an individual or group, an act of the powerful or powerless, and is a subjective concept which is perceived differently from different vantage points.
>
> (Jones, Bernath, and Rubli 2013, 15, my emphasis)

Using interviews, the project focuses on self-identified resistance and resistance that actors ascribe to other actors. The researchers' observations are also utilised in an effort to provide a distinction between the actors' and researchers' interpretations of what acts they consider to be resistance. The difficulty with this definition is that it requires intentionality on behalf of the actor and restricts the scope of analysis of resistance to the formal TJ process, discounting the fact that there may be competing and overlapping TJ *processes* at different levels (discussed further below). Resistance is extended to the powerful, not merely the powerless. However, the labelling of certain actions as resistance, either by respondents or the researchers, is a political act. While this definition by swisspeace does not take resistance to be a rejection of TJ it still focuses on actions that 'prevent or disrupt' these formal processes, thus maintaining the suggestion that resistant acts are deviant (which the project claims it is seeking to avoid).

While there have been numerous criticisms of everyday resistance literature, the primary challenge is that most literature defines resistance as an intentional or purposeful act (see Kalb 2006; Moore 1998, 349–351; Bayat 2000, 542–543). Obtaining evidence of the intentions behind an act and its meaning(s) to actor(s) was a methodological challenge I encountered in this project; for, as Scott explains, '[t]he very nature of the enterprise is such that the actor is unlikely to admit to the action itself, let alone explain what he had in mind' (1985, 290). For example, in formal TJ consultations in Nepal when victims were asked certain questions, many relayed their very personal experiences rather than answering the question (see Chapter 5). Could this be to ensure that they were given support or could it be a means to thwart or resist the structure and format of these consultations, or both? And if asked, would participants choose to admit or explain their intentions?

Some writers on resistance have abandoned the requirement for intentionality, and instead speak about both intended and unintended practices (for example, Jones, Bernath, and Rubli 2013); however, I argue that this conflates a range of actions.[10] Hence, in this book I consider resistance to be an intentional act. I acknowledge that I was not able to verify actors' intentionality in each of the examples I raise; hence I flag possible examples of resistance as one of the types of actions on the spectrum. While the issues raised regarding intentionality are valid, the continuum of actions on the spectrum ensures that actions are not too rigidly applied so as to reach an impasse.

Another challenge is distinguishing between survival/coping strategies and resistance, as well as trying to account for why certain actors choose not to resist (see, for example, Bayat 2000, 543; Fletcher 2001). This challenge is compounded because everyday struggles may be the reason and motivation for resistance. Bayat provides an example of poor families in Cairo who:

> tap electricity and running water illegally from the municipality despite their awareness of their illegal behavior. Yet, they do not steal urban services in order to express their defiance vis-a-vis the authorities. Rather, they do it because they feel the necessity of those services for a decent life because they find no other way to acquire them. But these very mundane acts when continued are followed by significant changes in the urban structure, social policy and in the actors' own lives. Hence, the significance of the unintended consequences of agents' daily activities.
>
> (2000, 543)

While such survival strategies are crucial, they are not necessarily indicative of resistance. With this in mind, a challenge is ensuring that resistance is not read into all acts and to avoid the tendency to romanticise, valourise, fetishise and essentialise resistance (Abu-Lughod 1990, O'Hanlon 1988, Kellner 1995). For example in the case of Nepal it is difficult to ascertain whether fake claims for victims' compensation such as those submitted by wives of the disappeared were resistance, survival/coping strategies, or a combination of the two (see Chapter 7). Thus, resistance is a possible action that actors exhibit in relation to TJ; however, it is important not to read resistance into acts by those deemed 'powerless,' particularly as specific acts may be a survival/coping strategy.

Given the limitations I have highlighted above, I take resistance and contentious action to be applicable to individual *and* collective actions, which need not be public nor require the state to be a party (although this is frequently the case with regard to TJ). Ultimately, locating actions on a spectrum assists to identify and analyse the various actors involved in TJ, their interests and the ways in which these actors mould TJ to pursue their agendas. I employ this action spectrum throughout the book, particularly in Chapters 6 and 7.

Notes

1 Accordingly, I was careful to keep an open mind and adopt 'theoretical agnosticism' rather than a blank slate (see Charmaz 2004, 501; Denscombe 2004, 111–112; Henwood and Pidgeon 2006).

2 In line with grounded theory I undertook theoretical sampling. This requires sampling to fill out and ascertain properties of a tentative category rather than achieve representativeness of the population (Charmaz 2004, 497).
3 I identified victims through victims' groups, Local Peace Committees, the International Committee of the Red Cross, human rights organisations and NGOs as well as by referral from other victims. Respondents, particularly victims' groups' leaders and NGO workers, frequently shared with me the stories of other victims they represented or knew. In one interview the leader of a victims' group spoke for almost one hour telling me his and other victims' stories, pausing only to give my research assistant a chance to convey the stories to me. Personal interview, 5 April 2012, Kathmandu. While this does not replace speaking directly with victims it allowed me to hear about stories that are not necessarily reflected in the interviews I conducted.
4 The Constituent Assembly was tasked with drafting the constitution by this date (see Chapter 4 for more details).
5 Some NGO workers advised that these ethnic clashes were possible though unlikely.
6 There were positive aspects of working with a research assistant in an unfamiliar context. These included research assistants providing another perspective about an interview, assisting with understanding some non-verbal language or providing insights into the local or wider context.
7 This was particularly evident in relation to my education qualifications stated on my business card. Education is traditionally a privilege of the upper classes in Nepal (Bista 2001).
8 Nepal is a relatively new democracy with varying opportunities and democratic spaces for groups to make claims. As the research of Lawoti on contentious politics during the 1990s in Nepal has demonstrated often contentious activities are linked to state-building episodes (Lawoti 2007a, c, b; Campbell 2005, 46).
9 In contentious politics anyone is capable of adopting scripts whereas for Scott hidden transcripts relate to the subaltern.
10 For example, swisspeace's definition of resistance (Jones, Bernath, and Rubli 2013, 15).

References

Abu-Lughod, Lila. 1990. 'The romance of resistance: Tracing transformations of power through Bedouin women.' *American Ethnologist* 17(1):41–55.

Al-Mohammad, Hayder, and Daniela Peluso. 2012. 'Ethics and the "rough ground" of the everyday: The overlappings of life in postinvasion Iraq.' *Journal of Ethnographic Theory* 2(2):42–58.

Amoore, Louise. 2005. 'Introduction: global resistance – global politics.' In *The Global Resistance Reader*, edited by Louise Amoore, 1–11. London: Routledge.

Bayat, Asef. 2000. 'From "dangerous classes" to "quiet rebels": Politics of the urban subaltern in the Global South.' *International Sociology* 15(3):533–557.

Bista, Dor Bahadur. 2001. *Fatalism and development: Nepal's struggle for modernization*. Hyderabad: Orient Longman Limited.

Campbell, John L. 2005. 'Where do we stand? Common mechanisms in organizations and social movements research.' In *Social Movements and Organization Theory*, edited by Gerald F. Davis, Doug McAdam, W. Richard Scott and Mayer N. Zald, 41–68. Cambridge: Cambridge University Press.

Charmaz, Kathy. 2001. 'Grounded theory: Methodology and theory construction.' In *International Encyclopedia of the Social & Behavioral Sciences*, edited by Neil J. Smelser, and Paul B. Baltes, 6396–6399.

Charmaz, Kathy. 2004. 'Grounded theory.' In *Approaches to qualitative research*, edited by Sharlene N. Hesse-Biber and Patricia Leavy, 496–521. Oxford: Oxford University Press.

Charmaz, Kathy. 2006. *Constructing grounded theory: A practical guide through qualitative analysis*. London: Sage.

Chester, Laurence. 2001. 'Unaccompanied asylum-seeking young people.' In *The Russell House companion to working with young people*, edited by F. Factor, V. Chauhan, J. Pitts, 163–169. Lyme Regis: Russell House Publishing.

Cohen, Louis, Lawerence Manion, and Keith Morrison. 2011. *Research methods in education*. 7th ed. London: Routledge.

Crow, Iain. 2000. 'The power of research.' In *Research training for social scientists*, edited by Dawn Burton, 68–80. London: Sage.

Das, Veena. 2007. *Life and words: Violence and the descent into the ordinary*. Berkeley: University of California Press.

Denscombe, Martyn. 2004. *The good research guide: For small-scale social research projects*. Berkshire: Open University Press.

Denzin, Norman K., and Yvonna S. Lincoln, eds. 2005. *The SAGE handbook of qualitative research*. 3th ed. Thousand Oaks, CA: Sage.

Eastmond, Marita, and Johanna Mannergren Selimović. 2012. 'Silence as possibility in postwar everyday life.' *International Journal of Transitional Justice* 6:502–524.

Ferme, M. C. 2001. *The underneath of things: Violence, history, and the everyday in Sierra Leone*. Berkeley: University of California Press.

Finnström, Sverker. 2010. 'Reconciliation grown bitter? War, retribution, and ritual action in Northern Uganda.' In *Localizing transitional justice interventions and priorities after mass violence*, edited by Rosalind Shaw, Lars Waldorf and Pierre Hazan, 135–156. Stanford, CA: Stanford University Press.

Fletcher, Robert. 2001. 'What are we fighting for? Rethinking resistance in a Pewenche community in Chile.' *Journal of Peasant Studies* 28(3):37–66.

Goldstone, Jack A. 1998. 'Social movements or revolutions? On the evolution and outcomes of collective action.' In *From contention to democracy*, edited by Marco G. Giugni, Doug McAdam and Charles Tilly, 125–145. Oxford: Rowman & Littlefield Publishers.

Henwood, Karen L., and Nick F. Pidgeon. 2006. 'Grounded theory.' In *Research methods in psychology*, edited by Glynis M. Breakwell, Sean Hammond, Chris Fife-Shaw and Jonathan A. Smith, 342–364. London: Sage.

Jones, Briony, Julie Bernath, and Sandra Rubli. 2013. Reflections on a research agenda for exploring resistance to transitional justice. www.swisspeace.ch/fileadmin/user_upload/Media/Publications/WP_3_2013.pdf

Jones, Briony, and Lisa Ficklin. 2012. 'To walk in their shoes: Recognising the expression of empathy as a research reality.' *Emotion, Space and Society* 5:103–112.

Kalb, Don. 2006. 'Uses of local knowledge.' In *The Oxford Handbook of Contextual Political Analysis*, edited by Charles Tilly and Robert E. Goodin, 579–594. Oxford: Oxford University Press.

Kellner, Douglas. 1995. *Media culture: Cultural studies, identity and politics between the modern and the postmodern*. New York: Routledge.

Lawoti, Mahendra. 2007a. 'Contentious politics in democratizing Nepal.' In *Contentious politics and democratization in Nepal*, edited by Mahendra Lawoti, 17–47. London: Sage.

Lawoti, Mahendra. 2007b. 'Democracy, domination and exclusionary constitutional-engineering process in Nepal, 1990.' In *Contentious politics and democratization in Nepal*, edited by Mahendra Lawoti, 48–72. London: Sage.

Lawoti, Mahendra. 2007c. 'Democratizing promoting and democratization hindering contentious politics: Lessons from Nepal.' In *Contentious politics and democratization in Nepal*, edited by Mahendra Lawoti, 322–336. London: Sage.

Locke, Karen. 2001. *Grounded theory in management research*. London: Sage.

Madge, Clare. 1993. 'Boundary disputes: Comments on Sidaway (1992).' *Area* 25 (3):294–299.

McAdam, Doug. 1996. 'Conceptual origins, current problems, future directions.' In *Comparative perspectives on social movements: Political opportunities, mobilizing structures, and cultural framings*, edited by Doug McAdam, John D. McCarthy and Mayer N. Zald. Cambridge: Cambridge University Press.

McAdam, Doug, Sydney G. Tarrow, and Charles Tilly. 2001. *Dynamics of contention*. Cambridge: Cambridge University Press.

Millar, Gearoid. 2010. 'Assessing local experiences of truth-telling in Sierra Leone: Getting to 'why' through a qualitative case study analysis.' *International Journal of Transitional Justice* 4:477–496.

Mills, Jane, Ann Bonner, and Karen Francis. 2006. 'The Development of constructivist grounded theory.' *International Journal of Qualitative Methods* 5(1):25–35.

Mittelman, James, and Christine Chin. 2000. Conceptualizing Resistance to Globalization. In Mittelman, James *The globalization syndrome: Transformation and resistance*. Princeton, NJ: Princeton University Press, 165–178.

Mohanty, Chandra. 1987. 'Under western eyes: Feminist scholarship and colonial discourses.' *Feminist Review* 30:61–88.

Moore, Donald S. 1998. 'Subaltern struggles and the politics of place: Remapping resistance in Zimbabwe's eastern highlands.' *Cultural Anthropology* 13(3):344–381.

O'Hanlon, Rosalind. 1988. 'Recovering the subject: Subaltern studies and histories of resistance in colonial South Asia.' *Modern Asian Studies* 22(1):189–224.

Obradovic′-Wochnik, Jelena. 2013. 'The "silent dilemma" of transitional justice: Silencing and coming to terms with the past in Serbia.' *International Journal of Transitional Justice* 7:328–347.

Oppenheim, Abraham N. 1992. *Questionnaire design, interviewing and attitude measurement*. London: Pinter.

Riaño-Alcalá, Pilar, and Erin K. Baines. 2012. 'Editorial note: Special issue on transitional justice and the everyday.' *International Journal of Transitional Justice* 6 (3):385–393.

Richmond, Oliver P. 2010. 'Resistance and the post-liberal peace.' *Journal of International Studies* 38(3):665–692.

Scott, James. 1985. *Weapons of the weak: Everyday forms of peasant resistance*. New Haven, CT: Yale Univerisity Press.

Scott, James. 1990. *Domination and the arts of resistance: Hidden transcripts*. New Haven, CT: Yale University Press.

Shaw, Rosalind. 2007. 'Memory frictions: Localizing the truth and reconciliation commission in Sierra Leone.' *International Journal of Transitional Justice* 1(2):183–207.

Shaw, Rosalind, and Lars Waldorf. 2010. 'Introduction: Localizing transitional justice.' In *Localizing transitional justice interventions and priorities after mass violence*, edited by Rosalind Shaw, Lars Waldorf and Pierre Hazan, 3–26. Stanford, CA: Stanford University Press.

Shaw, Rosalind, Lars Waldorf, and Pierre Hazan, eds. 2010. *Localizing Transitional Justice Interventions and Priorities After Mass Violence.* Stanford, CA: Stanford University Press.

Slater, Dan. 2010. *Ordering Power: Contentious politics and authoritarian Leviathans in Southeast Asia.* Cambridge: Cambridge University Press.

Snow, David A. 2004. 'Social movements as challenges to authority: Resistance to an emerging conceptual hegemony.' *Research in Social Movements, Conflicts and Change* 25:3–25.

Sultana, Farhana. 2007. 'Reflexivity, positionality and participatory ethics: Negotiating fieldwork dilemmas in international research.' *An International E-Journal for Critical Geographies* 6(3):374–385.

Theidon, Kimberely. 2014. '"How was your trip?" Self-care for researchers working and writing on violence'. http://webarchive.ssrc.org/working-papers/DSD_ResearchSecurity_02_Theidon.pdf.

Thomson, Susan. 2011. 'Whispering truth to power: The everyday resistance of Rwandan peasants to post-genocide reconciliation.' *African Affairs* 110(440):439–456.

Tilly, Charles, and Sydney G. Tarrow. 2007. *Contentious politics.* Boulder, CO: Paradigm Publishers.

van Dyke, Nella, Sarah A. Soule, and Verta A. Taylor. 2004. 'The targets of social movements: Beyond a focus on the state.' *Research in Social Movements, Conflict, and Change* 25:27–51.

Part II

3 Debating transitional justice

> International policy makers are on a roll; we have found the tools, we just need to use them. Unfortunately, we have yet to understand what they can do and their untoward effects … those working in this field must stop shying away from defining our goals … it is essential to stop repeating the assumptions about reconciliation, closure, justice and what 'victims want,' and address head on the differences among the disciplines that seem to inhibit a coherent approach …
>
> (Weinstein 2011, 9–10)

The evolution of TJ theory and practice has been encapsulated in debates among and between practitioners and scholars (Jeffery and Kim 2013, 8; see also Weinstein 2011, 3). This chapter provides an overview of the following key debates and areas of inquiry:[1] the definitions and understandings of justice; politics versus justice; the timing of TJ interventions; agency; a victim-centric approach; and, the victim/perpetrator binary. These debates are pertinent for two primary reasons. First, they outline the historical developments of TJ and in so doing provide a backdrop to how TJ arose in Nepal (see Jeffery and Kim 2013, 8). Second, they shape the issues with which TJ practitioners and scholars engage and accordingly they impact people's everyday lives in post-conflict countries. Specifically, they affect how TJ is implemented, particularly the categories that are created in practice, and the way justice is understood and delivered. Thus, they provide the opening for exploring TJ in Nepal and inform of the remainder of this book.

Definitions and understandings of justice

While the calls for justice abound in the aftermath of conflict or political transition, there is less clarity on the notions of justice underpinning such calls. As Chapter 1 discussed, this relates the way 'transitions' have been conceived of in TJ. McAuliffe explains:

> when transitions were being conceptualized during the wave of democratic revolutions in South America and Europe in the 1970s and 1980s, they were envisaged as relatively short-term episodes of legal-institutional

> reconstruction, as opposed to longer-term, deeper socioeconomic transformation. This view of transition in turn coloured the conception of justice as retributive or restorative, as opposed to distributive.
>
> (2015, 96; see Arthur 2009, 326)

Retributive and restorative justice offer different understandings regarding the subjects of crimes and which actors should be the focus of justice measures. Retributive justice aims to punish the perpetrators on behalf of the victims, which is regarded as backward-looking and perpetrator focused; whereas restorative justice aims to restore harmony and repair social relationships, which is regarded as forward-looking and victim-centric (see Jeffery and Kim 2013, 13–14; see also Walgrave et al. 2013, 160). In comparison, distributive justice seeks to guide the allocation of the benefits and burdens of social and economic activity in a given society. For the most part this is because the experiences and perceptions associated with this allocation are commonly identified as a key component of the underlying causes and drivers of conflict. Distributive injustice encompasses social, economic and cultural grievances and rights violations, including the perceived or real injustices in the distribution of resources, opportunities and power (Mani 2012).

TJ has been charged with not paying adequate attention to distributive justice. This lack of attention has been connected to TJ's origins in the human rights movement (Miller 2008, 277). While the Universal Declaration of Human Rights makes no division between human rights, over time there has been a tendency to separate and prioritise civil and political rights over economic, social, and cultural rights and this dichotomy has been imported into TJ processes (OHCHR 2008a, b; see Selim and Murithi 2011).[2] The emphasis on civil and political violations ultimately reflects a preoccupation with the *effects,* rather than the *causes* (often economic, social and cultural rights violations), of conflict (Sriram, Martin-Ortega and Herman 2009). A number of transitional contexts elucidate this point. The conflict in Nepal (1996–2006) was fought on grounds of distributive justice. Several studies have concluded that the primary causes of the conflict were economic and social grievances, including landlessness, poverty, uneven development, structural, identity-based exclusion and inequality (see Chapter 4). The post-election violence in Kenya (2007–2008), triggered by the irregularities in political elections, was fuelled by deep-seated disenfranchisement, discrimination and poverty (OHCHR 2008c). The South African apartheid was based on inequality and discrimination, including landlessness, a lack of healthcare and education (Barchiesi 1999; Seekings 2007). Also in Sierra Leone and Liberia, inequality, exclusion and poverty, including issues relating to land tenure and distribution, were deemed to be among the root causes of the conflict (Sierra Leone TRC 2005; Schmid 2009; TRC of Liberia 2009). It was these long-term structural injustices – based on inequality, political repression, and/or ethnic and religious divisions – which were often manipulated and mobilised to fuel the violence. In most, if not all, of these countries, civil and political rights abuses such as illegal detention, torture or murder were abundant. However, these types of civil and political abuses and injustices were sometimes the *symptoms* not the *causes* of the turmoil, while other civil and political rights violations such as endemic political corruption were inextricably linked to economic, social and cultural injustices.

Given this focus on civil and political injustices TJ approaches have been said to present human rights violations in an abstract manner, cut off from the dynamics of political, economic and social power. This issue is evident in the case of TJ commissions that are charged with producing a 'dominant script' that focuses on civil and political rights and on individual accountability (e.g. arbitrary or indefinite detention and severe assault), rather than on issues of distributive justice and economic, social and cultural rights and collective and structural factors (McEvoy and McGregor 2008, 8). Indeed, various truth commissions, including those in Chile, Argentina, Sierra Leone and South Africa, have been criticised for adopting an approach not suited to the context or to the aspirations and priorities of the victims, and for neglecting distributive justice (see Mani 2008).

In the last decade, calls to broaden the notion of justice from a focus on retributive and restorative justice to encompass distributive justice have gained traction (see OHCHR 2014). The rationale for addressing distributive justice is to prevent the recurrence of conflict by dealing with the economic, social and political violations and grievances that spurred the conflict, and to build sustainable foundations for lasting peace. For example, Mani (2002) proposes a broader conceptualisation of justice that encompasses *at least three* dimensions: legal justice or the rule of law; rectificatory justice or the restorative capacity of TJ; and distributive justice, which aims to address the root causes of conflict, the underlying social, political, economic or cultural injustices, including the perceived or real injustices in the distribution of resources, opportunities and power. This is a useful starting point to show the *various* dimensions of justice.

However the inclusion of distributive justice in TJ theory has implications for TJ practice. Some scholars and practitioners are concerned that if TJ widens its scope to investigate issues relating to distributive justice then this would expand, stretch and overburden TJ mechanisms. In response, I have argued that leaving these issues to be addressed by other actors in the post-conflict context fails to recognise there is a *continuum* of activities and actors across a range of fields that impact one another. The failure to recognise the continuum between TJ actors and these other actors fails to capitalise upon a synergy that could reinforce both TJ and other areas (e.g. development) (see Selim 2014; Selim and Murithi 2011). For Miller this is not just a question of pragmatism but of justice; implicit in the reluctance for TJ to address these issues is an 'assumption that the [TJ] instruments, and their inclusion or exclusion of economic considerations, have no practical effect on the questions of inequality, redistribution or development' (2008, 267).

The notion of justice underpinning TJ is not only criticised for its narrowness and exclusion of distributive justice but also because it encompasses male-defined conceptions of violence and harm (see O'Rourke 2008, 273). These critiques are salient in the context of Nepal. In one key study it was found that the majority (78%) of the victims of human rights violations were men; this could have been because women failed to 'identify violations other than the commonly perceived violations involving physical violence' (Aguirre and Pietropaoli 2008, 364); in fact, local organisations in Nepal estimate that up to 60 per cent of the victims and affected people were women (Thapa and Canyon 2017, 1) (see Chapter 4). Using a gender/feminist lens, Bell and O'Rourke (2007) and others question where women, feminism and gender are located in TJ and advocate for a gender justice approach to TJ (see, for example, Buckley-Zistel 2014, 7). Going beyond women's experiences as conflict victims, the literature is developing on women's diverse roles during conflict and in TJ processes; take, for example, Yarwood's edited volume, which presents nine national case studies of women's roles in TJ processes as beneficiaries, protagonists, participants and practitioners (2013, 2–3).

Critics also point to the simplistic assumptions about justice as well as the nature of conflict and transition (Kent 2010, 20; see also Nagy 2008; McEvoy 2008; Moon 2008). The TJ approach in South Africa is illustrative of these concerns. Scholars argue that the story of apartheid focused on gross human rights violations and omitted everyday horrors as well as the socio-political history including aspects of colonialisation and capitalism thereby limiting the parameters of those deemed to be perpetrators and beneficiaries of the regime (Wilson 2001; Mamdani 2000, 179; Miller 2008, 281; Leebaw 2008, 113).

A further critique is that it is not only the notion of justice that holds different meanings for actors but so too other terms such as 'truth', 'reconciliation', 'perpetrators' and 'violence' (see Olsen, Payne and Reiter 2010, 131). TJ mechanisms structure and significantly affect conceptions of these terms (Nagy 2008, 277–278). For some critics the quest to 'close the books' by providing one dominant narrative and truth is deeply problematic and 'should provoke careful interrogation of the story told and the way in which it is "corrected" during transition' (Elster 2004; Miller 2008, 287; for debates see Rushton 2006, 128, 133; McEvoy 2008, 19–20, Humphrey 2002, 108–111). The Serious Crimes Unit in Timor Leste, charged with investigating and prosecuting various conflict related crimes, is illustrative in this regard. Cohen and Lipscomb find that:

> A weak, shifting, and incomplete prosecution strategy also *inherently skewed the representation of the conflict* for the historical record and may have decreased the likelihood that certain types of victims, for example victims of gender-based violence, will receive justice through the courts in the future, as the likelihood that effective investigations can be completed in these cases wanes with time.
>
> (2012, 289, my emphasis)

What is more, it is argued that these terms have often been fetishised and are part of the liberal project where:

> justice represents the struggle for a 'depoliticized,' trustworthy rule of law; truth represents the rights of victims to tell their stories and thus to 'democratize history' and reconciliation represents the aspiration to a newly united citizenry in the postconflict state.
>
> (Miller 2008, 275)

To understand what justice means to people in the Nepali context I asked actors 'What does justice mean to you?' The responses are analysed in Chapter 7. I argue that people's conceptions of justice and needs in post-conflict Nepal are drawn from their everyday concerns about and experiences of injustice as well as what they encountered during the conflict. Related to understandings of justice is the relationship between politics and justice.

Politics versus justice

In the past, various TJ actors have sought to contain politics in one domain, separate from TJ, to minimise its impact on TJ operations. This was based on the aspiration and assumption that TJ processes are neutral, apolitical, technocratic and universalistic (for debates see Oomen 2005; McEvoy and McGregor 2008, 2, 6; Leebaw 2011, 92; Charlesworth and Chinkin 2000, 32; Buckley-Zistel 2009, 16; Nagy 2008, 279; McEvoy 2007). However, attempts to depoliticise TJ – particularly the two dominant approaches of retributive and restorative justice – dislodge violence from the political and historical context (Leebaw 2011) and also lead to unrealistically high expectations and undermine the credibility of international norms of accountability and justice (Newman 2002, 48). These issues are encompassed in what is often referred to as the politics versus justice dilemma or binary. Burgis-Kasthala argues that resorting to this binary – by emphasising the apolitical character of various TJ institutions – is in fact a 'useful way of understating and thus obfuscating its broader, political contribution' to TJ processes (2013, 514). For critical legalist Bhuta, the emerging legal 'expertise' of TJ disregards 'the extent to which an ostensibly *technical* model of "international justice" amounts to a particular mode of doing politics' (2005, 247). Taking this a step further, it is argued that the focus on law becomes a masquerade that emphasises a culture of impunity rather than eradicating it (Oomen 2005, 907).

More recently, there has been a shift from a separation between politics, justice, truth, peace and accountability to a holistic approach that sees these notions as being complementary and mutually reinforcing. Holistic approaches arguably displace the politics versus justice binary such that TJ policies in fact raise technical *and* political questions and decisions, among others (Newman 2002, 47; Apland 2012). By advocating for this holistic approach there seems to be an intention to pay attention to politics in TJ; however this book argues that TJ actors frequently encounter difficulties in linking TJ to politics, while also misreading politics and misconstruing where to locate it in Nepal (see Chapter 6).

A strong focus on legalism remains in TJ guidance notes and toolkit policy documents while the political aspects are frequently understated. See for example OHCHR's *Rule-Of-Law Tools For Post-Conflict States: National consultations on transitional justice* developed for UN missions, transitional administrators and civil society. This document in essence sidesteps the issue of decision-making by policy-makers after national consultations occur (OHCHR 2009). Actually 'it is becoming increasingly clear that a template of taking a "holistic approach" nevertheless leads to convergence of practices' which manifest in a 'distinguishable TJ template' irrespective of context and political particularities (Subotic 2012, 120). According to Leebaw, holistic approaches have not necessarily overcome these particular dilemmas 'but rather made them more difficult to evaluate to the extent that they have re-conceptualized the goals of transitional justice in apolitical terms' (2008, 98). Similarly to the critique of development projects:

> [w]hile there is a broad acceptance that politics matter, this is not an agenda that has been embraced evenly or broadly within and across different development agencies and organisations … [T]he notion of thinking of development as a technical problem that requires a (relatively) straightforward technical solution is deeply engrained in the way many development actors work. While donors may be paying more attention to politics, in many cases insisting they have internalised the importance of thinking politically and are working accordingly, "the default position is still technocratic".
>
> (Menocal 2014, 5)

In this book I demonstrate that Nepal provides a rich example of how actors engage with and mould TJ and the impact this has on the trajectory of TJ. The focus on national level politics obfuscates the dynamic activity at other levels that overlaps and intersects with and influences TJ on the ground. This focus thus provides an incomplete picture of actors and the interests involved in TJ, and how various actors mould TJ to their advantage. Related to the politics versus justice dilemma is the issue of timing.

Timing

In transitional contexts with a range of post-conflict priorities TJ advocates tend to pursue TJ processes sooner rather than later. States emerging from conflict are pressured to undertake TJ quickly and are offered expert advice about how to do so, particularly at a state level (Brahm 2007a, 62). The situation in Afghanistan provides a pertinent example, as it was only shortly after the US military campaign began in Afghanistan in 2001 that there was first talk of the possibility of a truth commission in Afghanistan; Hayner contends that it is without doubt that these discussions were prompted by international personnel in the region (Hayner 2002, 266–267). Asking whether TJ advocates should 'curb their enthusiasm', Mendeloff (2004, 362) explains that the truth-telling literature frequently does not distinguish between what is required immediately after conflict and the long-term concerns that are relevant to reconstruction. Even when these two phases are delineated, this does not minimise the pressure to establish truth-seeking mechanisms 'as quickly as possible'. For example, Bloomfield suggests '[t]he "right time" to deal with these matters never comes: they only become more difficult to deal with as time passes' (2003, 48).

Despite the push to quickly adopt TJ mechanisms, studies have revealed 'a lag between the transition and the adoption of mechanisms' (Olsen, Payne and Reiter 2010, 106). Trials take an average of four years to commence after transitions; although '[w]hile perpetrators are dealt with very quickly via amnesty, trial, or lustration, victims wait an average of 5.5 years to receive reparations, and 5.6 years to participate in a truth commission process' (Olsen, Payne and Reiter 2010, 106–107). Even when the aforementioned enthusiasm is curbed, pressure remains to pursue these norms; for example as Orentlicher, a leading TJ expert, asserts, it is 'preferable to say "not yet" than to reframe global norms in terms that suggest prosecuting atrocious crimes is nothing more than an option' (2007, 22). Underlying this tendency to pursue TJ in a short timeframe is the assumption that demands for truth and justice in post-conflict societies are inevitable; however, scholarship is revealing that local demands for justice may be absent or prioritised after 'other more pressing issues' (Subotic 2012, 125). When this situation arises in practice TJ advocates must then choose whether they will pursue TJ projects even with the lack of local demand or whether they will abandon or delay fighting impunity 'in order to take into consideration local needs' (Subotic 2012, 125).

Even if efforts are undertaken to ask local populations if and how the legacy of mass violence and human rights violations should be addressed it does not mean that there will not be difficulties encountered. Given that post-conflict spaces are complex, politically charged and fragile, it is also relevant that what may be 'seen as legitimate interests' in these weak, unstable post-conflict counties 'may deviate from interests in societies with more well-established institutions' (Hansen 2011, 21). As Mani explains:

> In the chaotic aftermath of divisive conflict, "public opinion" will not be a uniform, homogeneous, consensual single answer that is easy to uncover. Inevitably, there will be wide differences in opinion among different sectors of the local population, particularly on the extent, scope and type of justice desired, and several will insist on pursuing no accountability at all. However elusive, in all cases, there is a discernible, perceptible groundswell of public opinion that is audible to those who care to pay careful attention without leaping to conclusions or making sweeping generalizations.
>
> (2007, 26)

Indeed, given that transitional situations are dynamic, the compromises made early in the transition could be for the interim rather than 'endure permanently' (Sriram 2004, 203).

The issue of timing is also significant given that increasingly provisions for TJ mechanisms are included in peace agreements, as was the case in Nepal (see Chapter 5). However, peace agreements 'act like a snapshot of political and legal conditions at a point in time, but subsequent developments may fundamentally alter their terms' (Roht-Arriaza 2005, 9). What is more, studies have found that transitional countries appear to shift their TJ policies 'approximately six to eight years after the onset of the transition' (Fletcher, Weinstein and Rowen 2009, 206). In the case of Myanmar, Falvey (2010) contends that TJ decisions were often hastily made by political elites during the transition. Rather than making such hasty decisions, Falvey advocates for 'place-based engagement', which encompasses local actors being involved *before* the transition. Falvey argues that it is important to determine 'how communities affected by the violence talk about and understand the conflict', the priorities of these communities, and how these communities define justice (2010, 260; see also Shaw and Waldorf 2010, 24). Responding to these matters may lead to more effective TJ policies being developed. This is discussed further below.

This book demonstrates that the mindset to pursue TJ sooner rather than later was common during the initial stages of transition in Nepal. The rush to include TJ in Nepal hindered its capacity to be context-specific and victim-centric. Chapter 5 analyses how TJ provisions were included in the Comprehensive Peace Agreement and interrogates the ways that affected community members in Nepal were then invited to be involved in TJ policy and practice, including its design and implementation.

Agency

The pressure to initiate TJ processes as soon as possible after a conflict, among other issues, frequently results in TJ processes being orchestrated from 'above' by external actors (Kent 2010, 29; see also Rajagopal 2008, 1349; Oomen 2005; Sriram 2009, 98–99). External actors include international and regional organisations (e.g. UN), bilateral donors (e.g. USAID) and international NGOs (e.g. International Center for Transitional Justice). There has come to be a transnational network of scholars, activists and experts with an 'authoritative claim to policy relevant knowledge' (Haas 1992, 3; see also Baylis 2008). These actors 'descend en masse to a post-conflict country … possessing only scant knowledge of the local context' (Harwell and Le Billon 2009, 287), and notwithstanding, most of which promote the dominant state-centric TJ approach in *different* post-conflict settings. Baylis refers to these individuals as 'post-conflict justice junkies' who have worked in multiple post-conflict settings and who 'parachute' into different post-conflict contexts with little local historical or cultural knowledge (2008, 7). These TJ experts, scholars and practitioners have a limited understanding of the legal systems, local cultures and social and moral factors in part due to the lack of time spent in the country (McEvoy 2012, 312; see also Baylis 2008, 10). Clark and Palmer assert that 'the technical institutional approach views in-depth, society-specific knowledge as a luxury' (2012, 7); and they argue that '[i]f domestic political, social and cultural dimensions are considered important, it is as elements to be grafted on in the final stages of implementation' (2012, 7). Overlooking local knowledge can lead to 'the tendency to overreach and to simply deploy the tools and knowledge available, regardless of whether they are appropriate for the situation' (Baylis 2008, 11).

For Baylis, the knowledge[3] that post-conflict justice junkies bring to a new post-conflict posting is deeply influenced by the previous work setting's problems, approaches and techniques; this type of knowledge reveals the strengths post-conflict justice junkies provide in post-conflict settings as well as their Achilles' heel (2008, 7). Miller also exposes the dangers of the 'cross-fertilisation' of ideas by actors and elites who have participated in TJ processes elsewhere; many of whom have an interest in promoting and overplaying the successes of their work (2008, 271–272). Indeed given the tendency for ex-commissioners and scholars to become 'pervasive truth commission advocates' and 'consultants to, rather than fully external critics of, the [TJ] enterprise' the pool of people is often quite limited (Brahm 2007a, 69; see also Miller 2008, 290). Further to this, Clark and Palmer (2012, 7) explain:

> The narrow institutional approach to transitional justice elicits several discrete but connected problems. At the level of agents, the emphasis on global models affords immense power to international donors and consultants in shaping the transitional justice agenda, often to the detriment of domestic actors. Foreign generalists, who often lack a deep knowledge of particular transitional societies, wield significant influence because of their mastery of supposedly universal templates. Their models gain an international currency through a plethora of workshops and training courses and the funding of like-minded research and policy protects in transitional societies. The danger is that dissenting domestic voices – and a great deal of local insight, legitimacy and accountability to affected communities – are ignored.

Given this close relationship between scholarship, advocacy and practice, which has created 'a single feedback loop' (Duggan 2010, 317), we must ask whether it is possible to eschew the one-size-fits-all approach to TJ. Such an eschewal is necessary because the power afforded to these external actors diminishes the extent to which a deeply contextual approach to TJ is possible (discussed further below). Since this pool of individuals is predominately external to the post-conflict settings, this raises the issue of the extent to which local actors are truly involved in TJ processes.

There has been growing investigation of the 'local' in TJ literature (see, for example, Shaw and Waldorf 2010; Hinton 2011; de Feyter and Parmentier

2011; Riaño-Alcalá and Baines 2012).[4] Different understandings of 'local' have been posited. Millar contrasts the terms 'local' and 'global', explaining the local are 'those actors whose sphere of influence and operation is restricted and bounded by geography or culture' (e.g. rural women and marginalised communities), while global actors are 'those whose sphere of influence and operation extends across boundaries and peoples' (e.g. the UN and the World Bank) (Millar 2016, 32). Shaw and Waldorf adopt a levels-based definition of locality 'as a residual category characterized by both separation (from "the national," "the international," and "the global") and by the absence (of modernity)'; whereby the local is a 'standpoint based in a particular locality but not bounded by it' (2010, 6). Taking a place-based approach requires listening to affected community members' and victims' priorities and determining how these 'priorities intersect with those of international institutions and donors, and with the political interests of their own state' (Shaw and Waldorf 2010, 20). As McEvoy explains:

> the view 'from below' is really a way of providing a different vantage point in order to 'see' more clearly connections, accommodations and relationships with institutions and structures 'from above'. Neither does it suggest a facile or overly romanticised notion of the community as a site of harmony. Instead, it recognises community as a site of potential violence, hierarchy and unequal power relationships. Good practice emerges and is sustained in such places through a cold-eyed assessment of risks and local capacity and developing ways to protect against those risks and enhance existing skills and abilities.
>
> (2012, 311–312)

Advocates of local approaches warn that the tendency to fetishise the local should be resisted as it is not immune from power relations and gender, age and ethnic discrimination. Even worse, '[l]ocal practices may also be the product of manipulation, pragmatism or deceit by political elites' (Boesenecker and Vinjamuri 2011, 352).

Gready (2005) conceptualises locality in relation to justice, distinguishing between 'distanced justice' and 'embedded justice.' For Gready (2005, 8–9) distanced justice is ultimately alienating as it lacks local participation, undermines local systems and is geographically remote and thus invisible to communities. Conversely, embedded justice is, at a minimum, locally defined and owned, develops local legal systems and has 'high local visibility' (Gready 2005, 9; see also Schotsmans 2012, 277). Gready argues that 'justice needs to be embedded within and to engage the communities, cultures and contexts of conflict' (2005, 10). He contends that a key example of embedded justice is the *gacaca*[5] in Rwanda. This can be compared with the geographically remote International Criminal Tribunal for Rwanda trials with which few Rwandans were familiar. Writing before the commencement of the *gacaca* process, he argued that the *gacaca* process 'is potentially culturally embedded, participatory and restorative. In short, it is a revolution in transitional justice' (Gready 2005, 13). Gready's position stands in juxtaposition to the literature that reveals how these local practices were adapted and co-opted by the state (see, for example, Thomson and Nagy 2011, HRW 2011). For de Feyter, human rights claims should be 'ideally accommodated' by actors who are 'geographically close' to where those claims emerge (2011, 33). Local government institutions play a key role as 'the substantive guarantors' of international human rights as they are 'closer' to citizens than other public institutions (Papisca 2011, 85; see also de Feyter 2011, 37).

Other scholars also underscore the importance of local participation and decision-making. O'Rourke explains that:

> In contrast to a "one-size-fits-all" importation of transitional justice mechanisms, a community-based approach to transitional justice is said to entrust decision-making over the design, remit, conduct, character, and outcomes of the transitional justice process to members of a given community affected by violence.
>
> (2008, 271)

For Roht-Arriaza 'interweaving, sequencing and accommodating [of] multiple pathways to justice', including traditional or customary justice, might hold part of the answer to resist the local versus universal dilemma (2006, 8). Useful here is Schotsman's framing of local mechanisms where local 'does not necessarily refer to their [the mechanisms'] applicability in a limited geographical area, but rather to the *origins* of the mechanisms, stemming from a bottom up approach as opposed to external imposition' (2012, 264, my emphasis).

From the discussion above it is evident that the dominant TJ paradigm is frequently designed by external rather than local actors and this poses issues for TJ to be context-specific. This book explores the roles of various TJ actors in TJ in Nepal, I argue that the dominant role of external actors impacts the scope for voices of affected people to be heard and the capacity of communities – variously conceived – to engage with TJ. Through a deep contextual engagement this book examines the varied ways notions as justice, peace and conflict are understood and used in the context of Nepal. It also interrogates the opportunities for, and challenges of, understanding people's everyday lives and incorporating the voices of domestic actors, particularly victims, in the TJ process (see Chapters 5 and 6).

A victim-centric approach

Despite the critiques about the role of external actors, TJ has increasingly been framed as a *victim-centric* process by TJ policy-makers and practitioners (for debates see Clark 2011; Elster 2004; Humphrey 2003; Truth and Reconciliation Commission 2003; Robins 2011a, b, Sriram et al. 2012; UN 2010;

UN General Assembly 2011; UN Secretary General 2011). This has been particularly the case for two TJ mechanisms: truth commissions and reparations. Truth commissions focus on restorative justice and have been lauded as a means to provide recognition for victims and a space for victims to tell their stories without the strict legal requirements of prosecutions. While truth commissions are deemed more victim-centric than prosecutions a number of international criminal tribunals (e.g. Extraordinary Chambers in the Courts of Cambodia) as well as the International Criminal Court provide for victim participation in their proceedings in their guidelines and statutes (see, for example, the International Criminal Court's Rome Statute 2002). Also various human rights courts (e.g. Inter-American Court of Human Rights) have produced a rich body of case law which have 'blazed a trail' for victim-centred justice (Antkowiak 2011, 282; Taylor 2014, 6).

Similarly, reparations have been heralded as direct, tangible, victim-centred TJ mechanisms (see OHCHR 2014, 38–43). Reparations provide a way to redress the harm caused by gross human rights violations and are the only TJ mechanism 'that immediately and specifically targets victims' (OHCHR 2008d, 2). Human rights courts, particularly Inter-American Court of Human Rights, have played a key role in developing reparation jurisprudence (Moffett 2015, 379). From this case law five types of reparations have emerged: restitution; compensation; rehabilitation; measures of satisfaction; and guarantees of non-repetition. These types of reparations are encapsulated in the Basic Principles and Guidelines on the Right to a Remedy and Reparation for Victims of Gross Violations of International Human Rights Law and Serious Violations of International Humanitarian Law, adopted by the UN General Assembly in 2005. For proponents of reparations these principles 'constitute the beginning of a process of institutionalization and international involvement in the issue of reparations, the rights of victims, and the design and implementation of specific reparation programs' (García-Godos 2008, 116). Also relevant are the Updated Set of Principles for the Protection and Promotion of Human Rights through Action to Combat Impunity and related reports. In addition, the International Criminal Court's Rome Statute has reaffirmed the right to reparations for cases decided by the court – including establishing a Victims' Participation and Reparation Section responsible for handling victims' reparation claims – and the International Court of Justice makes decisions on reparations.

Critiques about whether TJ is victim-centric pertain to the inclusion of the local population in the design, planning and implementation of the TJ initiatives (see Lambourne 2009, 28–29). It also pertains to the ways in which victims participate in truth commissions that are arguably rigidly defined by actors other than victims or their representatives (for debates see Amnesty International 2007; Mani 2002; Dukalskis 2011; Brahm 2007b, 2009). What is more, the predominant thrust of evidence reveals that victims who were involved in truth commissions were rarely satisfied with the process and frequently had their expectations unmet (for debates see Theissen and Hamber

1998; Hamber 2000; Hamber et al. 2000; Wilson 2001; Stanley 2004, 2009). In addition, there are limited coherent policies and guidelines regarding what reparations entail in practice (for debates see UN General Assembly 2006; Magarrell 2007; UNDP 2012). To date, no reparations program has distributed the five types of reparations encapsulated in the Basic Principles (OHCHR 2008d, 9). Rather than defining reparations to comprise a wide range of measures that can provide legal redress for violations, in practice a narrow definition of reparations has been adopted to comprise 'whatever set of measures can be implemented to provide benefits to victims directly'; yet even with this narrow definition the challenges are significant (OHCHR 2008d, 9). In particular, '[t]he contexts in which reparations programmes are established are frequently characterized by weak institutional capacity, fractured social relations, very low levels of trust and a scarcity of financial resources' (OHCHR 2008d, 10). As Chapter 4 reveals, this is certainly the case in Nepal.

Indeed claims that TJ processes have a victim-centred approach have been contested. An extreme critique of the claim that TJ is victim-centric asserts that TJ is externally formulated and implemented and that this deprives local communities of agency; specifically, this approach frames locals as either victims to be rescued or perpetrators to be prosecuted, rendering them 'incapable or morally unworthy of positive contributions to peace-building' (Madlingozi 2010, 212). Building on broader critiques about how elites in the developing world 'instrumentalise global discourses of development, rights and liberal democracy to maintain the existing social structure rather than to change' TJ has also been charged with being an elite discourse (Ghale 2014). This critique has been raised in the context of Tunisia. Lamont and Pannwitz (2016, 278) argue the instrumentalisation of TJ was 'symptomatic of transitional justice constituting an elite discourse'. The authors explain that once national dialogue on transitional justice commenced it 'served to filter local voices into internationally established and pre-fixed normative frameworks' (Lamont and Pannwitz 2016, 280). Through the importation of a normative TJ framework and the application of lessons learned from other contexts, 'the social justice and dignity demands of the revolution, that centred around access to jobs, unemployment and inequality … were filtered into more traditional legal frameworks that centred around violations of civil and political rights' (Lamont and Pannwitz 2016, 280). In the context of Nepal, focusing on the language of human rights compared to needs, Robins argues that:

> Post-conflict efforts to create transitional justice mechanisms continue to be elite led and to marginalize victims and their agendas, and to be dominated by a narrow legalism that neglects the priorities of victims … [this research in Nepal] appears to confirm that the idea and meaning of rights in this transitional context is a product of the conjunction of victims with needs and a global discourse articulated by elites. However, the norms that emerge refer far more to priorities internal to the discourse

> itself than to the needs or agenda of victims … The result of rights language in Nepal emerging almost exclusively from dominant power groups is that it becomes an elite discourse, removed from the concerns of the marginalized and constrained by the political and other priorities of the privileged.
>
> (2012, 6–7)

For Robins, TJ is 'a global rights agenda that uses the language of giving agency to the marginalized actually serves to maintain a status quo that guarantees the position of ethnic and caste-based elites' (2012, 3). I examine these ideas further in Chapter 7.

The inclusion of participatory approaches

To address these concerns there has been growing momentum by practitioners, academics and policy-makers to take heed of the literature, knowledge and experience derived from development and participatory theory and practice (see Lundy and McGovern 2008a; McEvoy and McGregor 2008; Robins 2011a, b). Although relatively new in TJ discussions, participation has gained a mantra-like quality in development discourse and practice.[6] Participatory approaches in development emphasise that people are central to development. At the crux of participation is a concern with power, voice and rights (Cornwall 2003). Generally, advocates argue that participation is beneficial because it provides a means (the efficiency argument) and/or an end (the empowerment argument). A central component of this approach is that people who were once socially and economically marginalised in decision-making (deemed 'the powerless' or 'the lowers') should be given the space to identify and express their needs and the best ways to address those needs (Chambers 1994). It is argued that when local people are involved in a participatory process – when they take charge, organise, and take action – rather than simply being regarded as subjects, they are enabled to become agents of change with the ability to transform power and social relations by their own praxis (the empowerment argument) (Rahman 1993). The efficiency argument holds that participation is a tool that can be employed to achieve better project outcomes including increased effectiveness, sustainability and a reduction in time and money in the long term (Cornwall and Jewkes 1995; Gaventa and Cornwall 2006; Cleaver 2001).

A number of participatory models have been created or adapted.[7] A relatively common theme is that *information sharing* and *consultation* (usually in the lower or middle of most models) are tokenistic attempts at participation (this will be discussed further below). Although the rhetoric of participatory approaches has gained legitimacy, often it is only the language that has changed, with few stakeholders changing what they do (Chambers 1997). Claims that all stakeholders are participating as well as including all stakeholders in project descriptions and documents 'all too often boil down to situations in which only the voices and version of the local few are realised and heard' (Cornwall 2003, 1325).

Participatory approaches have been heavily criticised; although critics' opinions diverge regarding the flaws of participation (in theory, in practice or in both) (Cooke and Kothari 2001). Power relations are at the crux of participatory approaches, which in turn impact knowledge generation and sharing. Through participatory approaches Chambers (1994, 1439) argues, the transfer of knowledge is not just *from researchers/practitioners* to the locals but also *from locals* to the researchers/practitioners and *between locals*. This multi-directionality overcomes what is deemed to be 'legitimate' knowledge being solely derived from privileged experts (the 'uppers' or 'powerful'); this approach to knowledge has the effect of obscuring and under-privileging other forms of knowing and the voices of knowers (see Gaventa and Cornwall 2006, 124). However, critics argue participation privileges 'local' or 'indigenous' knowledge, which can legitimise a predetermined and externally derived development agenda, present external interests as local needs and deny the value of different forms of knowledge and expertise of various actors (Cooke and Kothari 2001). These critiques are valid and are pertinent with regard to the role of (external) experts and local actors in TJ.

Creating new 'spaces' in the metaphorical sense and a culture for meaningful participation is also an act of power (Chambers 2006, 2; Cornwall 2002). This raises the question of who creates, participates in and benefits from this space (Cornwall 2003). Although these temporary spaces may be created for a certain purpose, they may be conceived of differently by those who create, subscribe to and engage with them. It is not only important to consider the power exercised by researchers, practitioners and facilitators (e.g. who is invited to speak and who is excluded), but also the power local actors exercise (e.g. the extent to which people choose to participate and also who chooses not to participate, both of which can be conceived as acts with varying degrees of power). In fact, marginalised people may choose to exercise their agency and raise their voices by other means and in other domains (Cornwall 2003, 1329). Although the allure of romanticising the local is hard to resist, these new spaces are not immune from existing power relations and can, in fact, reproduce and further entrench unequal power relations without actually leading to changes in policies or structures and may even perpetuate the problems being addressed (Cornwall 2002, 5). The process can also provide a distorted view of people's aspirations and privilege voices of particular, but not necessarily representative, individuals or groups (Cornwall 2003, 1332; Cornwall and Jewkes 1995, 1673). Also, participants may be explicit about what they need but the researchers/practitioners may implement predetermined external agendas or measures that diverge from the participants' needs or they may even choose to withhold support. The danger is that participants' hopes and expectations are raised and that as opportunities are presented they exercise their voices and attempt to realise their rights, but ultimately there is lack of commitment and implementation. Even if these issues are addressed, the difficulty remains of how to translate the diversity of voices into a means of influencing policy. These problems will be explored in Chapters 5, 6 and 7.

In spite of the various critiques of participation in development there are increased calls for greater participation in TJ, particularly of victims. The UN has affirmed these views, but has placed particular emphasis on consultation. According to the UN Secretary-General, 'the most successful transitional justice experiences owe a large part of their success to the quality and quantity of public and victim consultations carried out' (UN 2004, 7). OHCHR (2009) contends that comprehensive processes of national consultations form a crucial part of TJ. National consultations are held to identify the needs and entitlements of affected communities, ensure a strong sense of local ownership, promote respectful dialogue and stakeholder articulation in the TJ process, reignite peace processes, trigger debates in the community and help victims and other members of civil society to develop local ownership of the TJ programme (OHCHR 2009, 2). In relation to victim-centric design and implementation of TJ, the UN explains that:

> National consultations, conducted with the explicit inclusion of victims and other traditionally excluded groups, are particularly effective in allowing them to share their priorities for achieving sustainable peace and accountability through appropriate transitional justice mechanisms.
>
> (2010, 6)

Another popular participatory approach in TJ has been public opinion surveys.[8] National human rights commissions have played a role but often these surveys have been conducted by NGOs and academic institutions (see AIHRC 2005; ICTJ 2006; International Center for Transitional Justice and the Human Rights Center 2004; Parmentier and Weitekamp 2013). OHCHR has also provided expertise and material support to governments, national human rights commissions and civil society (OHCHR 2009). Authors of a study that employed public opinion surveys argue that the consultative process in TJ has a number of benefits as it can mobilise civil society and the community, increase the impact of TJ 'mechanisms on sustainable human development,' 'influence the political agenda' and 'foster a sense of ownership and participation' (Vinck and Pham 2008, 399). For Parmentier, Rauschenbach and Weitekamp:

> population-based research provides valuable sources of information, as it brings to the surface empirically collected opinions, needs and concerns that are not based solely on theoretical assumptions. As such they constitute an additional source of information for academics and policy-makers about the strategies and mechanisms for dealing with the crimes

> of the past and reconstructing the future, and also allow further debate to take place in the countries concerned and beyond.
>
> (2014, 86)

These surveys are particularly crucial when the expectations and opinions of the local populations are not well known (Parmentier and Weitekamp 2013, 44–45).

Participatory approaches have been utilised to varying extents in TJ processes and timing has often been an issue. Many surveys are conducted *after* the initial decisions have been made rather than before initial design decisions (see Gibson and MacDonald 2001). Research has revealed that victims have frequently been dissatisfied with truth commissions (see Centre for the Study of Violence and Reconciliation & Khulumani Support Group 1998; Theissen and Hamber 1998; Hamber 2000; Hamber et al. 2000; Wilson 2001). Another issue is the agendas and approaches of those who use these participatory tools. Often surveys are designed by experts with limited knowledge of the local context, both within and beyond the conflict period (see Selim 2014). Again, this raises the issue of the extent to which external actors are involved in, and shape, TJ in a particular context.

Although some of the limitations of participation may be overcome, so far there are few examples of a comprehensive participatory approach in TJ. When participation does occur the focus is usually on consultation. In Chapter 5 I outline the various participatory activities in Nepal. To date, the limited literature on participation in TJ in Nepal has been focused on specific themes or types of victims. This book provides a broader outline of the participatory activities and analyses the extent to which these attempts have impacted the TJ trajectory. I argue that these activities provide opportunities for the voices of conflict-affected people to be heard in the TJ process; however, translating these voices into change is fraught with practical and political complexities.

The victim/perpetrator binary

While participation provides avenues for victims, among others, to be involved in TJ, another issue is how are victims defined and by whom. The notion of victimhood has primarily developed within Western criminological theory and policy-making, particularly since the aftermath of the Second World War. Victims' rights were framed as binary opposites to perpetrators' rights. As McEvoy and McConnachie explain, this perspective held that 'punishing the wicked' was 'the most satisfying method of honouring the righteous victim' (2012, 530). While victims are defined in a variety of legal and other instruments, the 1985 UN Declaration of Basic Principles of Justice for Victims of Crime and Abuse of Power was the first international articulation of a general description of victims. This definition encapsulated a number of distinctions regarding victims: direct/indirect (based on the proximity to harm); individual/collective (based on the number of victims); and first/second generation (based on familial relationship and time). This description served as the basis for the UN Commission on Human Rights' work regarding compensation, restitution and rehabilitation measures for victims of violations of gross human rights and fundamental freedoms, (see Shelton 2005; Bassiouni 2008). In 2005 the United Nations General Assembly adopted the Basic Principles and Guidelines on the Right to a Remedy and Reparation for Victims of Gross Violations of International Human Rights Law and Serious Violations of International Humanitarian Law (at times referred to as the Van Boven–Bassiouni Principles). These principles encapsulate the definitions of victim and victims' rights as well as international and state responsibilities and obligations with regard to reparations. In short, international law and norms provide victims with the right to truth, the right to justice and the right to reparation, which correspond with the main TJ mechanisms (truth commissions, prosecutions and reparation) (Waldorf 2009, 23–24).

The scope of the victim label is a point of contention. In South Africa over one-fifth of the victims' statements were deemed to be outside the scope of the official victim definition (Humphrey 2002, 110). In the truth commission in Chad, the fact that some of the worst victim torture cases were investigated actually 'discouraged some victims from giving evidence' and in so doing the truth commission provided 'an incomplete and therefore inaccurate record of atrocity' (Rushton 2006, 130). Moreover, at times individuals may deny the victim status attributed to them by others. Argentina provides a pertinent example where some kidnapped children of the disappeared (those who were adopted and raised by their kidnappers) not only deny claims of social, psychological or other harm but also actively *deny* their status as victims. Under the current conception of TJ this is problematic because '[i]f justice is what victims require, justice can only be achieved when victims consider themselves victims' (Gandsman 2012, 441). Thus, there are clear tensions and implications for ascribing and accepting the victim label. This will be explored further in Chapter 6.

Victims are frequently universalised, homogenised and festishised. Frequently, TJ experts and 'post-conflict justice junkies' treat victims homogeneously irrespective of the country they are from (see Baylis 2008). Falvey (2010, 268) stresses the importance of taking heed of different standpoints and experiences. He uses the case of Myanmar to illustrate this point. He writes:

> [A] male student activist who suffered torture and fled to Thailand may have very different ideas of justice from those of a female Karenni villager who has been displaced from her land, endured forced labor, and had a relative tortured and killed by the military. One may prioritize financial reparations, the other prosecutions.
>
> (Falvey 2010, 268)

Appreciation of these differences between and within ethnic groups is potentially rendered more significant due to the rise of ethnic identities in Nepal and issues that have surrounded attempts to adopt an ethno-federalist state structure (see Chapter 4).

Another issue is that the universalising human rights discourses that underpin much of the thinking about victimhood encourage a narrow or individualised focus on the origin of the harm or violence (Humphrey 2003, 185), such that individuals who are subjected to structural violence and inequalities are not usually considered to be victims. Also victims and perpetrators are not aligned in different communities, so there are fissures based on categorical differences (e.g. poverty, ethnicity, caste and language), which are important but not necessarily coherent units through which the conflict was experienced.

Despite the efforts and impact of victims' groups, victims' voices largely remain absent from the TJ literature. Recognising this Madlingozi (2010, 225) writes that:

> Despite the constant references to the need to have 'victims' voices be [*sic*] heard', to have 'victim-centered or bottom-up transitional justice processes', and to 'victim empowerment', transitional justice scholars and practitioners have not genuinely interrogated how their programmes and interventions have led to the dis-empowerment or empowerment of victims.

One reason for the limited number of published studies on the dynamics of victims' groups in post-conflict contexts is the difficulty with which their activities can be discerned or detected at the national and international level (Robins 2011a, 95). Furthermore, in the limited cases where the victims groups' views and agendas are included in TJ literature 'they remain largely submerged beneath discourses that come from various establishments' (Robins 2011a, 95).

Related to the issue of the victim label is the victim/perpetrator binary, which poses many challenges in TJ. The victim/perpetrator binary is criticised because it is argued that the strict dichotomisation can adversely impact peacebuilding, reconciliation and truth-telling efforts (Macdonald 2013, 53; see also Baines 2009, 164; Theidon 2006, 451). For many scholars the victim/perpetrator binary oversimplifies individuals' complex identities (Shaw 2010, 114; McShane and Williams 1992, 262; Bouris 2007). The problem is that the same 'constellation' of victims' characteristics is invoked and produced in *diverse* peacebuilding efforts (Bouris 2007, 48–49). Rather, in everyday life, individuals in post-conflict societies occupy often '"ambiguous" victim-perpetrator statuses', which include a range of classifications and identities (e.g. victims turned perpetrators, perpetrators turned victims, informants, bystanders, and forced perpetrators and combatants) (Baines 2009, 164; see also Theidon 2006). This was reiterated by Prieto's findings in Colombia that any approach that assumes a strict legalistic division between victims and perpetrators 'is factually inaccurate and inadequate for understanding the subject' (2012, 545).

The victim/perpetrator binary often leads to a deserving or worthy victim being juxtaposed with a culpable and blameworthy perpetrator. In many ways the act of prescribing the victim label (either to another or to oneself) puts the question of innocence and worthiness beyond purview, or least considerably out of the domain of TJ discussions conducted by TJ implementers and brokers. Approaches within the dominant TJ paradigm provide that 'victims' are entitled to reparations and 'perpetrators' should be subject to accountability mechanisms (Shaw 2010; Shaw and Waldorf 2010, 9–10). While victimisation and offending are usually perceived to be separate subfields within criminology (Costello 2010), criminological and psychological research reveals that assigning criminal responsibility is not clear cut. Factors that contribute to attributions of responsibility and blame include social class, ethnicity, physical attributes, influences and individual and situational factors and the impact of gender, particularly for sexualised crimes (see Hart, Ellis, and Paul 2007; Rye, Greatrix and Enright 2006). Notions of complicity and joint criminal enterprise also blur the line when assigning criminal responsibility. Complicity is where an individual is liable for an offense committed by another person when they contribute to the commission of the crime, while joint criminal enterprise 'imposes individual criminal responsibility on an accused for their participation in a group's common criminal plan' (Marsh and Ramsden 2011, 137). In various TJ contexts (e.g. Argentina, Colombia and South Africa) individual/corporate complicity has been raised (see Payne and Pereira 2016); while both liability doctrines have played a key role with regard to the allocation of guilt in international criminal tribunals (Danner and Martinez 2005). For example, in the International Criminal Tribunal for the former Yugoslavia joint criminal enterprise was 'repeatedly relied on in finding individuals guilty in cases before the tribunal' (Bogdan 2006, 63), however this application has been questioned (see for example Marsh and Ramsden 2011).

Research in non-TJ contexts also demonstrates that offenders and victims can often be the same individuals, encapsulated by the 'victim–offender overlap'. This is a 'phenomenon where a person's offending activity and victimization experiences are positively correlated' (Schreck and Stewart 2011); notably, 'the overlap is more persistent among some groups than others' (Reingle 2014). The above demonstrate the complicated ways victims' and offenders' roles and responsibilities intermingle and overlap during criminal incidents, and over time, which in turn complicates the victim/perpetrator binary.

It is apparent that greater attention is required in relation to the '"ambiguous" victim-perpetrator statuses' individuals in post-conflict societies occupy, which include a range of classifications and identities (Baines 2009, 164; see also Theidon 2006). This has implications for how we should define victims and perpetrators in different contexts (see Hansen 2011, 45). It also raises the question of whether a different vocabulary is required (see Rombouts 2002, 228). This book contributes to this discussion. Chapter 7 provides a detailed analysis of the victim/perpetrator binary in the context of Nepal and the Interim Relief Program, which is the main program put in place after the conflict through which victims have been officially recognised. I argue that victimhood is often connected with state support in Nepal; I also argue that the way TJ experts, implementers and brokers identify victims, based on the harm caused, does not always align with the way community members ascribe victimhood, which often is based on suffering. These key TJ debates and areas of inquiry inform the remainder of this book, particularly Chapters 6 and 7.

Notes

1 These debates and areas of inquiry tend to overlap.
2 Economic, social, and cultural rights include those human rights relating to housing, food, water, health care and education, while civil and political rights include those rights relating to freedom of speech and expression, participation in civil society and politics and ensuring an individual's physical integrity and safety.
3 Baylis classifies six types of knowledge that these 'post-conflict justice junkies' create: cultural knowledge, legal and technical knowledge, bureaucratic knowledge, analogical knowledge and networking knowledge' (2008, 7).
4 In relation to peacebuilding more broadly there have long been calls 'unscripted conversations' between the local recipients and local actors to discuss what type of peace they envisage for their local context (Richmond 2009, 329; Duffield 2007, 254; Cooper and Turner 2008).
5 *Gacacas* are traditional community justice mechanisms in Rwanda.
6 Throughout the 1980s and 1990s, the concept of participation metamorphosed from being 'part of a counter-hegemonic approach to radical social transformation' to being part of development orthodoxy (Leal 2007, 539).
7 The most well-known participation typology is Arnstein's ladder of participation. Each rung represents increased citizen power and control to plan and/or program. Arnstein differentiates between the ritual of participation and 'real power' that can affect the outcome arguing that 'participation without redistribution of power is an empty and frustrating process for the powerless' (1969, 216). Other models focus on the actors who employ participatory approaches (see Pretty 1995), the specific types of participants (e.g. children) or contexts (e.g. 'underdeveloped countries') and the interests of the actors involved (see White 1996); although sometimes these various participatory models have different end-points (e.g. transformative participation, citizen control, collective action or self-mobilisation).
8 Other mechanisms employed include participatory action research and collaborative oral history projects. For a detailed discussion, see OHCHR (2009). For further information, see also Aptel and Ladisch (2011), Lundy and McGovern (2008b), Lykes et al. (2003), ICTJ and UNICEF (2010), Iyodu (2011), OHCHR (2007), and Pillay and Goodfriend (2009).

References

Aguirre, Daniel, and Irene Pietropaoli. 2008. 'Gender equality, development and transitional justice: The case of Nepal.' *The International Journal of Transitional Justice* 2:356–377.

AIHRC. 2005. 'A call for justice: A national consultation on past human rights violations in Afghanistan.' 1–79. www.aihrc.org.af/media/files/ Reports/Thematic% 20reports/rep29_1_05call4justice.pdf.

Amnesty International. 2007. 'Truth, justice and reparation: Establishing an effective truth commission.' http://web.amnesty.org/library/print/ENGPOL300092007.
Antkowiak, Thomas M. 2011. 'An emerging mandate for international courts: Victim-centered remedies and restorative justice.' *Stanford Journal of International Law* 47: 279–332.
Apland, Kara. 2012. 'The power and politics of transitional justice.' Last modified 16 January 2012. http://justiceinconflict.org/2012/01/16/the-power-and-politics-of-transitional-justice/.
Aptel, Cécile, and Virginie Ladisch. 2011. *Through a new lens: a child-sensitive approach to transitional justice.* New York: International Center for Transitional Justice.
Arnstein, Sherry R. 1969. 'A ladder of citizen participation.' *Journal of the American Institute of Planners* 35(4):216–224.
Arthur, Paige. 2009. 'How 'transitions' reshaped human rights: A conceptual history of transitional justice.' *Human Rights Quarterly* 31:321–367.
Baines, Erin K. 2009. 'Complex political perpetrators: Reflections on Dominic Ongwen.' *Journal of Modern African Studies* 47(2):163–191.
Barchiesi, Franco. 1999. 'Socio-economic exploitation, meaning contestation and the TRC: Problematic Foundations for a discourse of social citizenship in post-apartheid South Africa.' International Conference on the TRC: Commissioning the Past, University of Witwatersrand, Johannesburg, 11–14 June.
Bassiouni, M. Cherif. 2008. 'Sources and subjects.' In *International criminal law: Sources, subjects and contents*, edited by M. Cherif Bassiouni, 1–70. Leiden: Martinus Nijhoff Publishers.
Baylis, Elena. 2008. 'Multiscalar civil society? Legal pluralism and inequality tribunal-hopping with the post-conflict justice junkies.' *Oregon Review of International Law* 10:361–390.
Bell, Christine, and Catherine O'Rourke. 2007. 'Does feminism need a theory of transitional justice? An introductory essay.' *International Journal of Transitional Justice* 1(1):23–44.
Bhuta, Nehal. 2005. 'Between liberal legal didactics and political manichaeism: The politics and law of the Iraqi special tribunal.' *Melbourne Journal of International Law* 6(2):245–272.
Bloomfield, David. 2003. 'The context of reconciliation.' In *Reconciliation after violent conflict: A handbook*, edited by David Bloomfield, Teresa Barnes and Luc Huyse, 40–48. Stockholm: International Institute for Democracy and Electoral Assistance.
Boesenecker, Aaron P., and Leslie Vinjamuri. 2011. 'Lost in translation? Civil society, faith-based organizations and the negotiation of international norms.' *International Journal of Transitional Justice* 5(3):345–365.
Bogdan, Attila. 2006. 'Individual criminal responsibility in the execution of a joint criminal enterprise in the jurisprudence of the ad hoc international tribunal for the former Yugoslavia.' *International Criminal Law Review* 6(1): 63–120.
Bouris, Erica. 2007. *Complex political victims.* Herndon: Kumarian Press.
Brahm, Eric. 2007a. 'Transitional justice, civil society, and the development of the rule of law in post-conflict societies.' *International Journal of Not-for-Profit Law* 9(4):62–72.
Brahm, Eric. 2007b. 'Uncovering the truth: Examining truth commission success and impact.' *International Studies Perspectives* 8(1):16–35.
Brahm, Eric. 2009. 'What is a truth commission and why does it matter?' *Peace and Conflict Review* 3(2):1–14.

Buckley-Zistel, Susanne. 2009. 'Transitional justice in divided societies – potentials and limits.' 5th European Consortium for Political Research General Conference, Potsdam University, Germany, 10–12 September.

Buckley-Zistel, Susanne. 2014. *Transitional justice theories.* London: Routledge.

Burgis-Kasthala, Michelle. 2013. 'Defining justice during transition? International and domestic contestations over the special tribunal for Lebanon.' *International Journal of Transitional Justice* 7(3):497–517.

Centre for the Study of Violence and Reconciliation & Khulumani Support Group. 1998. Submission to the Truth and Reconciliation Commission: Survivors' perceptions of the truth and reconciliation commission and suggestions for the final report.

Chambers, Robert. 1994. 'Participatory rural appraisal (PRA): Challenges, potentials and paradigm.' *World Development* 22(10):1437–1454.

Chambers, Robert. 1997. *Whose reality counts? Putting the first last.* London: Intermediate Technology Publications.

Chambers, Robert. 2006. 'Participatory mapping and geographic information systems: Whose map? Who is empowered and who disempowered? Who gains and who loses?' *Electronic Journal on Information Systems in Developing Countries* 25(2):1–11.

Charlesworth, Hilary, and Christine Chinkin. 2000. *The boundaries of international law.* Manchester: Manchester University Press,

Clark, Janine Natalya. 2011. 'Peace, justice and the International Criminal Court: Limitations and possibilities.' *Journal of International Criminal Justice* 9(3):521–545.

Clark, Phil, and Nicola Palmer. 2012. 'Introduction: Challenging transitional justice.' In *Critical perspectives in transitional justice*, edited by Nicola Palmer, Phil Clark and Danielle Granville, 1–16. Portland, OR: Intersentia.

Cleaver, Frances. 2001. 'Institutions, agency and the limitations of participatory approaches to development.' In *Participation: The new tyranny?*, edited by Bill Cooke and Uma Kothari, 36–55. New York: Zed Books.

Cohen, David, and Leigh-Ashley Lipscomb. 2012. 'When more may be less: Transitional justice in East Timor.' In *Transitional Justice*, edited by Melissa S. Williams, Rosemary Nagy and Jon Elster, 257–315. New York: New York University Press.

Cooke, Bill, and Uma Kothari, eds. 2001. *Participation: The new tyranny?* New York: Zed Books.

Cooper, Neil, and Mandy Turner. 2008. 'Conclusion: the political economy of peacebuilding – Whose peace? Where next?' In *Whose peace? Critical perspectives on the political economy of peacebuilding*, edited by Michael Pugh, Neil Cooper and Mandy Turner, 390–397. New York: Palgrave.

Cornwall, Andrea. 2002. 'Locating citizen participation.' *IDS Bulletin* 33(33):49–58.

Cornwall, Andrea. 2003. 'Whose voices? Whose choices? Reflections on gender and participatory development.' *World Development* 31(8):1325–1342.

Cornwall, Andrea, and Rachel Jewkes. 1995. 'What is participatory research?' *Social Science & Medicine* 41(12):1667–1676.

Costello, A. 2010. Offending and victimization. In *Encyclopedia of victimology and crime prevention*, edited by Bonnie S. Fisher and Steven P. Lab. Thousand Oaks, CA: Sage.

Danner, Allison Marston, and Jenny S. Martinez. 2005. 'Guilty associations: Joint criminal enterprise, command responsibility, and the development of international criminal law.' *California Law Review* 93(1):75–169.

de Feyter, Koen. 2011. 'The local relevance of human rights.' In *The local relevance of human rights*, edited by Koen de Feyter, Stephan Parmentier, Christine Timmerman and George Ulrich, 11–39. Cambridge: Cambridge University Press.
de Feyter, Koen, and Stephan Parmentier. 2011. 'Introduction: Reconsidering human rights from below.' In *The local relevance of human rights*, edited by Koen de Feyter, Stephan Parmentier, Christine Timmerman and George Ulrich, 1–10. Cambridge: Cambridge University Press.
Duffield, Mark. 2007. *Development, security and unending war*. London: Polity.
Duggan, Colleen. 2010. 'Editorial note.' *The International Journal of Transitional Justice* 4:315–318.
Dukalskis, Alexander. 2011. 'Interactions in transition: How truth commissions and trials complement or constrain each other.' *International Studies Review* 13(3):432–451.
Elster, Jon. 2004. *Closing the books: Transitional justice in historical perspective*. Cambridge: Cambridge University Press.
Falvey, Patrick. 2010. 'Local transitional justice practice in pretransition Burma.' In *Localizing transitional justice interventions and priorities after mass violence*, edited by Rosalind Shaw, Lars Waldorf and Pierre Hazan, 253–274. Stanford, CA: Stanford University Press.
Fletcher, Laurel E., Harvey M. Weinstein, and Jamie Rowen. 2009. 'Context, timing and the dynamics of transitional justice: A historical perspective.' *Human Rights Quarterly* 31(1):163–220.
Gandsman, Ari Edward. 2012. 'Retributive justice, public intimacies and the micropolitics of the restitution of kidnapped children of the disappeared in Argentina.' *International Journal of Transitional Justice* 6(3):423–443.
García-Godos, Jemima. 2008. 'Victim reparations in transitional justice – what is at stake and why.' *Nordic Journal of Human Rights* 26(2):111–130.
Gaventa, John, and Andrea Cornwall. 2006. 'Challenging the boundaries of the possible: Participation, knowledge and power.' *IDS bulletin* 37(6):122–128.
Ghale, Shradha. 2014. 'Whose discourse?' *The Kathmandu Post*. http://kathmandupost.ekantipur.com/news/2014-04-21/whose-discourse.html.
Gibson, James, and Helen MacDonald. 2001. *Truth–yes, reconciliation–maybe: South Africans judge the truth and reconciliation process*. Rondebosch: Institute for Justice and Reconciliation.
Gready, Paul. 2005. 'Analysis: Reconceptualising transitional justice: embedded and distanced justice.' *Conflict, Security & Development* 5(1):3–21.
Haas, Peter M. 1992. 'Introduction: Epistemic communities and international policy coordination.' *International Organization* 46(1):1–35.
Hamber, B. 2000. 'Does the truth heal: A psychological perspective on the political strategies for dealing with the legacy of political violence.' In *Burying the past: Making peace and doing justice after civil conflict*, edited by N. Biggar, 155–176. Washington, DC: George Town University Press.
Hamber, B., N. Mosikare, M. Friedman, and T. Mapea. 2000. 'Speaking out: The role of Khulumani victim support group in dealing with the past in South Africa.' Psychological programmes after war and dictatorship conference, Frankfurt, Germany.
Hansen, Thomas Obel. 2011. 'Transitionaljustice: Toward a differentiated theory.' *Oregon Review of International Law* 13(1):1–46.
Hart, Kristine J., Richard B. Ellis, and John Paul. 2007. 'Who's to blame?: Criminal justice and victim services students' assignments of criminal responsibility by gender.' *Quarterly Journal of Ideology* 30(1&2).

Harwell, Emily E., and Philippe Le Billon. 2009. 'Natural connections: Linking transitional justice and development.' In *Transitional justice and development: Making connections*, edited by Pablo De Greiff and Roger Duthie, 282–330. New York: SSRC Publications.

Hayner, Priscilla B. 2002. *Unspeakable truths: Facing the challenge of truth commissions.* New York: Routledge.

Hinton, Alexander L. 2011. *Transitional justice: Global mechanisms and local realities after genocide and mass violence.* New Brunswick, NJ: Rutgers University Press.

HRW. 2011. Justice compromised: The legacy of Rwanda's community-based Gacaca Courts. www.hrw.org/sites/default/files/reports/rwanda0511_cases.pdf.

Humphrey, Michael. 2002. *The politics of atrocity and reconciliation: From terror to Trauma.* London: Routledge.

Humphrey, Michael. 2003. 'From victim to victimhood: Truth commissions and trials as rituals of political transition and individual healing.' *The Australian Journal of Anthropology* 14(2):171–187.

ICTJ. 2006. *Colombian perceptions and opinions on justice, truth, reparations and reconciliation.* New York: ICTJ.

ICTJ, and UNICEF. 2010. *Children and truth commissions.* www.unicef-irc.org/publications/pdf/truth_commissions_eng.pdf.

Iyodu, Bernadette. 2011. Kenyan refugees included in transitional justice processes. In *Fahamu Refugee Legal Aid Newsletter.*

International Center for Transitional Justice and the Human Rights Center. 2004. Iraqi voices: Attitudes toward transitional justice and social reconstruction. In *Occasional Paper Series.* Berkeley: University of California Human Rights Center.

Jeffery, Renee, and Hun Joon Kim. 2013. 'New horizons: Transitional justice in the Asia-Pacific.' In *Transitional Justice in the Asia-Pacific*, edited by Renee Jeffery and Hun Joon Kim, 1–31. New York: Cambridge University Press.

Kent, Lia. 2010. 'Justica seidauk mai (justice is yet to come): Rethinking the dynamics of transitional justice in East Timor.' PhD, School of Social and Political Sciences, University of Melbourne.

Lambourne, Wendy. 2009. 'Transitional justice and peacebuilding after mass violence.' *International Journal of Transitional Justice* 3:28–48.

Lamont, Christopher K., and Hannah Pannwitz. 2016. 'Transitional justice as elite justice? Compromise justice and transition in Tunisia.' *Global Policy* 7(2):278–281.

Leal, Pablo Alejandro. 2007. 'Participation: The ascendancy of a buzzword in the neoliberal era.' *Development in Practice* 17(4–5):539–548.

Leebaw, Bronwyn. 2008. 'The irreconcilable goals of transitional justice.' *Human Rights Quarterly* 30:95–118.

Leebaw, Bronwyn. 2011. *Judging state-sponsored violence, imagining political change.* New York: Cambridge University Press.

Lundy, Patricia, and Mark McGovern. 2008a. 'The role of community in participatory transitional justice.' In *Transitional justice from below: Grassroots activism and the struggle for change*, edited by Kieran McEvoy and Lorna McGregor, 99–120. Oxford: Hart Publisher.

Lundy, Patricia, and Mark McGovern. 2008b. 'Whose justice? Rethinking transitional justice from the bottom up.' *Journal of Law and Society* 35(2):265–292.

Lykes, M. Brinton, Martin Terre Blanche, and Brandon Hamber. 2003. 'Narrating survival and change in Guatemala and South Africa: The politics of representation

and a liberatory community psychology.' *American Journal of Community Psychology* 31(1–2):79–90.
Macdonald, Anna. 2013. Local understandings and experience of transitional justice: A review of the evidence. http://eprints.lse.ac.uk/56354/1/JSRP_Paper6_Local_understandings_and_experiences_of_transitional_justice_Macdonald_2013.pdf.
Madlingozi, T. 2010. 'On transitional justice entrepreneurs and the production of victims.' *Journal of Human Rights Practice* 2(2):208–228.
Magarrell, Lisa. 2007. Reparations in theory and practice. www.ictj.org/sites/default/files/ICTJ-Global-Reparations-Practice-2007-English.pdf.
Mamdani, Mahmood. 2000. 'The truth according to the TRC.' In *The politics of memory: Truth, healing and social justice*, edited by Ifi Amadiume and Abdullahi An-Na'im, 176–183. London: Zed Books.
Mani, Rama. 2002. *Beyond retribution: Seeking justice in the shadows of war.* Cambridge: Polity.
Mani, Rama. 2007. 'Does power trump morality? Reconciliation or transitional justice?' In *Atrocities and International Accountability: Beyond transitional Justice*, edited by Edel Hughes, William A. Schabas and Ramesh Thakur, 23–41. Tokyo: United Nations University.
Mani, Rama. 2008. 'Editorial: Dilemmas of expanding transitional justice, or forging the nexus between transitional justice and development.' *International Journal of Transitional Justice* 2:253–265.
Mani, Rama. 2012. 'Towards integral justice for victims: Integrating the spiritual, cultural and aesthetic within transitional Justice.' 14th International Symposium of the World Society of Victimology, The Hague University, The Hague, 20–24 May.
Marsh, Luke, and Michael Ramsden. 2011. 'Joint criminal enterprise: Cambodia's reply to Tadić.' *International Criminal Law Review* 11:137–154.
McAuliffe, Padraig. 2015. 'Structural causes of conflict and the superficiality of transitional justice.' In *Theorizing Transitional Justice*, edited by Nir Eisikovits, Claudio Corradi and Jack Volpe Rotondi, 93–105. London: Ashgate.
McEvoy, Kieran. 2007. 'Beyond legalism: Towards a thicker understanding of transitional justice.' *Journal of Law and Society* 34(4):411–440.
McEvoy, Kieran. 2008. 'Letting go of legalism: Developing a 'thicker' version of transitional justice.' In *Transitional justice from below: Grassroots activism and the struggle for change*, edited by Kieran McEvoy and Lorna McGregor, 15–46. Oxford: Hart Publishing.
McEvoy, Kieran. 2012. 'Commentary on locality and legitimacy.' In *Critical perspectives in transitional justice*, edited by N. Palmer, C. Clarke and D. Granville, 311–318. Portland: Intersentia.
McEvoy, Kieran, and Kristen McConnachie. 2012. 'Victimology in transitional justice: Victimhood, innocence and hierarchy.' *European Journal of Criminology* 9 (5):527–538.
McEvoy, Kieran, and Lorna McGregor. 2008. 'Transitional justice from below: an agenda for research, policy and praxis.' In *Transitional justice from below: Grassroots activism and the struggle for change*, edited by Kieran McEvoy and Lorna McGregor, 1–14. Oxford: Hart Publishing.
McShane, Marilyn D., and Frank P. Williams. 1992. 'Radical victimology: A critique of the concept of victim in traditional victimology.' *Crime & Delinquency* 38(2):258–271.
Mendeloff, David. 2004. 'Truth-seeking, truth-telling, and postconflict peacebuilding: Curb the enthusiasm?' *International Studies Review* 6:355–380.

Menocal, Alina Rocha. 2014. *Getting real about politics: From thinking politically to working differently*. www.odi.org/sites/odi.org.uk/files/odi-assets/publications-opinion-files/8887.pdf

Millar, Gearoid. 2016. 'Respecting complexity: Compound friction and unpredictability in peacebuilding.' In *Peacebuilding and friction: Global and local encounters in post-conflict societies*, edited by Annika Björkdahl, Kristine Höglund, Gearoid Millar, Jaïr van der Lijn and Willemijn Verkoren, 32–47. New York: Routledge.

Miller, Zinaida. 2008. 'Effects of invisibility: In search of the "economic" in transitional justice.' *International Journal of Transitional Justice* 2:266–291.

Moffett, Luke. 2015. 'Transitional justice and reparations: Remedying the past?' In *Research handbook on transitional justice*, edited by Cheryl Lawther, Luke Moffett and Dov Jacobs, 377–400. Cheltenham: Edward Elgar.

Moon, C. 2008. *Narrating political reconciliation: South Africa's truth and reconciliation commission*. London: Lexington Books.

Nagy, Rosemary. 2008. 'Transitional justice as global project: Critical reflections.' *Third World Quarterly* 29(2):275–289.

Newman, Edward. 2002. '"Transitional justice": The impact of transnational norms and the UN.' In *Recovering from civil conflict: Reconciliation, peace and development*, edited by Edward Newman and Albrecht Schnabel, 31–50. London: Frank Cass Publishers.

O'Rourke, Catherine. 2008. 'The shifting signifier of 'community' in transitional justice: A feminist analysis.' *Wisconsin Journal of Law, Gender & Society* 23:269–291.

OHCHR. 2007. *Making peace our own: victims' perceptions of accountability, reconciliation and transitional justice in Northern Uganda*. New York: OHCHR.

OHCHR. 2008a. *Frequently asked questions on economic, social and cultural rights*. OHCHR. www.ohchr.org/Documents/Issues/ESCR/FAQ%20on%20ESCR-en.pdf.

OHCHR. 2008b. *Question of the realization in all countries of economic, social and cultural rights*. OHCHR. https://documents-dds-ny.un.org/doc/UNDOC/GEN/G11/121/76/PDF/G1112176.pdf?OpenElement.

OHCHR. 2008c. *Report from OHCHR fact-finding mission to Kenya, 6–28 February 2008*. OHCHR.

OHCHR. 2008d. *Rule-of-law tools for post-conflict states*. OHCHR. www.ohchr.org/Documents/Publications/RuleoflawVettingen.pdf.

OHCHR. 2009. Rule-of-law tools for post-conflict states: National consultations on transitional justice. www.ohchr.org/Documents/Publications/NationalConsultationsTJ_EN.pdf .

OHCHR. 2014. *Transitional justice and economic, social and cultural rights*. New York and Geneva: OHCHR.

Olsen, Tricia D., Leigh A. Payne, and Andrew G. Reiter. 2010. *Transitional justice in balance: Comparing processes, weighing efficacy*. Washington, DC: United States Institute of Peace Press.

Oomen, Barbara. 2005. 'Donor-driven justice and its discontents: The case of Rwanda.' *Development and Change* 36(5):887–910.

Orentlicher, D. F. 2007. '"Settling accounts" revisited: Reconciling global norms with local agency.' *International Journal of Transitional Justice* 1(1):10–22.

Papisca, Antonio. 2011. 'Relevance of human rights in the global space of politics: How to enlarge democratic practice beyond state boundaries and build up a peaceful world order.' In *The local relevance of human rights*, edited by Koen De Feyter,

Stephan Parmentier, Christine Timmerman and George Ulrich, 82–107. Cambridge: Cambridge University Press.

Parmentier, Stephan, Mina Rauschenbach, and Elmar Weitekamp. 2014. 'Repairing the harm of victims after violent conflict: Empirical findings from Serbia.' *International Review of Victimology* 20:85–99.

Parmentier, Stephan, and Elmar Weitekamp. 2013. 'Punishing perpetrators or seeking truth for victims: What does the population in Serbia think about dealing with war crimes?' *International Criminal Law Review* 13:43–62.

Payne, Leigh A., and Gabriel Pereira. 2016. 'Corporate complicity in international human rights violations.' *Annual Review of Law and Social Science* 12(1):63–84.

Pillay, Anu, and Lizzie Goodfriend. 2009. Evaluating women's participation in transitional justice and governance: A community dialogue process in Liberia. *Conflict Trends* 2(1):10–16.

Pretty, J. 1995. 'Participatory learning for sustainable agriculture.' *World Development* 23(8):1247–1263.

Prieto, Juan Diego. 2012. 'Together after war while the war goes on: Victims, ex-combatants and communities in three Colombian cities.' *International Journal of Transitional Justice* 6:525–546.

Rahman, Muhummad Anisur. 1993. *People's self-development: Perspectives on participatory action research*. London: Zed Books.

Rajagopal, Balakrishnan. 2008. 'Invoking the rule of law in post-conflict rebuilding: A critical examination.' *William & Mary Review* 49(4):1347–1376.

Reingle, Jennifer M. 2014. 'Victim-offender overlap.' In *The encyclopedia of theoretical criminology*, edited by J. Mitchell Miller, 911–913. Malden, MA: Wiley-Blackwell.

Riaño-Alcalá, Pilar, and Erin K. Baines. 2012. 'Editorial note: Special issue on transitional justice and the everyday.' *International Journal of Transitional Justice* 6 (3):385–393.

Richmond, Oliver P. 2009. 'Becoming liberal, unbecoming liberalism: Liberal-local hybridity via the everyday as a response to the paradoxes of liberal peacebuilding.' *Journal of Intervention and Statebuilding* 3(3):324–344.

Robins, Simon. 2011a. 'Addressing the needs of families of the Missing: A test of contemporary approaches to transitional justice.' PhD Post-war Recovery Studies, Department of Politics, University of York.

Robins, Simon. 2011b. 'Towards victim-centred transitional justice: Understanding the needs of families of the disappeared in postconflict Nepal.' *International Journal of Transitional Justice* 5(1):75–98.

Robins, Simon. 2012. 'Transitional justice as an elite discourse: Human rights practice where the global meets the local in post-conflict Nepal.' *Critical Asian Studies* 44 (1):3–30.

Roht-Arriaza, Naomi. 2005. 'Transitional justice and peace agreements.' *Role of the human in peace agreements*, Belfast, 7–8 March. www.ichrp.org/files/papers/63/128_-_Transitional_Justice_and_Peace_Agreements_Roht-Arriaza__Naomi__2005.pdf.

Roht-Arriaza, Naomi. 2006. 'The new landscape in transitional justice.' In *Transitional justice in the twenty-first century: Beyond truth versus justice*, edited by Naomi Roht-Arriaza and Javier Mariezcurrena, 1–16. Cambridge: Cambridge University Press.

Rombouts, Heidy. 2002. 'Importance and difficulties of victim-based research in post-conflict societies.' *European Journal of Crime, Criminal Law and Criminal Justice* 10 (2–3):216–232.

Rushton, Beth. 2006. 'Truth and reconciliation? The experience of truth commissions.' *Australian Journal of International Affairs* 60(1):125–141.

Rye, B. J., Sarah A. Greatrix, and Corinne S. Enright. 2006. 'The case of the guilty victim: the effects of gender of victim and gender of perpetrator on attributions of blame and responsibility.' *Sex Roles* 54(9):639–649.

Schmid, Evelyne. 2009. 'Liberia's truth commission report: economic, social, and cultural rights in transitional justice.' *PRAXIS – The Fletcher Journal of Human Security* XXIV:5–28.

Schotsmans, Martien. 2012. '"Blow your mind and cool your heart": Can tradition-based justice fill the transitional justice gap in Sierra Leone?' In *Critical perspectives in transitional justice*, edited by Nicola Palmer, Phil Clark and Danielle Granville, 263–287. Cambridge: Intersentia.

Schreck, Christopher J., and Eric A. Stewart. 2011. 'Victim-offender overlap and its implications for juvenile justice offending and victimization.' In *The Oxford handbook of juvenile crime and juvenile justice*, edited by Barry C. Feld and Donna M. Bishop, 47–70. Oxford: Oxford University Press.

Seekings, Jeremy. 2007. 'Poverty and inequality after apartheid.' 2nd After Apartheid Conference, University of Yale, New Haven, CT, 27–28 April.

Selim, Yvette. 2014. 'The opportunities and challenges of participation in transitional justice: Examples from Nepal.' *Journal of International Development* 29(8):1123–1148

Selim, Yvette, and Tim Murithi. 2011. 'Transitional justice and development: partners for sustainable peace in Africa?' *Journal of Peacebuilding and Development* 6(2):58–72.

Shaw, Rosalind. 2010. 'Linking justice with reintegration? Ex-combatants and the Sierra Leone experiment.' In *Localizing transitional justice interventions and priorities after mass violence*, edited by Rosalind Shaw, Lars Waldorf and Pierre Hazan, 111–132. Stanford, CA: Stanford University Press.

Shaw, Rosalind, and Lars Waldorf. 2010. 'Introduction: Localizing transitional justice.' In *Localizing transitional justice interventions and priorities after mass violence*, edited by Rosalind Shaw, Lars Waldorf and Pierre Hazan, 3–26. Stanford, CA: Stanford University Press.

Shelton, Dinah. 2005. 'The United Nations principles and guidelines on reparations: Context and contents.' In *Out of the ashes: Reparation victims of gross and systematic human rights violations*, edited by Koen De Feyter, S. Parmentier, M. Bossuyt and P. Lemmens, 11–33. Antwerpen: Intersentia.

Sierra Leone TRC. 2005. *Witness to truth: Final report of the TRC*. Sierra Leone: Sierra Leone TRC.

Sriram, Chandra Lekha. 2004. *Confronting past human rights violations: Justice vs peace in times of transition*. New York: Frank Cass.

Sriram, Chandra Lekha. 2009. 'Justice as peace? Liberal peacebuilding and strategies of transitional justice.' In *The liberal peace and the post-war reconstruction*, edited by Roger Mac Ginty and Oliver Richmond, 89–101. London: Routledge.

Sriram, Chandra Lekha, Jemima García-Godos, Johanna Herman, and Olga Martin-Ortega, eds. 2012. *Transitional justice and peacebuilding on the ground: Victims and ex-combatants*. Hoboken, NJ: Taylor and Francis.

Sriram, Chandra Lekha, Olga Martin-Ortega, and Johanna Herman. 2009. *War, conflict and human rights: Theory and practice*. London: Routledge.

Stanley, Elizabeth. 2004. 'Torture, silence and recognition.' *Current Issues in Criminal Justice* 1(5–25):5–25.

Stanley, Elizabeth. 2009. *Torture, truth and justice: The case of Timor Leste*. London: Routledge.

Subotic, Jelena. 2012. 'The transformation of international transitional justice advocacy.' *International Journal of Transitional Justice* 6:106–125.

Taylor, David. 2014.' Victim participation in transitional justice mechanisms: Real power or empty ritual?' www.impunitywatch.org/docs/IW_Discussion_Paper_Victim_Participation1.pdf.

Thapa, Lily, and Deon V. Canyon. 2017. The advancement of women in post-conflict Nepal. In *Online Occasional Paper*. Daniel K. Inouye Asia Pacific Center for Security Studies. http://apcss.org/wp-content/uploads/2010/03/17-Thapa-The-advancement-of-women-in-post-conflict-Nepal.pdf.

Theidon, Kimberely. 2006. 'Justice in transition: The micropolitics of reconciliation in postwar Peru.' *Journal of Conflict Resolution* 50(3):433–457.

Theissen, Gunnar, and Brandon Hamber. 1998. 'A state of denial: White South African's attitudes to the Truth and Reconciliation Commission.' *Indicator South Africa* 15(1):8–12.

Thomson, Susan, and Rosemary Nagy. 2011. 'Law, power and justice: What legalism fails to address in the functioning of Rwanda's gacaca courts.' *International Journal of Transitional Justice* 5(1):11–30.

TRC of Liberia. 2009. *Preliminary findings and determinations*. Liberia: TRC of Liberia.

Truth and Reconciliation Commission. 2003. 'The TRC report.' www.justice.gov.za/trc/report/index.htm.

UN. 2004. *The rule of law and transitional justice in conflict and post-conflict societies. Report of the Secretary-General*. New York: United Nations.

UN. 2010. Guidance note of the Secretary-General: United Nations' Approach to Transitional Justice. www.un.org/ruleoflaw/files/TJ_Guidance_Note_March_2010FINAL.pdf.

UN General Assembly. 2006. *Report of the Secretary-General: Uniting our strengths: Enhancing United Nations support for the rule of law*. New York: United Nations General Assembly.

UN General Assembly. 2011. *Report of the special rapporteur on the promotion of truth, justice, reparation and guarantees of non-recurrence, Pablo de Greiff*. Human Rights Council. www.ohchr.org/Documents/Issues/Truth/A-HRC-30-42.pdf.

UN Secretary General. 2011. The rule of law and transitional justice in conflict and post-conflict societies: Report of the Secretary-General. www.un.org/ruleoflaw/files/S_2011_634EN.pdf.

UNDP. 2012. *Fifth consolidated annual progress report on activities implemented under the United Nations Peace Fund for Nepal: Report of the administrative agent of the United Nations Peace Fund for Nepal for the period 1 January to 31 December 2011*. Multi-Partner Trust Fund Office, Bureau of Management United Nations Development Programme. http://mdtf.undp.org/document/download/9127.

Vinck, Patrick, and Phuong Pham. 2008. 'Ownership and participation in transitional justice mechanisms: A sustainable human development perspective from Eastern DRC.' *International Journal of Transitional Justice* 2(3):398–411.

Waldorf, Lars. 2009. Introduction. In *Disarming the past: Transitional justice and ex-combatants*, edited by Ana Cutter Patel, Pablo De Greiff and Lars Waldorf, 14–34. New York: Social Science Research Council.

Walgrave, Lode, Ivo Aertsen, Stephan Parmentier, Inge Vanfaechem, and Estelle Zinsstag. 2013. 'Why restorative justice matters for criminology.' *Restorative Justice* 1(2):159–167.

Weinstein, Harvey M. 2011. 'Editorial note: The myth of closure, the illusion of reconciliation: Final thoughts on five years as co-Editor-in-Chief.' *International Journal of Transitional Justice* 5:1–10.

White, Sarah. 1996. 'Depoliticising the development: The uses and abuses of participation.' *Development in Practice* 6(1):6–15.

Wilson, Richard A. 2001. *The politics of truth and reconciliation in South Africa: Legitimizing the post-apartheid state.* New York: Cambridge University Press.

Yarwood, Lisa (ed.). 2013. *Women and transitional justice: The experience of women as participants.* New York: Routledge.

4 The civil conflict

> Children used to play a game called 'thieves and police' but during the conflict children in Rolpa changed the name of the game to 'the Maoists and the army'.
> (Male interpreter, Rolpa, 10 September 2012)

The post-conflict environment in Nepal can be best understood in the context of the formation and continuation of economic, social and political injustices. While the conflict emerged from these injustices, it did not eradicate them. These factors impacted Nepali society, eventually catalysing the conflict. This chapter provides an overview of the evolution of the Nepali state (1768–1996), focusing on the role of the monarchy and Hinduism.[1] It then outlines the conflict (1996–2006) – including the causes, trajectory and impact – followed by the road to peace.

The evolution of the state (1768–1996)

From the Shah to the Rana regime

The monarchy and Hinduism were crucial components of the evolution of the Nepali state and national culture. The modern state of Nepal emerged in the late eighteenth century when Prithvi Narayan Shah, a king of the Gorkha region, unified several independent kingdoms. For almost two and half centuries royal families ruled Nepal and the kings were regarded as reincarnations of the Hindu god, Vishnu (Madeley 2009, 185).

Hinduism, as a religion and polity, legitimised the Shah dynasty of Gorkha (1768–1846) deeming the king sovereign lord, protector of subjects and territory, guardian and the source of spiritual power (Sharma 1997, 475). Despite the diversity and plurality of Nepal's religions, languages and traditions, the Shah regime and subsequent Ranas and Panchas rulers, sought 'to develop Nepal as a homogeneous, monolithic and unitary state providing protection for one language (Nepali), one caste group (hill Bahun-Chhetri), and one religion (Hindu)' (Hachhethu 2003, 7). It was on this basis that the Nepali national identity was developed. Disparity among hill high-caste groups and other social groups (including ethnic and caste groups such as *Janajati, Madheshya* and Dalit) increased through Hinduisation, institutionalisation of the caste system, the spread of a dominant national Nepali culture (*parbatiya*) and the centralisation of politics and administration (Hachhethu 2003, 7). Hinduisation created a feudal oligarchy (see Whelpton 2005, 49). Land ownership was directly related to the Hindu caste hierarchy, with the higher castes having larger ownership while lower castes had little or no ownership (Dahal 1995, 159).

In 1846 a military leader, Jang Bahadur, seized power and effectively relegated the then Shah monarch, King Tribhuvan, to a ceremonial role. Bahadur changed his name to Rana and the Rana family created strong political alliances, married into the royal family and made key government positions hereditary (Marshall Cavendish Corporation 2007, 529). The Rana period (1846–1951) further fermented exclusion by institutionalising the (Hindu) caste hierarchy through *Muluki Ain* (a national Civil Code) in 1854. The Code subsumed all Hindu and non-Hindu-groups, creating a rigid social hierarchy based on caste and ethnicity (von Einsiedel, Malone, and Pradhan 2012, 5). According to Hachhethu, '[b]y putting ethnic groups into the fold of Hindu based hierarchical caste system, the Code translated diversity into inequality' (2003, 5). During the Rana period, laws were promulgated that benefited ruling elites, the high-caste Bahuns and Chhetris, and institutionalised Hinduism and Nepali as the official religion and language, which effectively marginalised the myriad of other religions, languages and cultures (Thapa 2012, 39).

The Panchayat system

In 1951 an armed revolution was launched by the Nepali Congress (a major political party). Along with approximately 50,000 demonstrators, the Nepali Congress sought to oust the Rana regime to facilitate the return of King Tribhuvan, who had been exiled in India since November 1950. The subsequent 1951 Delhi agreement between King Tribhuvan, the Nepali Congress and the Ranas ushered in the first phase of experimentation with democratic reform (see Pfaff-Czarnecka 2004, 168). King Tribhuvan was restored to the throne and the leader of Nepali Congress, Matrika Prasad Koirala, became Prime Minister. The following decade of parliamentary democracy included the promulgation of the 1951 Interim Constitution and the 1959 Constitution of Nepal. According to Lawoti:

> With the end of the Rana regime and the advent of democracy in 1951, grievances and dissatisfaction began to be aired publicly. The marginalized groups started to mobilize and openly challenged the CHHE [Caste Hill Hindu Elite] domination of the state.
>
> (2012, 134)

King Mahendra succeeded King Tribhuvan in 1956 and dismissed the government in 1960. In 1962 King Mahendra promulgated a new Constitution that created a *Panchayat* system under an absolute monarchy, enshrined Nepali as the lingua franca and declared Nepal as a Hindu kingdom. Under this system political parties were banned and the King had executive powers. Thus, almost one century after the *Muluki Ain*,[2] the king and Hinduism were reinstated as the core aspects of Nepali nationalism (see Hachhethu 2003, 7).

The *Panchayat* period, which lasted for three decades, was characterised by components of the former regimes (Hinduism, the monarchy and the Nepali language). This period was encapsulated by slogans such as 'our king, our country' and 'one language, one dress, and one culture' and a government agenda of decentralisation, development and modernisation (Hachhethu 2003, 6–7; Pradhan 2003, 11). The *Panchayat* system preserved and reproduced an exclusionary Nepali national identity (Pandey 2010, 40). Throughout the *Panchayat* regime, marginalised groups were occasionally able to assert their identities and resist cultural homogenisation, but ultimately the ruling elites and upper castes were able to maintain their ethnic and cultural hegemony (Lawoti 2012, 134–135; Pradhan 2003, 10–13).

Thus, despite the democratic reforms in the 1950s, power remained concentrated in the monarchy and was held in place by a unitary national identity and the modernisation/development agenda. Over time, the increasing disparity between the elite upper class and marginalised groups grew, and this sowed seeds of discontent that led to the fracture of the polity in the 1990s.

The 1990 people's movement

In the context of the opening of democratic space, which provided room for dissent and mobilisation, ethnic consciousness and awareness increased (Hachhethu 2003, 11–14; Lawoti 2012, 135; Pradhan 2003, 13–17). The changes during this period prompted the government of Nepal, in 1989, to adopt the International Labour Organization Convention No. 169 on the rights of indigenous and tribal people. Nepal witnessed the rise of Dalit and caste/ethnic politics and the emergence of more conventional civil society actors making demands for the state to address the pervasive inequality, exclusion and discrimination (Gellner and Hachhethu 2008, 20–21; Shah 2003, 144). The right to self-determination and ethnic autonomy were core to these actors' demands for state restructuring (Tamang 2006, 285). There was particular focus on the development of various languages, on Nepal being declared a secular state, and on equitable access to political and economic resources (Pradhan 2003, 14–15). Twenty-one *Janajati* groups renamed themselves indigenous groups[3] and formed the Nepal Federation of Nationalities (NEFEN), later becoming the Nepal Federation of Indigenous Nationalities (NEFIN) in 1991, with the aim of 'documenting, preserving and promoting [the] cultures, languages, religion, customs, [and] traditions of the Indigenous Nationalities of Nepal and to assist them in developing and obtaining equal rights' (NEFIN 2004 quoted in Cailmail 2008, 8; see also Hangen 2010; Pradhan 2003, 16).

The *Panchayat* system was toppled by a popular movement (known as *Jana Andolan I*) leading Nepal into its second phase of democracy in 1990. The movement comprised various political parties from both ends of the political spectrum (including the Nepali Congress and the United Liberation Front) as well as protestors, who demanded that the multiparty system be restored. At the conclusion of the street protests, a select group of leaders from *Jana Andolan I*, the Nepali Congress and the United Left Front came together with representatives from the royal palace to draft the 1990 Constitution. The 1990 Constitution seemingly transformed Nepal from an absolutist monarchy, partyless system to 'a multi-ethnic, multi-lingual, democratic, independent indivisible, sovereign, Hindu and constitutional monarchical kingdom' (Nepal Constitution 1990, 3).

The Constitution prohibited discrimination based on caste, ethnicity, race or religion and bestowed protection on various communities to preserve their culture and language. Yet, despite these seemingly progressive provisions, the Constitution still declared Nepal to be a Hindu kingdom and Nepali to be the official language. Organised opposition to the declaration of a Hindu state predominately came from the Maoists, who sought a secular state, and the ethnic (*Janajati*) movement (see below) as well as from religious minorities (Toffin 2006, 233). Discontent was also widespread among non-elite, non-high caste groups on the basis of religion, ethnicity, language, caste and class. Onta contends that '[b]y declaring the Nepali language as the "language of the nation" and Nepal's "official language" and calling all other mother tongues spoken within Nepal "national languages," the Constitution gave at most a secondary status to these other languages' (2006, 319).

The introduction of multiparty democracy brought an 'awakening' of expectations regarding the transformation of the state, politics and societal forces (Pfaff-Czarnecka 2004, 167). As it became apparent that the changes were largely rhetorical, frustrations increased that these expectations would again not be realised (Lawoti 2008). The constitutional power-sharing arrangements between the king and parliament did not alleviate nor adequately address the inequitable political representation that existed along ethnic, religious, caste, gender and regional lines, and for the most part, the status quo of the disproportionate concentration of power and structures of political exclusion did not change with this democratisation process (Kievelitz and Polzer 2002, 26; Lawoti 2005). Upadhya asserts that '[t]hose who felt short-changed by the political transformations of 1951 and 1960 were particularly susceptible to the surge of frustration' (2003, 42). The historic apathy continued. In fact the marginalisation of minorities not only continued but grew (Gurung 2004).

Despite six years of democratic politics, 'the political system remained a reflection of the past legacy' characterised by inequitable political representation and disproportionate power remaining in the hands of a few political elites (Upadhyay 2008, 79; Kievelitz and Polzer 2002, 26). In the wake of three decades of the isolationist *Panchayat* regime and a series of short-lived governments, these frustrations were exacerbated by concerns regarding political instability. It was the disconnect between expectations and reality that brought the *Panchayat* regime 'to its knees in 1990' (Whelpton 2005, 154).

The civil conflict (1996–2006)

The causes of the conflict

As I have begun to demonstrate, the People's War (*Jana Yuddha*) in Nepal from 1996 to 2006 had many causes. The (qualitative and quantitative) literature on these causes of the conflict from a diverse range of disciplines is extensive although at times contradictory; however, 'the take-away is that a combination of grievances and opportunity set the structural stage for the conflict' (Shneiderman et al. 2016, 2057). I examine several main themes: poverty, a lack of economic opportunities and underdevelopment, political exclusion and ethnic cleavages.[4]

Poverty and a lack of economic opportunities and underdevelopment were key causes of the conflict. The Nepali state did not effectively engage with the Nepali countryside and this meant that vast segments of the population in remote areas experienced poverty, a lack of access to basic services and facilities (e.g. education, health and water) and less economic growth (including employment opportunities) (Lawoti 2010, 21). The correlation between poverty, social status and caste/ethnicity means that ethnic groups already economically and institutionally excluded were impacted the most (Friedman 2005, 70–71) (see below).[5]

Poverty has not only been presented as a cause of the conflict but a consequence of it. Poverty provided a legitimising discourse for violence while the conflict resulted in deepening poverty, particularly in the poorest areas. Poverty also was a factor in motivating people, mostly young people, to join the Maoists. Recruits earned approximately 3000 NPR per month (Kievelitz and Polzer 2002, 26). Do and Iyer (2010) contend this was due to the lack of opportunity/unemployment coupled with unfulfilled expectations and lower education status. It is notable, however, that the Maoist heartland in mid-western Nepal was not the poorest area of Nepal.

Despite recent improvements, Nepal remains one of the poorest countries in the world. In 2015 Nepal was ranked 144th out of 188 countries in the UNDP Human Development Index (UNDP 2016). Around one-third of the population lives on less than USD $14 per person per month (IFAD 2013, 1). The majority of rural households have little or no access to safe drinking water, sanitation, primary healthcare, education and other basic services (IFAD 2013, 1). According to IFAD the rural poor 'generally have large families, very small landholdings or none at all, and high rates of illiteracy. They are also concentrated in specific ethnic, caste and marginalized groups, particularly those of the lowest caste (Dalits), indigenous peoples (*Janajatis*) and women' (2013, 2). This will be discussed further in Chapter 7.

Political exclusion of marginalised groups also led to the conflict. Political power in Nepal was centralised in Kathmandu, which exacerbated the neglect of the periphery (Friedman 2005, 70–71; Hachhethu 2003, 8; Sharma and Donini 2010; Kievelitz and Polzer 2002, 26). A consequence of this centralisation was that other state agencies and local governments were ineffective and unresponsive because they lacked authority and resources (Lawoti 2010, 21). Not only was politics centralised in Kathmandu, it was concentrated predominately in the hands of male, upper caste hill Bahun, Chhetri and Newari elites. These groups disregarded issues in other areas (the mountains and Terai) and those that pertained to different castes, ethnic groups, classes and women, essentially excluding many Nepalis from meaningful participation and nation-building processes (Upreti 2007, 4). Dalits, who comprised over 20 per cent of the population, were extremely under-represented in the political landscape. Indeed, '[i]n occupying this position of marginalization and disempowerment, Dalits were quickly identified as a base of ready support for the Maoist insurgency' (Center for Human Rights and Global Justice 2005, 16).

Thus, even in the 1990s with 'the formal trappings of a democracy', Nepal remained politically exclusionary (Lawoti 2010, 19). For example, despite directives within the 1990 Constitution to increase people's participation through decentralisation, in practice the state remained centralised and it was into this vacuum that the Maoists entered with their agenda (Upadhya 2003, 52). Also, the winner-take-all 'majoritarian democracy' that was adopted severely limited the political space in governance for minority cultural and ideological groups, leading to further alienation (Lawoti 2010, 19). In fact, as noted above, the pervasive, deliberate and systematic exclusion of indigenous people actually increased during the post-1990 democratic era (Lawoti 2010, 10–11).[6]

The historical legacy of ethnic cleavages also contributed to the conflict. In multi-ethnic Nepal it was not ethnic *differences* that caused conflict but the ethnic *inequalities* between groups (horizontal inequalities), which led to violent group mobilisation (Brown et al. 2011, 114–119, Stewart 2002, Tiwari 2010). Horizontal inequalities (HIs) are multidimensional, encompassing the social, economic, cultural and political realms. Specifically, they include inequalities in ownership of assets and access to services (socio-economic HIs), inequalities in group distribution of political power (political HIs) and differences in the hierarchical status of different groups' norms, practices and customs (cultural status HIs) (Brown et al. 2011, 14). Given the historical legacy of Nepal, particularly the Hinduisation of the caste structure in Nepal as discussed above, these HIs have been attributed as being key causes of the conflict. This has been supported by Bray, Lunde and Mushred (2003) who conclude that the legacy of oppression of the lower castes catalysed and led to their support of the Maoists. Also Murshed and Gates' spatial-horizontal inequality study found that grievances (not greed) explained the intensity (but not the cause) of the conflict (2003). While these findings have been challenged,[7] the issue of ethnicity and ethnic mobilisation remains vital to understanding not only the causes of the conflict but also the current dynamics and social forces at play in Nepal (discussed further below).

Enter the Maoists

It was against this backdrop that the Maoists embarked upon an armed struggle with the aim of creating a secular republican state in Nepal, initially with very little support. The Maoists effectively tapped into over two centuries of fermented discontent, making the demands of marginalised groups their own (Lawoti 2012, 136). As Thapa explains, 'when the Maoists arrived on the scene, there was already a groundswell of grievances they could readily exploit with their all-embracing rhetoric that promised a sea change in social relations and an end to all forms of discrimination' (2012, 46). Unlike the political regimes of the past, the Maoist rhetoric cut through ethnic and class boundaries, calling for ethnic autonomy and the right to self-determination. The Maoists were able to exploit the frustrations of excluded groups and entice them to join their movement by promising them political space and, perhaps more importantly, access to modernity via economic resources and opportunities (Thapa 2012, 51; Shakya 2012, 122).

In fact, the Maoists' grievances in 1996 echoed the unfulfilled promises of the 1990 Constitution. They also covered some of the historical injustices of the traditional feudal culture that affected the Dalits, *Janajatis*, poor peasants and villagers (Riveros 2004, 6; Jha 2011, 89). Through an armed struggle the Maoists sought to establish a 'new people's democracy' (*naulo janbad*). The objectives of the insurgency were encapsulated in the 'Forty Point Plan' submitted to Prime Minister Sher Bahadur Deuba on 4 February 1996. The Forty Point Plan had three categories of demands: those relating to nationalism; political demands related to the public and wellbeing; and, economic and social demands, related to the people's living standards. The main objectives were to abolish the monarchy, to establish a people's republic committed to the principles of gender and caste equality, to set up a constituent assembly to draft a new constitution (something left-wing parties had demanded since the 1950s) and to provide services for poor rural areas. These demands were aimed at empowering disadvantaged groups (e.g. women, lower castes and other minorities) and counteracting injustice, social inequality, corruption and foreign domination of the country (Paffenholz 2006, 13).

By linking the insurgency to the causes of exclusion and discrimination the Maoists were able to justify their insurgency (Dhakal and Subedi 2006, 410). Tamang explains that '[i]nstead of condemning caste/ethnic based movements as reactionary, or viewing them simply as struggles by backward groups for sympathy, the CPN[-]M has come to recognize these movements as necessary allies' (2006, 284). Indeed, it was in the Maoists' vested interests to mobilise the socially excluded in their class war because of the many areas of convergence between the Maoist and indigenous agenda (Gurung 2005, 13).

The trajectory of the conflict

In October 1995 the Maoists began mobilising their cadres and expanding their support base in Rolpa and Rukum (OHCHR 2012, 38). The following month the police, loyal to the monarchy, launched Operation Romeo, a campaign that targeted Maoist sympathisers in Rolpa. Police actions included ill-treatment, torture, murder and rape and resulted in a large proportion of locals supporting or joining the Maoists. On 4 February 1996, a few days before the Forty Point Plan deadline, the Maoists proclaimed a People's War, which originated with attacks in Rolpa and Rukum (Mid-Western region), Sindhuli (Central region) and Gorkha (Western region). Based on the ideology of Marxism–Leninism–Maoism, the Maoists adopted a guerrilla strategy establishing bases in the rural and remote areas. As they gradually gained armed control of districts they were able to garner extensive political power (Center for Human Rights and Global Justice 2005, 2–3).

The conflict was initially concentrated in a few Maoist strongholds in western Nepal. Weapons were seized from armed people and local people were forced to pay revolutionary levies. Local people were also forced to help with construction and carrying supplies and some were forcibly recruited to join the rebels. I was told that if a family had more than one child then they were forced to send one child to join the Maoists.[8] The Maoist force gradually grew; as a Maoist Commissar told me:

> At first we had a little force. In the process of fighting we became a larger force. We became a bigger party through the conflict. As our power support increased we made an alternative local people's regime, even a court. We were a battalion then we became a brigade then a division.[9]

Initially, the Maoist insurgency was deemed to be a 'security problem' in the ambit of the police. However, the police were not well trained or equipped for counter-insurgency so this enabled the Maoist forces to widen their control (HRW 2004, 3). It is alleged that the police retaliated against Maoist attacks on police stations using methods that violated human rights (OHCHR 2012, 39–40). Security forces harassed those suspected of being Maoist supporters or informants. I was told that if someone was caught carrying long-life food items like chocolate or noodles they were suspected of providing these items to the Maoists who were hiding in the hills.[10] In May 1998 state forces launched a violent crackdown on the Maoists in the Western and Mid-Western regions in what was called Operation Kilo Sierra II. Operations such as these arguably helped to increase civilian support for the Maoists.

The role of humanitarian and human rights actors increased. In 1998 the International Committee of the Red Cross began monitoring the conflict and the following year it established a permanent presence in Nepal (OHCHR 2012, 41). Approximately two years later an independent national human rights institution, the National Human Rights Commission, was established;

the major functions of the commission included to conduct investigations into human rights violations and to continuously monitor the human rights situation in the country. In February 2001 the UN Special Rapporteur on extrajudicial, summary or arbitrary executions raised concerns about the unlawful killings and other human rights violations carried out by the Nepal Police and the Maoists (OHCHR 2012, 41). These are discussed further in Chapter 5.

Maoist political opponents, school principals and teachers, and those who disobeyed orders were among those who were publicly shamed, and the Maoists killed alleged informants or thugs. A Nepali NGO worker from Rukum, one of the worst affected districts, explained:

> People were very affected by the Maoists. Everyone saw killing and people's necks being cut and heard gunfire. There was torture, when people were cut they would put chilli or salt … If you followed a different ideology that was not the Maoists' you were forced to follow theirs, if you disagree, you were removed and your house was taken over by the Maoists; when people returned everything was gone … [T]hings were taken by Maoists and by locals.[11]

As has already been indicated, the Maoists were not solely responsible for the brutality. The security forces were involved in disappearances, torture and sexual assault among other human rights violations. A NGO worker described that her 27-year-old husband was travelling to Doti (a district in Nepal) to do an exam. On the way the army captured him and accused him of being part of the Maoists. In her words, 'they put him in mud with only his head outside'.[12] They beat him and planned to kill him the following day but instead they released him. Now she reports he is depressed and cries a lot, and that 'mentally he disappeared'.[13]

In regions controlled by the Maoists, local government structures were replaced by Revolutionary People's Councils (*Jana Adalat*) that arguably assumed state functions including those relating to health, education and the judiciary (Paffenholz 2006, 13; Pattanaik 2011, 103). A Maoist Commissar told me that these Councils mostly passed land rulings.[14] There was reportedly approximately 4,000 land transactions passed in Rukum and 3,500 of these transactions still remain contested (Basnet and Bk 2017). The Commissar also explained:

> If someone did something wrong then we would make a decision in front of a gathering of people. The main outcome was to take them to labour camp because we don't have permanent jails. If they commit a serious crime they must do hard work but if it is not serious then it might be one or two days' work in labour camp. They often constructed a bridge or a road or a track.[15]

The Maoists extorted cash from local elites and government employees. Police stations were targeted and seized weapons were used in the conflict. Institutions such as banks and NGOs were also targeted which resulted in many shutting their offices or drastically scaling down their work in certain areas. The number of police was dramatically reduced and frequently teachers and chairpersons of Village District Committees fled. Abductions and kidnappings were carried out. Schools in particular were targeted. In one village I met with a principal and teachers who explained that they were harassed during the conflict and that the Maoists had murdered one of their colleagues.[16] Another principal told me he was threatened and fled to India during the conflict.[17]

In 2001 the Army was deployed in 16 district headquarters (OHCHR 2012, 42) and the Armed Police Force (a paramilitary police force) was established. The Armed Police Force was created to support the Nepal Police in containing the insurgency. On 1 June 2001, according to the official story, Crown Prince Dipendra shot and killed King Birendra, the Queen and eight other members of the royal family and fatally wounded himself. The late King Birendra's brother, Gyanendra, ascended to the throne. The following month, in July 2001, Sher Bahadur Deuba became the Prime Minister and he announced a ceasefire with the Maoists, and the Maoists reciprocated leading to the first round of peace negotiations (OHCHR 2012, 44).

In September 2001 the formation of the People's Liberation Army (the Maoist army) was announced, although 'the Maoists had been developing their military capabilities since launching the "People's War" and had active combatants operating under a chain of command and engaging in military action long before officially forming the Army' (OHCHR 2012, 16). In November 2001 the Maoists resumed military operations and for the first time deliberately targeted an army barracks (in Dang). After the failure of the first round of peace talks in November 2001, the government declared a state of emergency, called the Royal Nepalese Army against the Maoist rebels (a measure that the king's brother, the late King Birendra, had always opposed) and promulgated the *Terrorist and Disruptive Activities (Control and Punishment) Ordinance* (TADO).[18] TADO granted wide powers to state security forces in relation to detention and empowering the Royal Nepalese Army to take over the counter-insurgency operations. Under the Ordinance the Maoists were now classified as a terrorist organisation. The insurgency, initially deemed to be a security problem in the ambit of the police, was now elevated to a military problem.

From this point the nature of the conflict changed dramatically. Conflict-related deaths and disappearances increased significantly with the escalation and spread of the conflict. The security forces adopted disappearances as a counterinsurgency tool (Tyynela 2014, 79). According to OHCHR:

> Faced with an often-unseen enemy, Security Forces used cordon and search operations, conducting house-to-house searches, often at night and

> in large numbers. During these operations, according to Amnesty International, Security Forces often arrested people whose names featured on lists provided by the local administration. The lists reportedly contained the names of people who were suspected of having provided food or shelter to the Maoists and who had attended Maoist meetings during the ceasefire. Allegations of human rights abuses increased dramatically following the declaration of the state of emergency and the mobilization of the army, particularly with respect to extrajudicial killings and disappearances by Security Forces.
>
> (2012, 46)

The armed revolution became increasingly violent with the Maoist insurgents targeting police officers, government officials, army depots and banks (Do and Iyer 2010, 736). By the latter half of 2003 the Maoists controlled several districts in eastern and western Nepal and in August 2004 managed to blockade Kathmandu for several days (Do and Iyer 2010, 737; see also Paffenholz 2006, 14). Attacks by the Maoists and the security forces continued.

Once the Maoists had most of the rural parts of Nepal under their control (by the government's own admission this was around January 2005), the Maoists declared a unilateral ceasefire and commenced talks with seven major political parties (the Seven Party Alliance[19]) 'to present a common front against the monarchy' (Do and Iyer 2010, 737). A 12-point agreement was brokered in India between the Maoists and the Seven Party Alliance in 2005. This paved the way for a popular uprising known as *Jana Andolan II*. On the nineteenth day of protests, as the movement garnered more public support and international support for King Gyanendra waned, King Gyanendra was forced to relinquish power and reinstate the dissolved parliament (on 24 April 2006). This created conditions for the Maoist ceasefire and another round of peace talks. The conflict concluded with the signing of the Comprehensive Peace Agreement between the Maoists and the Seven Party Alliance on 21 November 2006. Ultimately, the Maoists joined the transitional government, abandoning their call to arms and returned to mainstream politics. Details of the peace process will be discussed below.

Impacts of the conflict

The conflict impacted the majority of the country. Originating in four districts, by 2006 the conflict had spread to most of the 75 districts, with only two districts (Manang and Mustang) not reporting casualties (Tiwari 2007, 3). In relation to many human rights violations there has been difficulties determining which side (the security forces or the Maoists) were the culprits as people were frequently victimised by both sides because of suspicions that they were helping 'the enemy' (Pyakurel 2011, 77). Marginalised ethnic and caste communities were disproportionately affected by the conflict because, as noted above, these groups were more willing to support the Maoists and/or were targeted for Maoist recruitment which led to widespread victimisation by security forces (Advocacy Forum and ICTJ 2010, 46).

There are discrepancies between the figures relating to deaths, injuries and disappearances issued by the government (Ministry of Peace and Reconstruction) and those issued by humanitarian, human rights and international organisations (e.g. International Committee of the Red Cross, Informal Sector Service Centre and victims' groups) and to date no consensus has been reached (see, for example, Nepal Monitor 2011). Government figures have been revised several times based on data collected by a number of government task forces. According to the Informal Sector Service Centre, a leading Nepali human rights organisation, there were 15,027 fatalities with the state responsible for approximately two thirds of this figure (INSEC 2010, 13). The Ministry of Peace and Reconstruction has frequently revised the number of deaths, increasing it significantly in 2009 by 3,000 people, as more people, particularly those in the villages, lodged complaints about losing relatives during the conflict. In 2012 the Ministry of Peace and Reconstruction declared that 12,686 people were killed during the conflict (Ministry of Peace and Reconstruction 2014) although this figure has subsequently been revised. For a breakdown of fatalities according to OHCHR by the security forces (SF) and the Maoists (CPN-M) see OHCHR (2012, 54).

According to the United Nations Working Group on Enforced or Involuntary Disappearances, during 2003 and 2004 Nepal had the highest number of disappeared people in the world (Advocacy Forum 2010). The Ministry of Peace and Reconstruction and the International Committee of the Red Cross report that approximately 1,300 people were disappeared during the conflict (see Amnesty International 2014). However, the number of complaints to the National Human Rights Commission regarding disappeared people far exceeds the estimated number of missing people, with 3,397 reported disappearances by August 2010. In fact, some victims' groups (e.g. Society of the Families of the Disappeared) and local NGOs claim that this number is much higher (Nepal Monitor 2011). Interestingly, in my interviews I was told that some families of people working abroad in the Gulf falsely reported their loved ones disappeared (see Chapter 7). More recently, in August 2016, the International Committee of the Red Cross and the Nepal Red Cross Society provided an updated list of missing persons, which reported the number of conflict-related missing people was 1,334.

The majority of internally displaced persons were displaced from the Mid-Western region, where the conflict originated and the fighting was the most intense (Internal Displacement Monitoring Centre 2012). This is a major reason why I chose to conduct research in Rolpa, a Mid-Western district that was a Maoist stronghold (see Chapter 2). The reported numbers of internally displaced people during the conflict vary significantly with the Ministry of Peace and Reconstruction citing 89,000 people compared with the UN estimate of 50,000 people (Internal Displacement Monitoring Centre 2013). These figures do not include the thousands of people believed to have been displaced by post-conflict criminal and separatist violence in the Terai region (Internal Displacement Monitoring Centre 2013) (see Chapter 1).

Women fought in the conflict. Interviews with Maoist combatants indicate that the egalitarian ideology adopted by the Maoists – 'with its promise of gender equality, social justice and social inclusion – was tremendously appealing to women' (Goswami 2015, 3). However, the Maoists also forced families to contribute one member per family to join their forces so in some cases, particularly in rural, remote areas, women were forced to join the Maoists (Goswami 2015, 5). While the exact numbers of female combatants remains unknown, it is believed that 40 per cent of the Maoists combatants were women (Upreti and Kolås 2016, 3). Women performed combatant and non-combat military roles, including intelligence gathering and political mobilisation (Goswami 2015, 6). During the conflict (and afterwards in the cantonments) female combatants generally lived according to 'Maoist values'. Under these values women had much greater equality than prior to the conflict (e.g. they were able to marry outside of their ethnic group or caste) (see Pettigrew 2012); however, this posed difficulties once they left the cantonments. At the end of the conflict there were 3,846 female Verified Minors and Late Recruits, comprising approximately 20 per cent of the total number of combatants (Thapa and Canyon 2017, 2) (discussed below). Drawing on the research of Pettigrew, Shneiderman and Manchanda, Yadav argues (2016, 98 and 161) that the conflict 'created an enabling space for women's empowerment'. She explains:

> women's participation in the People's War has not only changed women's lives but it has also led Nepal towards radical social transformation. Despite the criticism that the Maoist revolution has not brought the promised changes to women's lives … the Maoist revolution has broadened women's horizons. It provided women with knowledge and skills to question doxic practices (the gender discriminatory practices which were never questioned before), which have opened up the possibility for women to critically reflect on their own status as well as the status of others. Such critical reflexivity is leading to changing performance among women and, due to the changing performance of women, the dominant image of womanhood is shifting.
>
> (Yadav 2016, 98)

Women were also subjected to detainment, torture and rape and were murdered by both the Maoists and the security forces during the conflict. While both sides are accused of committing sexual assaults, the majority of the allegations are against the Royal Nepalese Army, which used rape to punish female Maoist combatants and sympathisers (OHCHR 2012, 23). Despite the prevalence of other conflict-related human rights violations (e.g. enforced disappearances, killings and torture), there is little information about sexual violence. This is, in part, because there has been little attention given to these violations by organisations (including the National Human Rights Commission and national and international organisations) and because during the conflict there was limited reporting by females due to insecurity, cultural stigmatisation and fear of retaliation (Advocacy Forum 2010, 8, 45). Similarly, there is little known about the impacts of conflict-related trauma. This is particularly significant as there are an estimated 500,000 families affected; that is families with one or more family member killed, disappeared or displaced with many affected by psychological trauma. There are an estimated 9000 conflict widows, with only half having received monetary compensation (Thapa and Canyon 2017, 4) (see Chapter 7).

The conflict resulted in significant property loss and damage. Property was confiscated while in other instances people emigrated because of threats (Lawoti and Pahari 2010, 310–311). According to the Ministry of Peace and Reconstruction there were 12,657 incidents of private property seizure or damage. Public property (e.g. schools, police posts and government offices) was also damaged. In 2007, soon after the end of the conflict, the Ministry of Peace and Reconstruction estimated that the total destruction of government property was worth approximately 5 billion NPR. Ultimately, the conflict resulted in a heavy impact not only in terms of the loss of life but also economically and psychologically.

The road to peace

The Comprehensive Peace Agreement and the Constitution

Similar to the political practices of the 1990s, important decisions and agreements during the peace process were completed quickly. Lawoti asserts that much of the peace process was 'hashed out in 11th-hour backroom deals by a very small group of top leaders of the major parties' (2012, 140). He adds that most of these leaders were elite, upper caste, male and of advanced age (Lawoti 2012, 140). The document they produced, the Comprehensive Peace Agreement (CPA), contains a broad range of provisions including those relating to the Nepali army and the Maoists army, normalisation measures, the restructuring of the state and the resolution of problems related to ethnic, class, gender and regional differences (CPA 2006; ICG 2007, 10).

The interim government consisted of eight political parties, including the Maoists, who had taken the final step in transforming themselves from a rebel army to a mainstream political party by registering as a political party. This was a significant step in the consolidation of the peace process (Security Council Report 2007a). The month after the signing of the Comprehensive Peace Agreement, both sides came to an agreement with respect to the management and monitoring of the armies and their arms. This was formalised in the Monitoring of the Management of Arms and Armies agreement (8 December 2006), which was subsequently signed by the UN.

The Interim Constitution was endorsed by the Constituent Assembly on 1 January 2007 replacing the 1990 Constitution. The drafting of the Interim Constitution involved a 'more consultative process', with close to 4,000 submissions submitted to the 15-member drafting committee (Farasat and Hayner 2009, 19). The Interim Constitution declared Nepal 'an independent, indivisible, sovereign, secular, inclusive and fully democratic State' (Article 4) with a common aspiration for multi-ethnic, multi-lingual, multi-religious, multi-cultural characteristics (Article 3). It contains a number of provisions regarding citizenship, fundamental rights, the executive, the constituent assembly, legislative procedure and the judiciary. A notable inclusion was the right to equality, which prohibited discrimination on the grounds of gender, religion, race, caste, tribe, origin, language or ideological conviction, and with specific provisions on the prohibition against racial discrimination and untouchability (Articles 13 and 14), cornerstones of the former regimes. The Interim Constitution provides that the Constituent Assembly has a dual role of executive and legislative, and that it is charged with drafting Nepal's permanent constitution. As will be discussed below, this dual-structure led to a range of issues including lengthy delays in passing TJ-related legislation.

After being postponed twice the Constituent Assembly elections were held on 10 April 2008. As a surprise to many CPN-M, the Maoist political party, became the largest party, winning almost two-thirds of the 601 seats. Two major political parties in Nepal followed, with the Nepali Congress winning 110 seats closely followed by the Communist Party of Nepal (Unified Marxist-Leninist) with 103 seats. Despite its success, the CPN-M, not having won a clear two-thirds majority, was not able to govern in its own right. Thus they were forced into discussions to form a coalition government.

It was during the first meeting of the Constituent Assembly that Nepal's 240 year monarchy was abolished. By August 2008 a coalition government was formed (with the CPN-M, the Communist Party of Nepal (Unified Marxist-Leninist) and the ethnic-based Madhesi Peoples Right Forum), and Ram Baran Yadav (a member of the Nepali Congress party) was elected as the President and Prachanda (the CPN-M Chairman) was elected as Prime Minister of the Federal Democratic Republic of Nepal.

Thus, by 2008, there had been several ground-breaking achievements, including the official abolition of the monarchy, the elections for the Constituent Assembly and the declaration of Nepal as a federal democratic republic, all of which were major objectives of the Maoist insurgency. Ultimately, the Hindu monarchy and Hindu state were 'formally eliminated in the course of the peace process' (Lawoti 2012, 138). In short, '[w]hether referred to as an insurgency, a rebellion, a revolution, a movement, a conflict, or a civil war, the decade-long Maoist-led "People's War" dramatically altered the social and political landscape in Nepal' (Shneiderman et al. 2016, 2054).

However, while the conflict resulted in significant changes to the political landscape in Nepal, since then there has been significant stalling, fragmentation and paralysis. The Constitution referred to Nepal being a secular state and a republic but it was silent on federalism (Thapa and Ramsbotham 2017, 9). According to International Crisis Group (2016, 4), during this transition period:

> An ill-defined slogan of "federalism" took centre stage. The first Constituent Assembly (CA) was crippled by debate on its meaning. Mainstream parties were described as pro- or anti-federal, shorthand for whether they agreed with the analysis driving the demands for federalism and inclusion. The term became the repository of virtually all political and social anxieties related to the transition.

In particular the *Madhesis* sought two main amendments in the Constitution: a federal state to devolve power and proportional representation electoral system to increase marginalised groups' political representation.

In November 2011 the Supreme Court ruled that no further extensions of the Constituent Assembly's mandate were allowed. Despite a flurry of activity as the May 2012 deadline approached, no Constitution was produced, some four years after the process began. The Constituent Assembly was subsequently dissolved on 28 May 2012. After the dissolution, negotiations between the four main political forces – the Maoists, the Nepali Congress, the Communist Party of Nepal-Unified Marxist-Leninist and the United Democratic Madhesi Front – resulted in the 11-point agreement that provided for the appointment of the Chief Justice as the head of the interim government, marking the beginning of '[a] period of constitutionally dubious political arrangements' (Thapa and Ramsbotham 2017, 10).

The second Constituent Assembly elections were held on 19 November 2013. CPN-M lost popularity while Nepali Congress emerged as the largest party, winning 196 of the 575 elected seats. However '[d]espite promises of inclusion and broadening participation among Nepal's many ethnic and linguistic minorities during the run-up to the elections, the dominance of the male, high caste elite remains' (Adkin 2014). The Second Constituent Assembly was plagued with many of the same problems as its predecessor: 'Decisions were driven by dealmaking between senior leaders, personal calculations, little reasoned debate, and the ignoring or crushing of dissent within parties' (International Crisis Group 2016, 4). A few months after the 2015 earthquake, UCPN-M signed a 16-point deal on 8 June 2015. This agreement indicated the opposition party's intentions to provide a quick earthquake response and to speed up the promulgation of constitution and in turn paved the way to towards resolving certain issues regarding the constitution (International Crisis Group 2016, 5–6).

In the final months of the constitution drafting, as aspects of the draft became apparent, violent protests by *Tharus* and *Madhesis* groups, erupted in the southern part of Nepal. Many of these groups were concerned about the draft citizenship provisions and federal state structure. Sharing geographical and cultural affinities with people living on the other side of Nepal-India border, the *Tharus* and *Madhesis* groups 'have long complained about being treated unfairly by dominant hill caste groups, taunted and politically marginalised for appearing to be "more Indian and less Nepali"' (Acharya 2016). The ongoing violence and protests led to the deaths of over 40 people.

Amid the escalating violence, and after over seven years of wrangling, the Constitution of Nepal came into effect on 20 September 2015. The Constitution was endorsed by 90% of the Second Constituent Assembly (538 out of 598 Constituent Assembly members). The Preamble states Nepal will become a 'federal democratic republican system of governance' and Article 4 states 'Nepal is an independent, indivisible, sovereign, secular, inclusive democratic, socialism-oriented federal democratic republican state'. The Preamble also asserts the 'determination to create an egalitarian society on the basis of the principles of proportional inclusion and participation, to ensure equitable economy, prosperity and social justice'. The Constitution provides for a mixed electoral system: First Past the Post and Proportional Representation. There are a number of key provisions on social inclusion. According to Article 10.1, no Nepali citizen shall be denied the right to citizenship. The Constitution also provides the right to social justice for groups who have historically been marginalised and excluded, including 'gender and sexual minority people', indigenous communities and low-caste Dalits (Article 42). The death penalty was abolished. With regard to the conflict the Preamble notes '[r]emembering the glorious history of historical peoples' movements and armed struggles time and again and the sacrifice made by people for national interest, democracy, progressive change, and recognizing the martyrs, the disappeared citizens and the victims' (Constitution of Nepal 2015). Pushpa Kamal Dahal, the Maoists' leader, hailed the adoption of the constitution 'a victory of the dreams of the thousands of martyrs and disappeared fighters' (Haviland 2015).

Despite a number of progressive provisions, there remain major concerns. The move from unitary to a federal system with seven states has caused alarm among particular ethnic groups who share provinces with hill districts, fearing the historically predomination by high caste, hill people will continue. The decrease in the percentage of proportional representation from the Interim Constitution is also feared to favour high caste, hill people. Additionally the Constitution has different provisions for men and women on citizenship by naturalisation; these provisions have been heavily criticised as discriminatory both to women and ethnic minorities in the south, with higher proportions of cross-border marriages. Some liberal and religious groups are also displeased about the secular provisions which 'they say cement the primacy of a conservative, exclusivist strain of Hinduism that the Constitution provides for Nepal to be a secular' (International Crisis Group 2016, 2).

After the promulgation, anti-constitution turmoil and unrest continued in the Terai. Within a few days of the adoption of the constitution, an umbrella grouping of Madhesi parties, the United Democratic Madhesi Front (UDMF), instigated a blockade at checkpoints along Nepal-India border. The UDMF were seeking changes to the recently adopted Constitution. After limited consultation, in early 2016, two constitutional amendments were passed. The amendments focused on delineation of constituencies and inclusive representation in state organs; however a number of groups, particularly Madhesi parties, have expressed that these changes inadequately address their grievances (International Crisis Group 2016, i). Indeed, according to International Crisis Group (2016, i), the constitution 'has deepened ethnic, social and political fractures' in Nepal. Not long after the amendments were passed the blockade came to an end; it lasted for 135 days and resulted in economic hardship particularly for the poor and those affected by the earthquake (International Crisis Group 2016, 21).

The role of third parties

External actors played a role in the peace process in Nepal. The content presented in this section is discussed in more detail in Chapters 5 and 6 but warrants highlighting here because it will assist the understanding of the initial period of the peace process. India has multiple interests in Nepal and a great deal of influence on Nepali actors. It was actively engaged behind the scenes throughout the conflict, during the peace process (see Farasat and Hayner 2009) and more recently during the blockade. For example, India supported and hosted peace talks, which led to the 12-point Understanding (see Whitfield 2012, 157). Geopolitically, it was in India's interests to ensure that Nepal remained stable. While '[n]o other international actor has had more influence' on the peace process, India has had varying degrees of success facilitating the relationship between the *Madhesis* and the government of Nepal (Adhikari 2017, 27–29).

China, Nepal's other neighbour, did not recognise the Nepalese rebels to be waging guerrilla warfare in line with that advocated by Mao Tse Tung; instead it classified the rebels as 'anti-government outfits' (Cottle and Keys 2007, 173). It is reported that China did not offer support to the Maoists and, in fact, it may have provided arms to the government of Nepal. In the latter part of the conflict India and China diplomatically denounced the Maoist insurgency in Nepal as terrorist activity (Cottle and Keys 2007, 174). This made post-conflict relations with the new government of Nepal difficult. Throughout the peace process China's involvement 'has been indirect and discreet, in line with its policy of "non-interference" and acknowledge of India's primacy in Nepal' (Adhikari 2017, 29). The roles of other countries, such as the UK and US, are outlined in Chapters 5 and 6.

Individuals also played a significant role. This was especially the case for individuals connected with the US-funded Nepal Transition to Peace (NTTP). The NTTP was 'an initiative conceived not only as a resource for the political parties on the peace process, but also as a negotiating space for the different stakeholders' (Farasat and Hayner 2009, 16). A key player in the NTTP was Hannes Siebert, a South African expert. Also significant was Günther Baechler, a Swiss peacebuilding advisor who positioned himself as 'a resource to, and informal facilitator between, the different groups engaged in dialogue' (Farasat and Hayner 2009, 16).

Two UN missions – the Office of the United Nations High Commissioner for Human Rights (OHCHR) and United Nations Mission in Nepal (UNMIN) – also played a role in the peace process. Towards the end of the conflict, in May 2005, a human rights mission was sent by OHCHR to monitor the human rights situation, advise the government on the promotion and protection of human rights and to observe whether international humanitarian law was being upheld. According to Rawski and Sharma (2012, 182) the presence of OHCHR provided crucial protection for human rights defenders, aided the expansion of political space for pro-democracy supporters and, through OHCHR's monitoring role during the April 2006 street demonstrations, contributed to the success of the People's Movement (*Jana Andolan II*). In the early stages of the peace process the major political parties leveraged the international legitimacy lent by the UN's presence (Adhikari 2017, 30). However, Nepal's neighbours, India and China, were not in favour of the organisation's presence in Nepal. The scope of OHCHR's mandate and the mandate's renewal was the source of contestation (discussed in Chapters 5 and 6).

In addition to OHCHR's ongoing role, the CPN-M and Seven Party Alliance sought political (technical) assistance in the peace process from the UN. A formal invitation was issued in July 2006 and by late August 2006, a political office, UNMIN, was established in Nepal (pursuant to Security Council Resolution 1740). UNMIN was headed by Ian Martin as Personal Representative of the UN Secretary General. The UN's role was further detailed in subsequent peace agreements between the two sides. Within a few weeks of signing the CPA, the Maoists and the government signed the Agreement on Monitoring of the Management of Arms and Armies (AMMAA) with the UN on 8 December 2006 (discussed below). This was consolidated into the CPA. Notably UNMIN was 'an experiment – a political mission was set up at the outset rather than as a follow-on from a peacekeeping mission' (Security Council Report 2008b). The Mission's five tasks covered three areas: monitoring the ceasefire code of conduct, monitoring arms and armed personnel and monitoring the Constituent Assembly elections and providing technical assistance to the Electoral Commission areas (UN Security Council 2007; ICG 2007, 28–29). Given this varied mandate, the mission included a range of personnel including military officers, electoral experts and observers, and police and civil administration teams.

UNMIN played a key role in the Disarmament, Demobilisation and Reintegration (DDR) process. Once the AMMAA was signed, combatants began moving into cantonments and weapons were seized. In total, there were 28 PLA cantonments throughout the country (seven cantonments that were military quarters and the remainder were sub-cantonments), many of which had rudimentary conditions. A total of 2,855 weapons from the NA and 3475 weapons from the Maoists were handed over. The overall number of combatants was uncertain. There were discrepancies between the Maoist leadership's public statements compared to their leaked confidential statements; there were also claims that at the end of the conflict the Maoists were actively recruiting in order to increase their numbers. Not all PLA personnel entered the cantonments; some of the experienced combatants joined the Young Communist League (YCL) while senior commanders and commissars maintained their ranks (International Crisis Group 2011, 5).

In early 2007 UNMIN commenced registration and verification. Over 30,000 combatants were registered in March 2007 and 19,602 combatants were later verified as members of the PLA. UNMIN sought to ensure two key factors: that the combatants were recruited before the signing of the ceasefire and were adults. Approximately 4,000 combatants were deemed to Verified Minor and Late Recruits (VLMRs) and were 'disqualified' (see Chapter 7). Although these combatants were no longer permitted to remain in the cantonments, due to political haggling, it took several years before they were formally discharged. These combatants received cash payments (both from both the UN and Maoists) totalling approximately 22,000 NPR (see Robins, Bhandari and Ex-PLA Research Group 2016). In early 2010 a United Nations Inter-Agency Rehabilitation Programme (UNIRP) was launched. This programme included education, vocational skills training and micro-enterprise development, and encompassed approximately half of the disqualified VMLRs. Other rehabilitation programs were conducted by various UN agencies and aid agencies (e.g. GIZ) with varying degrees of success.

The DDR process was fraught with delays and difficulties and the application of DDR to the combatants was disputed. For example, Pushpa Kamal Dahal, the Maoist leader, stated that since the PLA represented popular sovereignty the DDR process should instead be applied to the Nepalese Army (Caramés and Sanz 2009, 94). The Maoist leadership also maintained that the CPA 'contained parallel commitments with regard to the two armies: "professionalisation of the PLA [through integration] and democratisation of the Nepal Army"' (International Crisis Group 2011, 5). Although the Committee for the Recommendation for the Formulation of the Plan for the Democratisation for the Army and Improvement of the Security Apparatus issued a detailed plan in August 2010, this report resulted in little discussion after its release (Sudheer 2017, 44). Indeed, as the International Crisis Group (2011, i) explains:

> It is tempting to see integration and rehabilitation … as a largely technical issue, but it is deeply political. The peace process viewed both armies as equals; neither was presented as having been defeated. All parties signed up to bring the PLA into the security forces, including the national army, which in turn was to undergo a process of reform to make it smaller, more inclusive and more accountable.

It was not until November 2011 that the political impasse gave way leading to a seven-point agreement signed by the major political parties and the leader of the United Madhesi Democratic Front. In effect, the agreement provided that ex-combatants would have the option to choose from: a rehabilitation package; integration into the Nepalese Army; or, a voluntary retirement with a cash package (ranging from 500,000 to 800,000 NPR depending on their rank). By the time ex-combatants were offered this choice their number had decreased to around 17,000, owing to a large number of them being absent or 'self-integrating' into society, or moving overseas. Very few ex-combatants (6) chose the rehabilitation option, while 1,422 registered their interest for army integration (close to 1,000 ex-combatants were eventually integrated). The majority of the ex-combatants (15,624) opted for voluntary retirement option with the cash package. After six years the cantonments were officially closed in October 2012. Ex-combatants will be further explored in Chapter 7.

Returning to the role of UNMIN, after escalating resistance from a range of actors, including major political parties and the Nepali Army, its mandate was not renewed and it ceased operations in Nepal on 15 January 2011. The UN acknowledged calls from observers that the international community had failed to comprehend the underlying subtleties and tensions of the political situation in Nepal (Security Council Report 2008a). However, the UN also contended that it was due to an increased understanding of the complexity of the situation and dynamics in the Nepal that required UNMIN to continue operations in Nepal. The UN frequently cited completing the mandate as a reason for possible extension of UNMIN. However, there was limited clarity about how 'completion' would be achieved. For example, in relation to arms monitoring, it was unclear whether 'adequate progress' was the point at which the special committee was fully functioning or whether it would be achieved when decisions were made about the future of combatants and implementation was underway (Security Council Report 2009).

Among the Security Council members there were divergent views on UNMIN's mandate, term and role in the peace process. China strongly held the position that the UN should not be involved in facilitating the political process beyond the original UNMIN mandate, arguing that the Nepali government's wishes were paramount, whereas the UK and the US held that UNMIN should remain to complete its mandate, despite the delays and setbacks (Security Council Report 2007b). Differences between Security Council members were also evident in relation to the degree of support that should be provided for the peace process, the type of UN presence required upon UNMIN's withdrawal and the degree of pressure the UN should put on the government to release minors from the cantonments (Security Council Report 2009). India, while not a member of the Security Council, generally felt that 'UNMIN's position contradicted India's' (Adhikari 2017, 30). The EU, Nepal's largest aid donor, supported Nepal's requests for an extension of UNMIN's mandate (Security Council Report 2008a). Against this backdrop Chapter 5 examines the TJ process in Nepal.

Notes

1 This is sometimes referred to as 'sanskritisation' which is the process when low caste (e.g. Hindu or tribal) groups alter their rituals, customs, ideology and way of

life to imitate the higher caste (Srinivas 1965 cited in Bahadur 2007, 5). However, the usefulness of this concept has been called into question (Bahadur 2007, 6).

2 The *Muluki Ain* remained in force but references to caste were removed in 1963.

3 This was done in response to the UN declaration of the World Indigenous Peoples Year in 1993 and for the Decade of Indigenous People from 1995–2004.

4 For further information see Shneiderman et al. (2016), Friedman (2005, 71–72), Do and Iyer (2006), Hatlebakk (2009), and Tiwari (2010). Studies on the causes of the conflict have found that the conflict was due to poverty, underdevelopment and the failed policies of the government (Thapa 2002, 2003; Thapa and Sijapati 2004; Gersony 2003; Do and Iyer 2007). Others have found that economic factors such as landlessness, inequality and a lack of opportunity were the driving factors (Deraniyagala 2005; Murshed and Gates 2005; DFID 2003; Bohara, Mitchell and Nepal 2006; Macours 2006).

5 The 2011 Census reveals that there is 47% poverty among Dalits, 44% in hill *Janjatis*, 41% in Muslims and 35–40% in *Madhesis* compared to 19% in *Brahmin/Chhetri* and 14% in *Newar* (see Shukla 2011, 240).

6 This is compared to the *Panchayat* and the first parliamentary democratic period (1959–1960).

7 For example, Gersony (2003) argues that ethnic and caste divisions were not a major cause of the conflict, and Gurung (2005, 13) concludes that no correlation exists between the intensity of the insurgency and the density of socially excluded parts of the population, but that there is a correspondence between the level of poverty and the area of insurgency.

8 Personal interview, 9 September 2012, Rolpa.

9 Personal interview, 9 September 2012, Rolpa.

10 Personal interview, 11 September 2012, Rolpa.

11 Personal interview, 22 March 2012, Dang.

12 Personal interview, 21 September 2012, Dadeldhura.

13 Personal interview, 21 September 2012, Dadeldhura.

14 Personal interview, 9 September 2012, Rolpa.

15 Personal interview, 9 September 2012, Rolpa.

16 Personal interview, 11 September 2012, Rolpa.

17 Personal interview, 10 September 2012, Rolpa.

18 TADO was subsequently adopted by Parliament as the *Terrorism and Disruptive Activities Act* (2002).

19 The Seven Party Alliance comprised the Nepali Congress, the Unified Marxist–Leninist, the Nepal Congress (Democratic) Party, the Nepal Workers and Peasants Party, the United Left Front, the Nepal Sadbhavana Party (Anandi Devi) and Janamorcha.

References

Acharya, Anurag. 2016. 'Nepal: A costly constitution.' *Al-Jazeera*. www.aljazeera.com/indepth/opinion/2016/12/nepal-costly-constitution-161207093116670.html.

Adhikari, Aditya. 2017. International support for peace and transition in Nepal. In *Two steps forward, one step back: the Nepal peace process*, edited by Dr Alexander Ramsbotham, Deepak Thapa, 27–31. www.c-r.org/downloads/Accord-26-Nepal-WEB_0.pdf.

Adkin, Ross. 2014. 'Nepal tries again to write its own constitution.' *The Diplomat*, 12 March 2014. https://thediplomat.com/2014/03/nepal-tries-again-to-write-a-constitution/.

Advocacy Forum. 2010. 'Review of implementation of the recommendations made by the UN Working Group on Enforced or Involuntary Disappearances after its visit to Nepal in December 2004.' www.advocacyforum.org/downloads/pdf/publications/af-briefing-series-1-disappearance.pdf.

Advocacy Forum, and ICTJ. 2010. 'Across the lines: The impact of Nepal's conflict on women.' www.ictj.org/sites/default/files/ICTJ-Nepal-Across-Lines-2010-English.pdf.

Amnesty International. 2014. 'Nepal: Deliver justice for "disappeared"'. Last modified 29 August 2014. www.amnesty.org/en/for-media/press-releases/nepal-deliver-justice-disappeared-2014-08-29.

Bahadur, Amar. 2007. 'Sanskritization and caste opposition: A case study of Dalits Pokhara.' *Himalayan Journal of Sociology and Anthropology* III, Sept. 2008:1–10. www.nepjol.info/index.php/HJSA/article/view/1492/1466.

Basnet, Devendra, and Ganesh Bk. 2017. 'CPN (Maoist Center) validating war-era land transactions in Rukum.' *myRepublica*. www.myrepublica.com/news/21356/.

Bohara, Alok, Neil Mitchell, and Mani Nepal. 2006. 'Opportunity, democracy and the exchange of political violence: A subnational analysis of conflict in Nepal.' *Journal of Conflict Resolution* 50(1):108–128.

Bray, John, Leiv Lunde, and Murshed S. Mansoob. 2003. 'Nepal: Economic drivers of the Maoist insurgency.' In *The political economy of armed conflict: Beyond greed and grievance*, edited by Karen Sherman and Jake Ballentine, 107–132. Boulder, CO: Lynne Riener.

Brown, Graham K., Corinne Caumartin, Arnim Langer, and Frances Stewart. 2011. 'Addressing horizontal inequalities in post-conflict reconstruction.' In *Rethinking transitions: Equality and social justice in societies emerging from conflict*, edited by Gaby Ore Aguilar and Felipe Gomez Isa, 11–30. Cambridge: Intersentia.

Cailmail, Benoit. 2008. 'The fall of a Hindu monarchy: Maoists in power in Nepal.' *Asie Visions*, 12.

Caramés, A. and Sanz, E. 2009. 'Eritrea: Demobilization and reintegration, 2002–present.' In *Analysis of disarmament, demobilization and reintegration (DDR) programmes in the world during 2008*, edited by A. Caramés and E. Sanz. Bellaterra: School for a Culture of Peace.

Center for Human Rights and Global Justice. 2005. The missing piece of the puzzle: Caste discrimination and the conflict in Nepal. www.ifri.org/sites/default/files/atoms/files/the_fall_of_a_hindu_monarchy.pdf.

Constitution of Nepal. 2015 (official English translation by the Ministry of Law, Justice and Parliamentary Affairs of Nepal) www.constitutionnet.org/sites/default/files/nepal_constitution_-_official_translaiton_eng_mljpa.pdf.

Cottle, Drew, and Angela Keys. 2007. 'The Maoist conflict in Nepal: A Himalayan perdition?' *Australian Journal of International Affairs* 61(2):168–174.

CPA. 2006. *Comprehensive Peace Agreement*. Concluded between the Government of Nepal and the Communist Party of Nepal, signed on 21 November 2006.

Dahal, Dilli Ram. 1995. 'Ethnic cauldron, demography and minority politics: The case of Nepal.' In *State, leadership and politics in Nepal*, edited by Dhruba Kumar. Kathmandu: Centre for Nepal and Asian Studies.

Deraniyagala, Sonali. 2005. 'The political economy of civil conflict in Nepal.' *Oxford Development Studies* 33(1):47–62.

DFID. 2003. *Economic aspects of insurgency in Nepal*. London: Department for International Development.

Dhakal, Ameet, and Jhalak Subedi. 2006. 'The Nepalese private sector: Waking up to conflict.' In *Local business, local peace: The peacebuilding potential of the domestic private sector*, edited by Jessica Banfield, Canan Gündüz and Nick Killick, 405–431. London: International Alert.

Do, Quy-Toan, and Lakshmi Iyer. 2006. 'An empirical analysis of civil conflict in Nepal.' *Center on Institutions and Governance Working Paper* No. 12. www.alnap.org/system/files/content/resource/files/main/no12-iyer.pdf.

Do, Quy-Toan, and Lakshmi Iyer. 2007. 'Poverty, social divisions, and conflict in Nepal.' *World Bank Policy Research Working Paper* 4228 May. http://documents.worldbank.org/curated/en/871141468323682873/pdf/wps4228.pdf.

Do, Quy-Toan, and Lakshmi Iyer. 2010. 'Geography, poverty and conflict in Nepal.' *Journal of Peace Research* 47(6):735–748.

Farasat, Warisha, and Priscilla Hayner. 2009. *Negotiating peace in Nepal: Implications for Justice*. Brussels: Institute for Peacebuilding / International Centre for Transitional Justice. https://ictj.org/sites/default/files/ICTJ-IFP-Nepal-Negotiating-Peace-2009-English.pdf.

Friedman, Lindsay. 2005. *The conflict in Nepal: A simplified account*. Kathmandu: Shtrii Shakti.

Gellner, David N., and Krishna Hachhethu. 2008. 'Introduction.' In *Local democracy in South Asia: Microprocesses of democratization in Nepal and its neighbours*, edited by David N. Gellner and Krishna Hachhetu, 13–22. London: Sage.

Gersony, Robert. 2003. *Sowing the wind: History and dynamics of the Maoist revolt in Nepal's Rapti hills*. Portland, OR: Mercy Corps International.

Goswami, Roshmi. 2015. *UNSCR 1325 and Female Excombatants – Case Study of the Maoist Women of Nepal*. New York: UN Women. http://wps.unwomen.org/pdf/research/ROSHMI.pdf.

Gurung, D. B. 2004. 'Maoist insurgency: Politico-historical, socio-cultural, and economic implications – II.' *The Telegraph* (Nepal), 24 March. www.nepalnews.com.np/contents/englishweekly/telegraph/2004/mar/mar24/national.htm#2.

Gurung, Harka. 2005. 'Social exclusion and Maoist insurgency.' National Dialogue Conference on ILO Convention 169 on Indigenous and Tribal Peoples, Kathmandu, 19–20 January.

Hachhethu, Krishna. 2003. 'The question of inclusion and exclusion in Nepal interface between state and ethnicity.' The Agenda of Transformation: Inclusion in Nepali Democracy, Kathmandu, Nepal, Social Science Baha, Kathmandu, Nepal, 24–26 April.

Hangen, Susan I. 2010. *The rise of ethnic politics in Nepal: Democracy in the margins*,. London: Routledge.

Hatlebakk, Magnus. 2009. 'Explaining Maoist control and level of civil conflict in Nepal.' Institute (CMI Working Paper WP 2009:10). www.cmi.no/publications/3498-explaining-maoist-control-and-level-of-civil.

Haviland, Charles. 2015. 'Why is Nepal's new constitution controversial?' *BBC World News*. www.bbc.com/news/world-asia-34280015.

HRW (Human Rights Watch). 2004. 'Between a rock and a hard place: Civilians struggle to survive in Nepal's civil war.' www.hrw.org/reports/2004/nepal1004/nepal1004.pdf.

ICG (International Crisis Group). 2007. 'Nepal's constitutional process.' https://d2071andvip0wj.cloudfront.net/128-nepal-s-constitutional-process.pdf.

IFAD (International Fund for Agricultural Development). 2013. 'Enabling poor rural people to overcome poverty in Nepal.' www.ifad.org/en/web/knowledge/asset/39429831.

INSEC (Informal Service Sector Center). 2010. *Annual report*.
Internal Displacement Monitoring Centre. 2012. 'Around 50,000 people remain displaced.' Last modified 11 April. www.internal-displacement.org/idmc/website/countries.nsf/(httpEnvelopes)/1949E98C81942B55C12571FE004D8821?OpenDocument.
Internal Displacement Monitoring Centre. 2013. 'Nepal IDP figures analysis.' www.internal-displacement.org/south-and-south-east-asia/nepal/figures-analysis.
International Crisis Group. 2011. *Nepal: From two armies to one. Crisis Group Asia Report*, No. 211, 18 August. www.crisisgroup.org/ne/file/1453/download?token=_Bh13FSM.
International Crisis Group. 2016. Nepal's divisive. new constitution: An existential crisis. *Asia Report*, No. 276, 4 April. www.crisisgroup.org/file/82/download?token=k1qlhquX.
Jha, Nalin Kant. 2011. 'Mainstreaming of the Maoists: Challenges and prospects.' In *State and democracy in Nepal: Emerging paradigm, issues and challenges*, edited by B. C. Upreti, 87–97. New Dehli: Kalinga Publications.
Kievelitz, Uwe, and Tara Polzer. 2002. 'Nepal country study on conflict transformation and peace building.' http://nepalconflictreport.ohchr.org/files/docs/2002-00-00_report_gtz_eng.pdf.
Lawoti, Mahendra. 2005. *Towards a democratic Nepal: Inclusive political institutions for a multicultural society*. New Delhi: Sage.
Lawoti, Mahendra. 2008. 'Exclusionary democracy in Nepal, 1990–2002.' *Democratization* 15(2):363–385.
Lawoti, Mahendra. 2010. 'Evolution and growth of the Maoist insurgency in Nepal.' In *The Maoist Insurgency in Nepal: Revolution in the Twenty-First Century*, edited by Mahendra Lawoti and Anup K. Pahari, 3–30. Abingdon: Routledge.
Lawoti, Mahendra. 2012. 'Ethnic politics and the building of an inclusive state.' In *Nepal in Transition: From people's war to fragile peace*, edited by Sebastian von Einsiedel, David M. Malone and Suman Pradhan, 5. New Dehli: Cambridge University Press.
Lawoti, Mahendra, and Anup K. Pahari. 2010. 'Violent conflict and change: Costs and benefits of the Maoist rebellion in Nepal.' In *The Maoist insurgency in Nepal: Revolution in the twenty-first century*, edited by Mahendra Lawoti and Anup K. Pahari, 304–326. Abingdon: Routledge.
Macours, Karen. 2006. 'Relative deprivation and civil conflict in Nepal.' *Himalayan Journal of Development and Democracy*, Special Issue, 39–40. http://digitalrepository.unm.edu/cgi/viewcontent.cgi?article=1014&context=hprc.
Madeley, John. 2009. 'Religion and the state.' In *Routledge handbook of religion and politics*, edited by Jeffrey Haynes, 174–191. London: Routledge.
Marshall Cavendish Corporation, ed. 2007. *The world and its peoples: Eastern and Southeastern Asia*. New York: The Brown Reference Group.
Ministry of Peace and Reconstruction. 2014. 'Emergency peace support project.' www.epsp.gov.np.
Murshed, Mansoob S., and Scott Gates. 2003. 'Spatial horizontal inequality and the Maoist insurgency in Nepal.' *Review of Development Economics* 9(1):121–134.
Nepal Constitution. 1990. 'Constitution of the Kingdom of Nepal VS 2047.' *Himalaya, The Journal of the Association for Nepal and Himalayan Studies* 11(1):19–68.
Nepal Monitor. 2011. 'Recording Nepal conflict: Victims in numbers.' Last modified 23 July 2011. www.nepalmonitor.com/2011/07/recording_nepal_conf-print.html.

OHCHR. 2012. *The Nepal conflict report*. www.ohchr.org/Documents/Countries/NP/OHCHR_Nepal_Conflict_Report2012.pdf.

Onta, Pratyoush. 2006. 'The growth of the Adivasi Janajati movement in Nepal after 1990: The non-political institutional agents.' *Studies in Nepali History and Society* 11(2):303–354.

Paffenholz, Thania. 2006. 'Nepal: Staying engaged in conflict. Experiences and lessons learnt from Conflict Sensitive Programme Management (CSPM) in fragile context with armed conflict.' www.sdc-conflict-and-humanrights.ch/en/Home/Discussions_and_Lessons_Learnt/Experiences_from_SDC_and_Partners/media/Nepal_Staying_engaged.pdf.

Pandey, Nishchal Nath. 2010. *New Nepal: The fault lines*. London: Sage.

Pattanaik, Smruti S. 2011. 'Maoist in power: From rebel to ruler.' In *State and Democracy in Nepal: Emerging Paradigm, Issues and Challenges*, edited by B.C. Upreti, 98–121. New Dehli: Kalinga Publications.

Pettigrew, Judith. 2012. 'Unexpected consequences of everyday life during the Maoist insurgency in Nepal.' *Journal of International Women's Studies* 13(4):100–112.

Pfaff-Czarnecka, Joanna. 2004. 'High expectations, deep disappointment: Politics, state and society in Nepal after 1990.' In *Himalayan people's war: Nepal's Maoist rebellion*, edited by Michael Hutt, 166–191. Bloomington: Indiana University Press.

Pradhan, Rajendra. 2003. 'Ethnicity, caste and a pluralist society.' In *State of Nepal*, edited by Kanak Mani Dixit and Shastri Ramachandaran, 1–21. Kathmandu: Himal Books.

Pyakurel, Uddhab P. 2011. 'The vision of the Jana Andolan II for a future of Nepal.' In *State and democracy in Nepal: Emerging paradigm, issues and challenges*, edited by B. C. Upreti, 68–86. New Delhi: Kalinga Publications.

Rawski, Frederick, and Mandira Sharma. 2012. 'A comprehensive peace? Lessons from human rights monitoring in Nepal.' In *Nepal in transition: From people's war to fragile peace*, edited by Sebastian von Einsiedel, David M. Malone and Suman Pradhan, 175–200. New Dehli: Cambridge University Press.

Riveros, Natalia. 2004. 'Towards conflict transformation in Nepal: A case For UN Mediation.' www.monitor.upeace.org/pdf/Peacemag-Nepal.pdf.

Robins, Simon, Ram Kumar Bhandari, and Ex-PLA Research Group. 2016. *Poverty, stigma and alienation: Reintegration challenges of ex-Maoist combatants in Nepal: A participatory action research project with ex-PLA fighters in Nepal*. Berghof Foundation. www.berghof-foundation.org/fileadmin/redaktion/Publications/Grantees_Partners/Final_Report_Ex-PLA_Nepal_May_2016.pdf.

Security Council Report. 2007a. 'May 2007 monthly forecast.' Last modified 27 April 2007. www.securitycouncilreport.org/site/c.glKWLeMTIsG/b.2701397/k.8580/May_2007BRNepal.htm.

Security Council Report. 2007b. 'October 2007 monthly forecast.' Last modified 28 September 2007. www.securitycouncilreport.org/site/c.glKWLeMTIsG/b.3454435/k.8AB4/October_2007brNepal.htm.

Security Council Report. 2008a. 'January 2008 monthly forecast.' Last modified 21 December 2007. www.securitycouncilreport.org/site/c.glKWLeMTIsG/b.3750609/k.87B5/January_2008brNepal.htm.

Security Council Report. 2008b. 'October 2008 monthly forecast.' Last modified 29 September 2008. www.securitycouncilreport.org/monthly-forecast/2008-10/lookup_c_glKWLeMTIsG_b_4559905.php.

Security Council Report. 2009. 'April 2009 monthly forecast.' Last modified 30 March 2009. www.securitycouncilreport.org/site/c.glKWLeMTIsG/b.5053253/k.6D7F/April_2009brNepal.htm.
Shah, Saubhagya. 2003. 'From evil state to civil society.' In *State of Nepal*, edited by Kanak Mani Dixit and Shastri Ramachandaran, 137–160. Kathmandu: Himal Books.
Shakya, Sujeev. 2012. 'Unleashing Nepal's economic potential: A business perspective.' In *Nepal in transition: From people's war to fragile peace*, edited by Sebastian von Einsiedel, David M. Malone and Suman Pradhan, 114–128. New Dehli: Cambridge University Press.
Sharma, Jeevan Raj, and Antonio Donini. 2010. 'Towards a "great transformation"? The Maoist insurgency and local perceptions of social transformation in Nepal.' http://fic.tufts.edu/assets/great-transformation.pdf.
Sharma, Priyag Raj. 1997. 'Nation building, multi-ethnicity, and the Hindu state.' In *Nationalism and ethnicity in a Hindu kingdom: The politics of culture in contemporary Nepal*, edited by David N. Gellner, Joanna Pfaff-Czarnecka and John Whelpton, 471–494. London: Routledge.
Shneiderman, S., L. Wagner, J. Rinck, A. L. Johnson, and A. Lord. 2016. 'Nepal's ongoing political transformation: A review of post-2006 literature on conflict, the state, identities, and environments.' *Modern Asian Studies* 50(6):74.
Shukla, Deeptima. 2011. 'Fighting poverty: Exploring linkage between development and democracy in Nepal.' In *State and democracy in Nepal: Emerging paradigm, issues and challenges*, edited by B. C. Upreti, 233–247. New Dehli: Kalinga Publications.
Stewart, Frances. 2002. 'Horizontal inequalities a neglected dimension of development.' www.crise.ox.ac.uk/pubs.shtml.
Sudheer, Sharma. 2017. 'Army and security forces after 2006.' In *Two steps forward, one step back: the Nepal peace process*, edited by Dr Alexander Ramsbotham and Deepak Thapa, 41–45, Issue 26, Conciliation Resources. www.c-r.org/downloads/Accord-26-Nepal-WEB_0.pdf.
Tamang, Mukta S. 2006. 'Culture, caste and ethnicity in the Maoist movement.' *Studies in Nepali History and Society* 11(2):271–301.
Thapa, Deepak. 2002. 'The Maobadi of Nepal.' In *State of Nepal*, edited by Kanak Mani Dixit and Shastri Ramchandran, 77–99. Kathmandu: Himal Books.
Thapa, Deepak. 2003. *Understanding the Maoist movement of Nepal*. Kathmandu: Centre for Social Research and Development.
Thapa, Deepak. 2012. 'The making of the Maoist insurgency.' In *Nepal in transition: From people's war to fragile peace*, edited by Sebastian von Einsiedel, David M. Malone and Suman Pradhan, 37–57. New Dehli: Cambridge University Press.
Thapa, Deepak, and Ramsbotham, Alexander. 2017. *Two steps forward, one step back: the Nepal peace process*, Issue 26, Conciliation Resources. www.c-r.org/downloads/Accord-26-Nepal-WEB_0.pdf.
Thapa, Deepak, and Bandira Sijapati. 2004. *A kingdom under siege: Nepal's Maoist insurgency, 1996 to 2003*. Kathmandu: The Printhouse.
Thapa, Lily, and Deon V. Canyon. 2017. 'The advancement of women in post-conflict Nepal.' In *Occasional Paper*: Daniel K. Inouye Asia Pacific Center for Security Studies.

Tiwari, Bishwa Nath. 2007. 'An assessment of the causes of the conflict in Nepal.' Second Annual Himalayan Policy Research Conference, Nepal Study Centre, Madison.

Tiwari, Bishwa Nath. 2010. 'An assessment of the causes of conflict in Nepal.' In *The Maoist insurgency in Nepal: Revolution in the twenty-first century*, edited by Mahendra Lawoti and K. Anup, 241–262. Abingdon: Routledge.

Toffin, Gerard. 2006. 'The politics of Hinduism and secularism in Nepal.' *Studies in Nepali History and Society* 11(2):219–240.

Tyynela, John. 2014. 'Can truth commissions strengthen peace processes?' www.kofiannanfoundation.org/app/uploads/2013/11/ictj-report-kaf-truthcommpeace-2014.pdf.

UN Security Council. 2007. 'Resolution 1740(2007).' www.un.org/press/en/2007/sc8942.doc.htm.

UNDP. 2016. *Hum dev for everyone: Briefing note for countries on the 2016 Human Development Report Nepal*. New York: UNDP. http://hdr.undp.org/sites/default/files/2016_human_development_report.pdf.

Upadhya, Sanjay. 2003. 'A dozen years of democracy: the games that parties play.' In *State of Nepal*, edited by Kanak Mani Dixit and Shastri Ramachandaran, 39–61. Kathmandu: Himal Books.

Upadhyay, Prakash. 2008. 'Quandary in Nepal: A conflict perspective.' *Himalayan Journal of Sociology & Anthropology* 3:73–85.

Upreti, Bishnu Raj. 2007. 'Addressing structural causes of conflict and promoting peace through a conflict-sensitive development approach: Some lessons from Nepal.' International Conference Centre for International Studies and Cooperation (CECI), Kathmandu, 16–18 January.

Upreti, Bishnu Raj, and Åshild Kolås. 2016. 'Women in Nepal's transition. In *PRIO policy brief*.' Oslo: PRIO. www.prio.org/utility/DownloadFile.ashx?id=72&type=publicationfile.

von Einsiedel, Sebastian, David Malone, and Suman Pradhan. 2012. 'Introduction.' In *Nepal in transition: From people's war to fragile peace*, edited by Sebastian von Einsiedel, David M. Malone and Suman Pradhan, 1–33. New Delhi: Cambridge University Press.

Whelpton, John. 2005. *A history of Nepal*. Cambridge: Cambridge University Press.

Whitfield, Teresa. 2012. 'Nepal's Masala peacemaking.' In *Nepal in transition: From people's war to fragile peace*, edited by Sebastian von Einsiedel, David M. Malone and Suman Pradhan, 155–174. New Dehli: Cambridge University Press.

Yadav, Punam. 2016. *Social transformation in post-conflict Nepal: A gender perspective, Routledge research on gender in Asia series*. Abingdon: Routledge.

5 The transitional justice process in Nepal

> In 2006, most Nepalese were only just beginning to hear about transitional justice. The question was whether it could work in Nepal to hold people accountable for abuses committed during the insurgency.
>
> (Rausch 2017, 2)

This chapter outlines the TJ process in Nepal. It discusses the TJ provisions and legislation, the TJ commissions and other TJ mechanisms. Next, it provides my actor typology that maps the key actors involved in the TJ process. I identify four main groups of actors: TJ experts, TJ brokers, TJ implementers and victims. This typology assists with understanding the various actors involved and identifying which actors are making claims and on whose behalf. It also provides a useful means of examining the ways these actors interact with each other and engage with transitional justice. Finally, it outlines various participatory activities across a range of themes and types of victims.

The national transitional justice agenda

Transitional justice provisions and legislation

TJ discussions predominantly arose during the peace negotiations.[1] The TJ provisions were principally contained in the Comprehensive Peace Agreement (CPA) and the Interim Constitution.[2] These TJ provisions were drafted with limited consultation with victims and other TJ actors (discussed further below and in Chapter 6). The CPA included provisions relating to the disappeared and the human rights violations during the conflict. Both sides agreed to provide, remarkably within 60 days of signing the CPA, the details of those disappeared or killed during the conflict (Article 5.2.3). A National Peace Rehabilitation Commission was to be established to normalise the situation arising from the conflict, maintain peace and conduct rehabilitation work for victims and conflict-related Internally Displaced Persons (Article 5.2.4). Both parties also guaranteed not to encourage impunity and to provide the right to relief for families of those disappeared and torture victims (Article 7.1.3). In particular, the CPA prescribed that a Truth and Reconciliation Commission

(TRC) would be created 'to probe into those involved in serious violation of human rights and crimes against humanity in [the] course of the armed conflict for creating an atmosphere for reconciliation in the society' (Article 5.2.5).[3]

The CPA lacked guidance on timeframes and sequencing of events/actions, including how to form the prescribed investigative bodies and determine their respective mandates. With regard to disappearances the Supreme Court issued a directive order to establish a Commission of Inquiry into Enforced Disappearances (CIEDP) in June 2007.[4] Although the government responded rapidly and announced the formation of the CIEDP (on 21 June 2007) the commission was not in compliance with the Supreme Court ruling or international standards (Farasat and Hayner 2009, 24). In December 2007 the CPA signatories reiterated commitment to the CPA in a 23-point agreement. This agreement reiterated unfulfilled commitments including those relating to the disappeared and the TRC (ICTJ and Advocacy Forum 2008).

The Interim Constitution also outlined the specific state responsibilities in relation to the conflict. The government and Maoists together insisted that a clause in the penultimate version – which would have empowered the government to promulgate retrospective laws on crimes against humanity – was removed from the final version (Farasat and Hayner 2009, 19–20). The Interim Constitution reiterated the provision to establish a high-level TRC to 'investigate the facts regarding grave violation of human rights and crimes against humanity committed during the course of conflict, and create an atmosphere of reconciliation in the society' (Part 4[s]). The government was to make arrangements for appropriate relief, recognition and rehabilitation for the families of those killed, disabled or injured during the course of armed conflict (Part 4[p]). The state was also held responsible for the relief for families of victims of those disappeared but this was made contingent upon the report of the CIEDP (Part 4[q]). The Constitution also prescribed that the state was to establish conflict rehabilitation programs for internally displaced persons, to rebuild damaged infrastructure and to provide relief for private and public property damaged as a result of the conflict (Part 4(r)). On the basis of these provisions, and following the 2007 Supreme Court's directive order, the newly established Ministry of Peace and Reconstruction drafted bills for the establishment of a TRC and the CIEDP.

The draft TRC and CIEDP bills were made public in July 2007 and November 2008, respectively. The draft bills were heavily criticised by civil society, OHCHR and victims' groups for being drafted without consultation (ICJ 2009). It was only *after* the bills were made public that consultations by the Ministry of Peace and Reconstruction were held with of some victims, victims' groups and civil society (discussed below). The bills were first tabled in early 2010.[5] While it was envisaged that separate parliamentary sub-committees were to review each bill, in mid-2011 a seven-member thematic subcommittee was established to finalise both bills (MPTF 2011, 4). Notably, OHCHR advice to this committee focused on international experiences and lessons learned rather than on obligations under international law (MPTF 2011, 4). Months later an informal task group comprising three major political parties (UCPN-M, Nepali Congress and CPN-UML) was established so that once political consensus was reached then this would be reflected in the draft bills; arguably '[t]his development effectively took the legislative process out of the hands of the thematic committee' (MPTF 2011, 4). The following month two of the three parties (UCPN-M and Nepali Congress) came to an agreement that a blanket amnesty would be granted for conflict-related crimes committed by the state and the Maoists. This led to widespread criticism from victims' groups, NGOs and donors. However, human rights advocate and director of Advocacy Forum, Mandira Sharma (2017, 34) notes that as early as 2007 human rights organisations were 'aware of tacit agreement among the political parties to forget the past and condone impunity'.

In a significant departure from the initial TJ design in May 2012 the government replaced the two pending bills regarding these commissions with an ordinance for a single TJ mechanism with wide powers to grant amnesty. I was informed that families of the disappeared were concerned that specific provisions relating to those disappeared would be overlooked or disregarded if a single commission was established. The ordinance was declared unconstitutional by the Supreme Court. The Court ordered that separate commissions were required to investigate enforced disappearances and truth and reconciliation, and that the TRC bill was to be revised in consultation with victims, activists and legal experts and detailed changes were to be made to ensure the bills were in line with the victims' rights to justice and due process (Advocacy Forum 2014a; Adhikari et al. 2014, 66).[6]

There have been similar examples of tussling between the government and various TJ actors. In August 2012, during the period when the Constituent Assembly had been dissolved, the Council of Ministers provided the President with an ordinance for establishing one commission: the Commission on Investigation of Disappeared Persons, Truth and Reconciliation. The ordinance contained a number of issues; particularly problematic were those pertaining to granting amnesties and Commission-initiated reconciliation. This ordinance lapsed before it was made law. Again in March 2013, the President of Nepal promulgated a revised ordinance (the 2013 Ordinance).[7] Among the problematic provisions was a provision that empowered the Commission to grant amnesties for 'serious crimes.' There was no consultation with the National Human Rights Commission or community members. In fact, according to OHCHR, '[t]he text was negotiated amongst the four main political parties as part of a political compromise that would facilitate national elections' (OHCHR 2013, 2). Victims and TJ brokers filed writ petitions at the Supreme Court. These petitions challenged the ordinance's constitutionality, particularly with regard to the victims' rights to remedy in the Interim Constitution. It also challenged the ordinance's compliance with international law (e.g. with respect to Article 2 of the International Covenant on Civil and Political Rights) (ICJ 2014, 4, 7).

On 1 April 2013 the Supreme Court stayed the implementation of the 2013 ordinance. However, later that month slightly revised TRC and CIEDP bills were reintroduced in the Constituent Assembly. Again activists, national and international human rights groups, victims groups and donors among other actors criticised the bill for contravening Supreme Court orders and, in effect, providing amnesty and encouraging reconciliation in a manner that is contrary to victims' wants and international practice. In January 2014 the Supreme Court held that the revised ordinance violated Nepal's Interim Constitution, international human rights law, previous rulings by the Court and 'accepted principles of justices' and 'was an obstacle to transitional justice'.[8] The Court ordered the government to address a number of issues. Specifically, the government was instructed to form two commissions (a 'Truth and Reconciliation Commission' and a 'Commission of Inquiry on Enforced Disappeared Persons'), to criminalise disappearances and to ensure no amnesty provisions were established. Pursuant to the Court's recommendation a team of experts was established to assist with the drafting of the legislation. The team comprised government officials, experts, human rights lawyers and victims but the team was only given two weeks to draft recommendations and these recommendations appear to have had a limited influence on the bill (Bisset 2014, 3).

A slightly modified version of the draft legislation was passed by the Constituent Assembly on 25 April 2014. The *Commission on Investigation of Disappeared Persons, Truth and Reconciliation Act* (2014) (the TJ Act) was approved by the President on 11 May 2014. The Act provides for the creation of two commissions: a Truth and Reconciliation Commission and Commission of Inquiry on Enforced Disappeared Persons. The TJ Act also provides for the establishment of a Special Court with the authority to rule on conflict-related crimes, although the court's functions and its relationship with other TJ mechanisms are unclear. In particular, it is not specified whether cases must be heard by one of the commissions before being heard by the Special Court (Bisset 2014, 5).

Activists, donor and other actors have stressed that the TJ Act does not comply with the Court's previous rulings (HRW 2014). A number of issues have been raised, including that the TJ Act:

- provides amnesties for gross violations of international human rights and serious violations of international humanitarian law;
- provides the Commission with the power to initiate reconciliation between victims and perpetrators without their consent, which may put pressure on victims to 'reconcile';
- provides the government with the power to appoint commissioners and staff, which brings in to question the commissions' independence and partiality;
- fails to define key terms (e.g. 'serious violation of human rights,' 'act of disappearing a person' and 'reparation,') which may provide scope for evasion of conflict-related violations; and,

- fails to clarify the relationship between the NHRC and the commissions, which may weaken the NHRC and create coordination and cooperation issues (see Bisset 2014, Budhathoki 2014).

Petitions have been filed at the Supreme Court challenging the Act (discussed below).

The TJ Act provides that both commissions have a two-year tenure, with the possibility of extension. There are to be at least five commissioners, with at least one female commissioner and one from the NHRC. The commissioners are required to be Nepali citizens with a minimum bachelor's degree. Applicants who are affiliated with political parties and have been involved in armed conflict are ineligible. Also, applicants are ineligible if they have been convicted for a criminal offence or a human rights violation. The commissions have a mandate to investigate cases that have been lodged with the commission or those that it deems to lay within its jurisdiction. It is the responsibility of the government to implement the commissions' recommendations and the NHRC is authorised to alert ministries of the progress of implementation. A Recommendation Committee was established to nominate the chairperson and commissioners for both commissions; although emblematic of the political climate the Committee was plagued with issues.[9]

The transitional justice commissions

The TJ commissions were set up on 10 February 2015. A few weeks later, on 26 February 2015, the Supreme Court annulled the amnesty provision of the TJ Act in favour of 234 victims who had challenged the Act.[10] The Court stated that the amnesty provision went against the Court's earlier verdicts, constitutional provisions as well as principles of justice, and international law. According to OHCHR (2016) '[t]he Court held that any provisions of the Act that serve to compromise this judicial role are invalid, including the power to grant amnesties, powers to divert such cases from the courts or to otherwise interfere in such cases'.

There had been minimal progress to establish the commissions before the 2015 earthquake devastated parts of Nepal and effectively stalled the commissions' work. The earthquake was a magnitude of 7.8, and it struck near Kathmandu on 25 April 2015. Nearly 9,000 people were killed, 22,000 were injured and 600,000 structures were damaged or destroyed. An aftershock, with a magnitude of 7.3, which struck close to Kathmandu on 12 May 2015, killed more than 100 people and left 1,900 injured.[11] Over one quarter of the population is estimated to have been affected by the earthquakes.

Later that year at the UN Universal Periodic Review in November 2015, major donors, including Switzerland, Denmark, Norway, Germany and the UK, reaffirmed Nepal should pursue a credible TJ process and comply with the Supreme Court's orders as well as international laws and practice. This was the first time India formally raised the issue of transitional justice at the Universal Periodic Review. As part of its response the government of Nepal noted that there were bills before Parliament and some of the issues raised were 'already taken care of' (The Kathmandu Post 2015b). In December 2015 the TRC sought conflict dossiers from the Nepalese Army, the former rebel party UCPN (Maoist), the Nepal Police and the Armed Police Force, among others (Nagendra Adhikari 2016).

It was not until February 2016 that TJ commissions' regulations were endorsed, approximately six months after they had been provided to the government for approval. A number of provisions were removed from the proposed regulations. For example, the power of the CIEDP to confiscate the passports of, and arrest, accused. The government had not approved funding for the commissions; notwithstanding the commission had begun holding discussions with victims and other stakeholders and drafting the registration complaints' procedure (Rai 2016c). On behalf of CIEDP, Dr Pathak wrote to the UN Secretary-General Ban Ki-moon, 'complaining about the United Nations' indifference towards Nepal's transitional justice mechanisms and sought its technical, financial and expert support to carry out CIEDP's work' (Pandey 2016b). In response, the UN officially informed the government it could not support the TJ mechanisms '[i]n the absence of steps by the Government of Nepal to ensure that the enabling law and procedures of the CIEDP and TRC are in compliance with its international legal obligations' (OHCHR 2016) and stated that an essential requisite for their support was the amendment of the TJ Act in line with Nepal's obligations under international law.

A key issue that has arisen for the TJ commissions is the lack of staff. In late 2015, the government authorised 100 positions for the TRC (although the TRC had requested 144) and 70 positions for the CIEDP. However, as of February 2016, there were only 27 TRC staff and 25 CIEDP staff (Rai 2016b). The Chairman of the CIEDP explained the lack of staff was in part because the government was not issuing staff allowances usually provided to government staff that transfer to another government office (Rai 2016b).

The commissions and various TJ actors have continually lobbied the government with regard to TJ. For example, in late 2015 the TRC Chairman submitted an eightpoint amendment proposal to the Ministry of Law, Justice and Parliamentary Affairs with regard to the statutory limitations for rape. Also, in early 2016 the CIEDP Chairman Lokendra Mallik sought the Ministry to address the criminalisation of enforced disappearances, which was required for CIEDP to investigate conflict-related enforced disappearances and recommend actions against the perpetrators. Chairman Mallik lamented that without the criminalisation of enforced disappearances the commission would have limited jurisdiction to recommend reparation (The Kathmandu Post 2015a); he also stated that '[t]he government is in a deep slumber. It has done nothing to bring such laws. How can we function in the absence of such laws' (Pandey 2016c). Despite the active petitioning to the Supreme Court (for a detailed discussion see Wagle 2015) and subsequent rulings, the government has yet to respond to the Supreme Court directions to introduce and amend legislation.

Ongoing concerns have been raised about the commissions by the NHRC, the Supreme Court, conflict victims, civil society representatives and the international community. These included concerns about the commissions' impartiality and efficiency, the infighting between TRC members, as well as concerns with the government's cooperation with the TJ commissions, namely the delay in the government amending the TJ Act and the lack of human and financial support provided. The TRC Chairman, Surya Kiran Gurung, threatened to quit if the government did not amend the existing TJ Act to comply with the Supreme Court's verdict as well as international norms and principles. In June 2016, almost ten years after the CPA was signed, the former Prime Minister, Sher Bahadur Deuba was charged with conflict-related human rights violations. A complaint jointly lodged with the TRC by six families of the deceased, accused Deuba of mobilising the Nepal Army to kill Maoist cadres at Ansrang, after a truce for peace talks (Business Standard 2016).

The CIEDP and the TRC began collecting conflict-related complaints from the victims of insurgency in April 2016. Given the low number of complaints registered on the first day concerns were raised about whether information about registration had been properly disseminated (Parajuli 2016). Challenges included 'reaching out to families of all the victims, especially those living away from urban centres; convincing victims' families that justice will be delivered; and assuring the witnesses that security and confidentiality would be maintained' as well as the absence of a law to criminalise enforced disappearances and torture (Parajuli 2016). In some districts the police and the army requested the details of those people who registered their cases; however, these requests were denied by the commissions (Pandey 2016e). There have been reports that various security personnel have exerted pressure and intimidation on complainants and commission members. The Nepal Army requested the Local Peace Committees in Rukum and Jumla provide details of complaints filed against it and reportedly sent plain-clothes officials to monitor complaints filed against it (Nepal 2016). The Maoists have also sought information from the Ministry of Home Affairs on complaints against high-ranking Maoists (Nepal 2016). The Conflict Victims Common Platform monitored the complaints in 15 districts and noted a number of issues with the ways the Local Peace Committees treated victims and recorded their complaints (Nepal 2016). According to Nepal (2016):

> Victims have reported that peace committee secretaries were unable to manage situations when people victimized by opposing sides arrived at the same time to submit their complaints. Those unable to write have at times been narrating their experience to a room full of strangers, or worse, people linked to their perpetrators.

The CIEDP published the list of 2,886 individuals reportedly disappeared during the conflict and has sought additional information 'from the public, civil society, political parties, rights organisations, government bodies, national and international organisations' (Rai 2016a). The TRC has received almost 60,000 complaints but there are an estimated total of 70,000 complaints by victims, if the complaints filed with NHRC and various district offices (e.g. police and administration) are also considered (myRepublica 2017).

As the commissions approached the end of their two-year mandate the concerns with TJ commissions and the government's cooperation intensified. A TRC member, Madhabi Bhatta, was reported to have said: 'Either TRC's tenure has to be extended or it should be dissolved' (Pandey 2016d). In a joint statement by TRIAL International REDRESS HimRights Advocacy Forum JuRI-Nepal (Justice and Rights Institute-Nepal) stated:

> For the mechanisms to fulfill their tasks, extending their mandate must go hand in hand with legal improvements: the criminalization and retroactive application of crimes of torture, enforced disappearance and use and recruitment of child soldiers, as well as the lifting of statutes of limitations for rape, murder and torture. Legal ambiguity on the relationship between the criminal justice system and the transitional justice bodies should also be clarified … The bodies will also have to clarify their internal policies and processes: under which criteria will cases be recommended for prosecution? Which safeguards are in place to prevent political interference? How will reparation packages operate and what will be their scope? How will victims and witnesses be protected from potential reprisals?
>
> (Trial International et al. 2017)

The commissions completed their two-year mandate on 9 February 2017 and, pursuant to an emergency cabinet meeting, were granted a one-year extension until February 2018. The day after the extension was granted the Parliamentary Committee on Social Justice and Human Rights directed the government to amend the TJ Act to be in line with the Supreme Court rulings (myRepublica 2017). At the time of writing this had yet to occur.

Other transitional justice mechanisms

The TRC and CIEDP have been the focus of TJ efforts with limited progress on other TJ mechanisms. There have been a number of attempts by the various governments in Nepal to promote army personnel accused of conflict-related crimes. Also, amnesties have been sought for high-ranking personnel and politicians (e.g. Maoist Constituent Assembly member Balkrishna Dhungel). There has been a mass withdrawal of conflict-related cases, with some estimates at over 1,000 'politically motivated' cases withdrawn by the government, pursuant to Article 5.2.7 of the Comprehensive Peace Agreement. On 5 May 2016 the two ruling coalition partners – CPN-UML and UCPN-M – agreed to a nine-point deal, which included provisions to implement the constitution, socio-economic transformation and post-earthquake reconstruction and notably an amnesty provision 'to immediately initiate the process to withdraw or give clemency on insurgency-era cases and other politically-motivated cases filed on various occasions' (myRepublica 2016). The agreement was highly criticised by the national and international organisations (see, for example, HRW 2016). A writ petition lodged on 9 May 2016, which sought an interim order by the Supreme Court on the nine-point agreement, was quashed by the Supreme Court (The Himalayan Times 2016). In July 2016 the Attorney General Hari Phuyal explained that the Nepal security agencies, the CPN-Maoist Centre leaders and the Maoist security agencies had agreed that there would be no amnesty for serious offences, highlighting the TJ commissions would only recommend prosecution in exceptional cases (Kamat 2016).

Until 2013 there had been no vetting of abusive officials/personnel. However, in response to the 2012 Supreme Court ruling the army introduced regulations to prevent human rights violators from serving as UN peacekeepers; although it is unclear whether the regulations have been implemented (Advocacy Forum 2012, 2014b). Criminal charges have only been filed in a handful of cases (see ICJ 2014, 9–11) and some senior alleged perpetrators have had visa restrictions imposed by other countries. Politicians continued to evaded calls to commence criminal prosecutions by maintaining that conflict-related cases were to be dealt with by the TRC. In January 2013 Nepal Army Colonel Kumar Lama was held in the UK under the universal jurisdiction for charges of torture committed during the conflict. Col Lama was acquitted of both counts of torture in August and September 2016, respectively and he reportedly (re)joined the Nepal Army immediately after his return from London (for further details see Chapter 6).

To date there have not been any reparations provided. However, in October 2016 the TJ commissions prepared draft guidelines on reparations. With regard to murder, the TRC came up with 16 categories (in relation to the nature, circumstances, contexts and methods of the killing) and proposed 18 reparation schemes for families and dependents in murder cases, including free education, vocational training, and psychological counselling (Pandey 2016a). Other reparation packages were suggested for six other types of conflict-related crimes: torture, rape and sexual violence, abduction, maiming, seizure of property and forcible eviction and displacement (Pandey 2016a). The draft reparation guidelines also included a public apology from the government or responsible individuals from the conflict parties, a declaration of Martyrs' Day in the name of the victims and naming local infrastructure after the victims. These draft guidelines are set to be reviewed by the TRC and other concerned parties, including victims' groups' representatives (Pandey 2016a).

During the conflict there were various ad hoc programs of relief for those deemed to be conflict victims. The details of these programs have been outlined in an Advocacy Forum report entitled *Discrimination and irregularities: The painful tale of interim relief in Nepal* (Marg 2010). In the early part of the conflict these programs included a relief program for victims of the Maoists in 1999 and the Victims of Conflict Fund in 2002. By October 2004, two years before the end of the conflict, the government had spent 1.1 million NPR on the compensation of families of civilians and police personnel who were killed by the Maoists (Marg 2010, 9). Although there were other funds allocated for IDP rehabilitation and immediate relief in 2003 and 2004 they do not appear to have been disbursed (Marg 2010, 9). In August 2004 a taskforce was formed with the mandate to formulate a program to provide relief to IDPs. However, in October 2004, a 15-point relief package for 'conflict victims' was announced by the government. The program included a range of relief provisions including a monthly allowance for displaced persons above 60 years (300 NPR), an education allowance for children of the deceased or displaced persons (1,000 NPR), vocational training and income-generating skill development programs, a one-off family allowance (2,000–4,500 NPR) and loans for small businesses (Marg 2010, 10). This program was short-lived: it was abandoned four months later when King Gyanendra took power in February 2005. The subsequent National Policy on Internally Displaced Persons, 2006 and the Procedural Directives of National Policies Relating to the Internally Displaced, 2007 were not fully implemented; by July 2010 only 2,500 families who were displaced (out of the 52,000 cases recorded by the MoPR) had received relief (Marg 2010, 10, 20).

In June 2007 a MoPR special taskforce was formed to collect data about the names of people killed, disappeared, injured, abducted, illegally detained, orphaned or who suffered property loss or damage. As part of this process the taskforce was mandated to collect data from other sources including the ICRC, the NHRC and INSEC, although over time the taskforce only relied on data from the District Administrative Office (ICTJ 2011a, 10). In the same month the Supreme Court ordered the government to provide immediate interim relief to victims of 'physical and mental torture' (Marg 2010, 6).

In 2008 the government commenced an Interim Relief Program. The program was funded from a World Bank grant ($50 million USD) for post-conflict recovery in Nepal. By July 2010 1.4 million NPR (approximately $19.2 million USD) had been spent on interim relief (Marg 2010, 12). In total, $23 million USD was spent on relief programs and the remaining $27 million USD was allocated to reintegration packages for ex-combatants (see discussion on 'real' victims in Chapter 6) (Carranza 2012, 11). Pursuant to the Citizens' Relief, Compensation and Economic Assistance Procedure, 'conflict victims' are regarded:

> as those who depended on individuals killed in conflict, those who lost their body parts during conflict, those who were displaced, those who disappeared and their families, those abducted by the conflicting parties and those suffering damage to lives and property.
>
> (Nepal Monitor 2011)[12]

Relief was provided in the form of monetary assistance, education scholarships, medical treatment and skills development training. Table 5.1 provides a summary

Table 5.1 Relief provided by the government through the Relief and Rehabilitation Unit as of November 2010

Categories of violations eligible to receive IRP	*Total number/unit of victims identified by the Ministry of Peace and Reconstruction Task Force*	*Total number/unit of victims who received Interim Relief Program*
Deceased persons	16,009	13,964
Kidnapped/disappeared persons	1219	221
Property loss/damage	11,775	4238
Disappeared persons	1292	1197
Support to people with disabilities	4305	1292
Destroyed infrastructure	5100	1480
Assistance to widows	9000	3668

Source: ICTJ 2011a, 7.

of the relief provided by the Relief and Rehabilitation Unit in the MoPR as of November 2010. The Interim Relief Program will be explored in Chapter 7.

It can be seen that over the ten years since the signing of the CPA, the trajectory of TJ has altered significantly. Many contend that 'those accused of the gravest crimes can still feel untouchable' (ICG 2009, 30). Indeed, the ongoing efforts 'to grant pardons suggest that interim arrangements may enable the political elite to sweep past misdeeds under the carpet' (ICG 2007, i). Political parties have used the idea of 'consensus' to prevent the courts from pursuing conflict-era human rights violations (see, for example, Adhikari et al. 2014, 7). What remains underexplored is the ways the various actors, including the government, have engaged with and sought to mould TJ, the focus of the following chapter.

Transitional justice actor typology

Before providing details of the participatory activities conducted in relation to TJ in Nepal, it is important to provide an outline of the key actors involved. In this section I categorise the various actors involved in TJ in Nepal based on the functions of TJ actors and the levels/arenas (international, national and local) where the contestation happens. This typology assists with understanding the various actors involved in TJ in Nepal and identifying who is making claims and on behalf of whom. It also provides a useful means to examine the ways these actors interact with each other and engage with TJ. By characterising the functions of these actors and the arenas in which these actors operate, I avoid the issue of grouping the majority of TJ actors against victims (see Chapter 1). Four main groups of actors are identified: the TJ experts, those who produce TJ discourse and knowledge; the TJ brokers, those who operationalise TJ on the ground; TJ implementers, those who implement TJ on the ground; and victims.[13] Details of the programs and activities these actors have conducted will be discussed below.

TJ experts

As discussed in Chapter 3, to date TJ discourse has primarily been constructed by actors external to post-conflict countries. The combined efforts of this heterogeneous group of TJ experts have led to the establishment of the norms of accountability, justice and peace, which have been replicated throughout the world (see Teitel 2003; Triponel and Pearson 2010; Orentlicher 2007; Balasco 2013). The impact of TJ experts has been instrumental in the evolution of TJ. TJ experts are predominately human rights experts and organisations based in the headquarters of various international organisations in the Global North. Crucially, activism by TJ experts 'has succeeded in framing states' choice as one of which model of justice to adopt, not whether any should be adopted at all' (Subotic 2012, 118).

Generally, TJ experts advocate for a combination of judicial and non-judicial TJ mechanisms: truth commissions, prosecutions, reparations and institutional reforms (see Chapter 1). Arguably, the authority of these actors 'comes from their technical expertise and the moral imperative of responding to atrocities' whereby the 'language of "best practice" justifies the transfer of norms as knowledge transfer' (Apland 2012). TJ experts are often in control of the financial resources for TJ and are well connected to the media (Ramji-Nogales 2010, 19). According to Subotic (2012, 108), TJ experts create TJ templates, set the tone of TJ debate and dictate the TJ options from which transitional states choose. Through the production of these 'models of TJ', TJ experts have produced 'a self-reinforcing cycle that further institutionalizes their professional authority' (Subotic 2012, 106, 118).

At the transnational level the transitional justice social movement comprises TJ experts who make claims on behalf of victims, which raises significant issues (see Chapters 6 and 7). Of concern is that the 'limited repertoires' in effect narrow the range of TJ options (Sriram 2007, 591). Usually TJ experts support truth commissions over other mechanisms that might provide similar outcomes (Daly 2008, 23). In addition, states' and other TJ actors' responses to the calls for justice by TJ experts may be made simply to appease the movement's actors. TJ experts may also find themselves mobilising alongside other TJ actors 'which may create tensions with local actors pursuing different strategies' and may need to change their agendas 'to avoid co-optation by political leaders and competition with local individuals and organizations' (Rowen 2012, 711). This is particularly evident with regard to the TRC in Nepal (see Chapter 6).

TJ experts include the Office of the High Commission on Human Rights (the UN's lead organisation on TJ), the International Centre for Transitional Justice (a specialist INGO that focuses on accountability for mass atrocities and human rights abuse) the International Commission for Jurists, TRIAL, the United States Institute of Peace and the International Committee of the Red Cross.[14] I outline these organisations' TJ-related programs and activities, as they are indirectly involved in shaping TJ in Nepal (they also have country offices in Nepal which I locate in the category 'TJ brokers,' discussed below).

The International Centre for Transitional Justice is a specialist INGO that focuses on accountability for mass atrocity and human rights abuse through TJ mechanisms. Its founders were actively involved in TJ measures in transitional countries; for instance Alex Boraine and Paul van Zyl were involved in South Africa's Truth and Reconciliation Commission and David Tolbert was involved in the International Criminal Tribunal for the former Yugoslavia. This is an example of the transfer of personnel between TJ expert organisations and TJ mechanisms around the world that in turn impacts the ways national and local actors articulate their claims. While organisations such as the International Centre for Transitional Justice have gained prominence, little is known about 'how they adapt to change and how they learn from policy failures' (Subotic 2012, 111–112).

The International Centre for Transitional Justice Director of Research, Pablo de Greiff, was appointed as the first UN Special Rapporteur on the Promotion of Truth, Justice, Reparation and Guarantees of Non-recurrence in May 2012. The four elements of the Special Rapporteur's mandate (truth, justice, reparation and guarantees of non-recurrence) are expected to:

> ensure accountability, serve justice, provide remedies to victims, promote healing and reconciliation, establish independent oversight of the security system and restore confidence in the institutions of the State and promote the rule of law in accordance with international human rights law.
>
> (OHCHR 2014)

With regard to Nepal there was correspondence between the Special Rapporteur and government in 2012 and 2013 (see, for example, UN General Assembly 2013). The Special Rapporteur along with other UN Special and Chief Rapporteurs released a joint statement expressing their concerns about the TJ legislation that was passed in April 2014 (discussed above). This came a few months after the UN Human Rights Council urged Nepal to address conflict-related violations and provide reparations to victims, and just one month after the UN Secretary-General urged Prime Minister Sushil Koirala to form a Truth and Reconciliation Commission in line with international standards.

Another TJ expert is the United States Institute for Peace (USIP). As the field of TJ was gaining increased prominence, Neil Kritz at USIP edited an early piece of TJ literature entitled *Transitional Justice: How Emerging Democracies Reckon with Former Regimes* (1995). USIP is a US federal, nonpartisan conflict management centre that seeks to prevent and mitigate international conflict. Its Rule of Law team provides advice and assistance to individuals, organisations and governments working on TJ issues and conducts research, consultation and workshops. USIP has also produced a DVD on truth commissions entitled *Confronting the Truth: Truth Commissions and Societies in Transition* that outlines various countries' experiences with truth seeking. This DVD was shown at USIP's and the Ministry of Peace and Reconstruction's consultations in Nepal (discussed below).

The International Commission for Jurists is an INGO composed of eminent lawyers and judges from all regions of the world. It seeks to promote and protect human rights through the rule of law by using its '*legal expertise* to develop and strengthen national and international justice systems' (ICJ 2017, my emphasis). The transfer of personnel between TJ expert organisations is again evident as the former International Commission for Jurists Nepal Country Representative was a former OHCHR Nepal employee.

TRIAL, a Swiss association based in Geneva, aims to put the law at the service of victims of international crimes, including war crimes, genocide, crimes against humanity, torture and forced disappearances. TRIAL became partners with Lawyers Forum for Human Rights (LAFHUR), a Nepalese NGO, with the stated aim 'to combine their respective expertise in order to help victims obtain redress in the most efficient way' (TRIAL 2014). Despite concluding its partnership with the Committee for Social Justice, a local victims' organisation in May 2010, TRIAL indicates that its local partnerships have led to the filing of the first cases before the UN Human Rights Committee. TRIAL, along with ICTJ, the International Commission for Jurists, Human Rights Watch, Advocacy Forum – Nepal and seven other local organisations working with victims of human rights violations and their families, submitted a briefing note to the UN Special Rapporteur (TRIAL 2012).

As had been the case in many post-conflict contexts, TJ experts played a prominent role in the TJ process in Nepal (as will be discussed in Chapter 6).

TJ implementers

Since the inclusion of TJ provisions in the CPA, TJ has largely been undertaken at the national government level. This category of TJ actors generally comprises national politicians, the Supreme Court and relevant government ministries and agencies. It is notable that a number of the relevant ministries and agencies were established after the conflict so their infancy impacts their capacity to implement TJ measures. Also, the Interim Government and various Committees established to draft relevant TJ legislation largely comprise members from the same political parties that would be investigated and punished through the TJ process. Over three-quarters of the first Constituent Assembly members were from the three largest political parties that were involved in the conflict; also Pushpa Kamal Dahal, the leader of the Maoists during the insurgency, was the Prime Minister until 2009 (see Bhandari 2011, 14–15; ICG 2009, 21).

Fullard points to 'elite pact politics' as one of the major reasons that there has not been an effective TJ process. She states:

> Neither the Nepalese state nor the CPN-M will be enthusiastic about an impartial scrutiny of their actions, the disclosure of the grim facts of disappearances, or the potential for criminal justice proceedings against them or their members. Both parties have indicated support for some kind of amnesty that will cover actions undertaken in pursuit of political goals ... As a result, it is questionable whether either side has the political will to seriously pursue a project of accountability for disappearances and past crimes. Instead, they may attempt to construct, manage and direct a process that 'passes for' or mimics transitional justice in form rather than substance.
>
> (2008, 12–13)

Although the second Constituent Assembly has a different makeup, similar interests and political pacts remain evident.

The Ministry of Peace and Reconstruction is the focal government body tasked to deal with TJ. The Ministry conducted consultations regarding the draft bills on the Truth and Reconciliation Commission and the Commission on Disappearances (with the assistance of TJ brokers such as OHCHR) and designed and implemented the Interim Relief Program (see Chapter 7). Another TJ implementer is the National Human Rights Commission (NHRC), an administrative body tasked with protecting and promoting human rights. During the conflict the Commission monitored and investigated conflict-related human rights violations. I was told in 2012 that the Commission is still working through a backlog of cases.[15] The NHRC has made a range of recommendations regarding investigation and criminal punishment of perpetrators but as of August 2010 the government had implemented only 34 of the 386 recommendations (NepalNews 2010). Through the range of its activities the NHRC forms the practical link between international standards and their operationalisation, representing the government's efforts to promote and embed international norms in domestic structures (Cardenas 2004, 53). In January 2012 the *Human Rights Commission Act* was adopted in Nepal. The legislation changed the Commission from a constitutional body to an administrative branch of the government; this has implications for the jurisdiction and independence of the Commission (Redress 2014). A worker at the Commission informed me that since September 2013, when the tenure of the commissioners came to an end, the NHRC had struggled to function as it was effectively leaderless.[16] After a one-year delay the government appointed the NHRC chairperson and commissioners in November 2014.

Local Peace Committees are also involved in implementing TJ. The decision to establish Local Peace Committees in Nepal arose from the Nepal Transition to Peace Project under the Nepal Peace Trust Fund, a donor trust fund (see below). This Fund was managed by the Ministry of Peace and Reconstruction and included international community involvement, via donors and government ministries, which provided legitimacy and assisted with providing funds (Sapkota 2017, 25). According to the manager of the Fund, Bishnu Sapkota (2017, 25), this fund lacked transparency and required more inclusive funding priorities. Ultimately local actors did not determine the local peace strategy; according to victims' group leader, Ram Bhandari, this strategy 'was designed from the top down, based on political negotiation and donors' recommendations' (2011, 15).

In the absence of effective local government and in the wake of the CPA, Local Peace Committees began to be established in July 2007. According to the terms of reference (Section 4.1) these committees were temporary mechanisms tasked with promoting and facilitating the peace process at the local level until the new Constitution was adopted (ICTJ 2011a, 9). Local Peace Committees were mandated to assist with implementing the CPA; promote local dialogue to mitigate or resolve conflicts; encourage reconciliation, healing, and mutual trust; observe local political and social developments; gather data on conflict victims and conflict damage and monitor interim relief and reconstruction programmes.

Despite having a broad mandate the majority of Local Peace Committees narrowly focused their activities on reviewing victims' applications for interim relief (discussed in Chapter 7). According to the Terms of Reference drafted by the MoPR, each committee was to be composed of up to 23 members including representatives from political parties, civil society, the local Chamber of Commerce and Industries, as well as representatives of victims and two people from various indigenous and ethnic groups, with the Local Peace Committee coordinator rotating every six months. The composition of Local Peace Committees provided opportunities for victims and local representatives to raise local concerns and identify priorities and potentially innovative and responsive proposals regarding TJ-related issues. They also provided opportunities for victims and community members to be involved in decision-making – a key component of meaningful participation. However, frequently decisions were made by the committee co-ordinator – usually a political party representative – based on party interests (see Chapter 7). Bishnu Sapkota explains that the failure to establish the National Peace and Rehabilitation Commission – envisaged to be a neutral, inclusive national body to oversee the implementation of the CPA – led to the Ministry of Peace and Reconstruction becoming partisan, and in turn the Local Peace Committees effectively became 'district branches of the MoPR despite their stated roles as autonomous peacebuilding mechanisms' (2017, 24).

The Supreme Court, another TJ implementer, has made numerous directives in relation to TJ. As early as 2007 the Supreme Court ordered that the government establish a Commission of Investigation on Enforced Disappeared Persons to provide compensation to torture victims and to draft laws regarding the protection of disappeared persons and the criminalisation of torture and to implemented the Geneva Conventions. It also ordered the government to address the needs of the internally displaced, return captured property and provide compensation to victims. In 2012 the Court ordered the government to establish a mechanism to vet the promotion of security personnel. The Court has also made orders regarding the government's withdrawal of conflict-related cases. With a number of writ petitions lodged, the Court has been quite active with respect to various TJ measures in Nepal (for further details on the Supreme Court's jurisprudence on TJ see Wagle 2015).

TJ brokers

While TJ discourse has been driven by TJ experts at the international level, at the national level there is another category of actors: the TJ brokers. TJ brokers are largely 'downloaders' of the international norms and work locally to diffuse these norms (see Boesenecker and Vinjamuri 2011). These actors vary in terms of their relationship to TJ experts; they include in-country human rights organisations, country offices of TJ experts and national NGOs. In Nepal TJ brokers have largely focused on accountability (e.g. criminal prosecutions and the International Criminal Court) and the Truth and Reconciliation Commission and the Commission of Investigation on Enforced Disappeared Persons.

TJ brokers are usually human rights organisations.[17] Frequently, these organisations are led by elite, educated, upper class males, a stark difference to many of the victims and affected community members (Robins 2012, 24). These organisations conduct brokerage, which produces 'a new connection between previously unconnected or weakly connected sites' (Tilly and Tarrow 2007, 215; see also Tarrow 2005, 190–192). Pertinently, these actors use brokerage to bring previously unconnected groups (e.g. certain victims) into TJ discussions (see McAdam, Tarrow, and Tilly 2009; Merry 2006). However, there are significant variations in TJ brokers' locations and methods, which have 'important consequences for the contention in which they participate' (McAdam, Tarrow, and Tilly 2001, 142). At times some TJ brokers actively merge people with different interests but they can also deliberately keep people separated (see McAdam, Tarrow, and Tilly 2001, 142). As Chapter 7 demonstrates this has occurred with various human rights organisations seeking to unite victims from both sides of the conflict.

Of significance is that brokerage produces new advantages for the actors involved but particularly for brokers. Over time 'brokerage establishes biases toward [the] use of the same connections instead of other possible connections that would, in principle, produce different sorts of collective interaction' (McAdam, Tarrow, and Tilly 2001, 142, see also 157). This selectivity can be seen with respect to how various victims' groups are called upon as the voice of victims in Nepal (see Chapter 7). These victims' groups, among other actors, are 'certified', another contentious politics mechanism, whereby external authorities validate actors, including their performances and claims

(McAdam, Tarrow, and Tilly 2001, 121). Indeed these certified groups are 'political actors that have rights to exist, to act, to make claims, and/or to draw routinely on government-controlled resources' (McAdam, Tarrow, and Tilly 2001, 146).

An example of brokerage in Nepal is encapsulated in the following response by the district coordinator of a Nepali regional human rights organisation:

> Truth and Reconciliation Commissions are compulsory for peace processes. The alternatives only free perpetrators ... by ignoring international standards, making a weak Truth and Reconciliation Commission and Commission on Disappearances and saying the peace process is complete without prosecutions, how is this justice? It will again fuel conflict ... [The TJ process is] now led by human rights activists and civil society.[18]

Along with TJ experts, TJ brokers have led the call for adopting and pursuing TJ in Nepal. A leading TJ broker is Advocacy Forum, a human rights organisation founded by a group of lawyers in 2001. This organisation has been particularly influential with regard to TJ. The organisation seeks to promote the rule of law and accountability for human rights violations, uphold international human rights standards in Nepal and redress injustice (Advocacy Forum). The organisation was involved in ensuring the OHCHR country office was established in Nepal in 2005. In relation to TJ, the organisation's activities are focused on establishing TJ mechanisms 'to ascertain the actual truth by identifying and prosecuting the perpetrators', ending the culture of impunity and strengthening the rule of law, providing reparations to victims and creating a 'conducive environment for reconciliation in order to provide justice for the victims' (Advocacy Forum 2014a). In particular, the organisation exerts pressure at the national and international level to establish TJ mechanisms in line with the international standards, enhances the capacity of various stakeholders on TJ related issues, unifies 'conflict victims to facilitate their access to justice via capacity building measures', and advocates and lobbies for a reparation programs for the victims (Advocacy Forum 2014a).

Advocacy Forum supports Conflict Victims' Society for Justice, a victims' association that has formed a victims' network in 20 districts. Advocacy Forum works in coordination with the Conflict Victims' Society for Justice and Accountability Watch Committee. Again, demonstrating the involvement of human rights organisations in TJ, the Accountability Watch Committee is composed of organisations and individuals working in the areas of human rights, the rule of law and accountability. It is predominately composed of current or former workers from human rights organisations (barring two victims and activists).[19] A lawyer in this group, who works for International Commission for Jurists, frequently provides written briefs on the TJ progress in Nepal to TJ brokers and foreign governments and development agencies (the latter are usually TJ sponsors and funders).

The Informal Sector Service Centre (INSEC), a leading human rights organisation, is another key player in Nepal. INSEC has human rights reporters in each of the 75 districts with five regional offices. The organisation issues Human Rights Yearbooks many of which include details of the numbers of conflict victims. INSEC has advocated for the ratification of the International Criminal Court's Rome Statute (including coordinating the National Coalition for the International Criminal Court), monitored human rights and actively campaigned, lobbied and advocated for TJ and human rights issues at the local, national and international level. District INSEC officers have visited affected communities to verify victims' stories.[20] I was told the organisation's main goal was 'how to get victims justice and how to get justice from those who don't want to give it.'[21]

OHCHR Nepal (hereafter OHCHR for the sake of clarity) was also a key TJ broker. In 2009, pursuant to funding from the UN Peace Fund Nepal, OHCHR launched its nation-wide 'Peace through Justice' project (OHCHR 2009). The immediate objective was to assist the government 'to establish effective transitional justice mechanisms and support the society built on respect for the rule of law and human rights, including through the active participation of the marginalized groups, [and] women at the grassroots level' (UNDP 2014b). The project was designed to ensure that civil society organisations were 'key collaborative partners' and victims were both participants and beneficiaries (MPTF 2011, 16). Table 5.2 summarises the UN's key program with respect to TJ.

Further details of these activities will be provided throughout the remainder of this book.

ICTJ's country office in Nepal (hereafter ICTJ for the sake of clarity) is also a key TJ broker. ICTJ has been involved in Nepal since 2006. The former head of ICTJ, Lucia Withers, was a former OHCHR employee. ICTJ reportedly works 'at the national and grassroots level to further transitional justice in Nepal' (ICTJ 2015). To date, ICTJ has provided technical assistance, training and advocacy for local activists, government officials and parliamentarians on truth-seeking and/or reparations and provided educational material on gender and TJ (in partnership with UN Women Nepal). It has conducted a number of studies with victims (see below). A recent program report stated that the range of activities include 'building informed constituencies among policy makers, civil society, victims, and the international community', providing technical assistance to policy-makers on the design and implementation of TJ processes, influencing policy-makers (e.g. by providing NGOs with international comparative experience and technical expertise) and supporting the coordination and development of strategies for NGOs and victims' groups (ICTJ 2015). Demonstrating the close working relationship between most TJ experts and brokers, one respondent informed me that the closure of the OHCHR country office did not pose a huge challenge as ICTJ head office frequently provided research and policy input to OHCHR in New York so the skills, knowledge and contacts remained.[22] One of ICTJ's national partners is Advocacy Forum.

Table 5.2 Summary of OHCHR's Peace through Justice project

Output	*Examples of activities*
1. MoPR conducting effective preparations for the creation of the commissions and providing necessary support in the on-going work of the commissions	• Drafted and reviewed TJ legislation • Conducted regional consultations on TJ legislation, district meetings and thematic cluster meetings • Conducted workshops on TJ for government officials from relevant ministries • Organised a study trip to South Africa for three members from the MoPR to meet with people involved in establishing the South African TRC • Established the TJ Resource Centre
2. Transitional justice commissions working effectively and in accordance with international human rights standards	• Organised 'interaction' with international consultant on accountability and amnesty with civil society and various organisations and individuals • Conducted meeting on TJ and gender • Screened TJ documentary for civil society • Conducted meetings with Constituent Assembly members
3. Mapping documents with research and analysis on conflict related international human rights and humanitarian law	• Drafted and produced conflict report • Compiled conflict dataset reference archive
4. Civil society and national institutions are supporting the work of the commissions	• Provided one grant to ICTJ and 24 grants to 47 national organisations, activities included docudramas on TJ, street drama performances, conflict victims' profiles, information kits and television talk shows, training of psycho-social counsellors and radio programmes

Sources: Adapted from MPTF 2011, Phuyal and Pokhrel 2012, UNDP 2014b.

ICTJ has conducted training on TJ. The training utilised the ICTJ Trainer's Manual on Transitional Justice (2011b). As Figure 5.1 reveals the topics covered include truth-seeking, reparations, prosecution, institutional reform and gender. The manual employs an 'experimental learning approach' and provides comprehensive information on the TJ process in Nepal and context-specific activities. One of its main purposes is to ensure that '[p]articipants … gain information about the meaning and origin of transitional justice, its approaches and [the] different strategies it engages' (ICTJ 2011b, 6, see also 12).

The manual will be discussed further in Chapter 7.

Figure 5.1 Photo of author's copy of the *ICTJ Trainers' Manual on Transitional Justice*
Source: author.

UN Women is also a TJ broker. The Gender and TJ Network in Nepal was established by UN Women and ICTJ in partnership with various NGOs. The network spans ten districts; notably these districts were chosen because UN offices already existed there. The network seeks to include 'gender perspectives of justice in [the] transitional phase of Nepal' (WHR 2012b). One member of this network is Women for Human Rights (WHR). This NGO contends that its most important activity in this regard has been the facilitation role it plays between relevant government ministries and conflict-affected women concerning pensions, compensation and other relevant services (WHR

2012a). These services have been provided to over 1500 'conflict effected [*sic*] single women' (WHR 2012b). WHR has developed a legal toolkit for conflict-affected women, which includes details of relevant government agencies and international organisations.

Along with UN Women, the UNDP is another UN agency that plays a role in TJ in Nepal. The UNDP Enhancing Access to Justice for Consolidation of Peace project (August 2008 – December 2012) aimed to target TJ, 'gender justice' and access to justice at the local level (UNDP 2010a). UNDP partnered with UN Women to implement the TJ component. The UNDP provides that the 'objective of the project is to raise national capacity to carry out transitional justice processes through enhancing [the] execution of court decisions, victims' support and [the] witness protection programme, and [providing] technical assistance to the Ministry of Peace and Reconstruction' for the establishment of the TRC and CIEDP (UNDP 2010a, 6). Project outputs covered a range of activities and included strengthening the coordination of NGOs and government institutions (e.g. NHRC), supporting victims participating in TJ and the criminal justice system, training about TJ for district level women's organisations, supporting the establishment of a TRC secretariat and providing assistance to the TRC (UNDP 2010a, 23). This project was implemented in 'Central level justice agencies' and in 11 districts (UNDP 2014a).

Since the end of the conflict, the International Committee of the Red Cross Nepal (hereafter ICRC for the sake of clarity) has sought to address the humanitarian consequences of the conflict. It prioritised its work on issues related to the disappeared. This includes encouraging the government to help families of the disappeared, supporting forensic work (e.g. exhumations and the identification of remains) and providing psychosocial, economic and legal assistance to the families of missing persons (e.g. helping to establish the National Network of Families of Disappeared and Missing).[23] The ICRC's local partner is the Nepal Red Cross. I was informed that ICRC focused on the organisation's experience and knowledge and left human rights organisations to pursue justice, as it was important to share tasks.[24] A former ICRC worker, Simon Robins, has been involved with families of the disappeared (discussed below).

While this list is by no means exhaustive it indicates that the pool of experts and brokers is highly legalistic and often working in partnership, leaving little space for tailoring TJ to the local context. This is particularly problematic given that donors and funders rely on a limited range of actors that are neither representative of those affected nor attuned to context specificities. These issues will be discussed in Chapters 6 and 7.

Victims

In this book, I take this group of actors to encompass victims,[25] victims' representatives and victims' groups, predominantly although not exclusively at the local level.[26] Until relatively recently there had been little written about victims' groups in Nepal, most of which were formed after the conflict ended in 2006. Some victims' groups represent victims of both sides, while others focus on certain types of victims. According to a victims' group leader Ram Bhandari (2011, 44) the trajectory of victims' groups was as follows: in 1999 the Society of Families of those Disappeared by the State was the first group formed by families of the disappeared. This group was later renamed the Society of the Families of Warriors Disappeared by the State and it comprised family members of those disappeared by the state. Another victims' group was formed for people who were victimised by Maoist forces, called the Maoist Victim Association. In Bardiya a victims' group called the Conflict Victims' Committee was originally for families of the disappeared but now includes victims from both sides of the conflict. This transformation also occurred with the Committee for Social Justice in Lamjung district. In 2008 the Conflict Victim Society for Justice was formed as an umbrella group with approximately 20 district networks. With the support from ICRC, a families of the disappeared network was formed called the National Network of Families of Disappeared and Missing. According to Bhandari, many of the victims' groups see each other as competitors, particularly with regard to obtaining funding from donors (2011, 77).[27]

Efforts to develop a national level umbrella network Solidarity Campaign for Justice, which included the involvement of the above-mentioned associations, were arguably hampered by internal divisions and external constraints (Bhandari 2011, 58).[28] However, in a recent development, the Conflict Victims Common Platform (CVCP) was launched on 25 November 2014. The Platform – formerly headed by Bhandari – 'is a loose network of 13 victims' associations, supported by the UN (CVCPNepal 2014, see also UN 2014). CVCP is intended to help victims overcome internal divisions, to assist with reframing the TJ debate in Nepal and to '[s]upport efforts to formulate a common position and demands' (UN 2014, see also UNRCO 2014, 5). The CVCP is discussed further in Chapter 7.

Some victims' groups have the institutional backing of specific organisations, usually TJ brokers (e.g. Advocacy Forum and the ICRC). These organisations have helped to make these victims' groups more visible, given them greater recognition and provided varying degrees of financial and technical support. For example, various victims' groups are involved with the Transitional Justice Advocacy Group, which is 'a loose network of organisations working on human rights and TJ issues' (Bhandari 2011, 22). These victims' groups provided victims' perspectives on the TJ bills with the technical support of ICTJ (Bhandari 2011, 22). However Bhandari is highly sceptical of victims' groups sponsored by human rights organisations and points to the influx of aid and expertise by TJ experts and TJ brokers as one of the reasons that the victims' movement in Nepal has fragmented and weakened (Bhandari 2011, 17–18, 23, 57–58). According to an ICTJ report by Fullard (2008, 23), victim organisation has been constrained by the division of victims along lines of political affiliation. It has also been constrained because victims in Nepal

> are overwhelmingly from poor and marginalized communities with few resources or education, [and are] occupied with the daily struggle for subsistence, and [are] not a political force. They are often located in distant remote rural areas, mitigating against easy mobilization and unity.
>
> (Fullard 2008, 23)

Chapter 7 explores these issues further.

Examples of participation in Nepal

In light of the actor typology, this section provides examples of participatory activities that have been carried out in Nepal.[29] This section reveals how actors in the typology engage with one another; in particular it demonstrates the ways in which certain actors in the typology – especially TJ brokers – seek to engage with victims and communities regarding TJ. There has been a great deal of participation in Nepal over a range of TJ issues and by many actors. Where possible I have sought to draw attention to the following key questions: what are the stated reasons for employing participation?[30] When does participation occur? and Who is participating and how? I will analyse who benefits from the participatory process and/or from its outcomes in Chapter 6.

TRC and CIEDP

The majority of participation in TJ in Nepal has been in relation to the TRC and CIEDP. Following the CPA the first participatory activity I have been able to trace was conducted by the TJ broker, United States Institute of Peace, to address a perceived need for more information about international experiences and practices of TJ. From 10 to 17 July 2007 the United States Institute of Peace conducted a weeklong series of roundtable sessions including civil society organisations, victims' groups, government representatives, political parties and the media. These consultations took place in the same week that the Ministry of Peace and Reconstruction released the draft TRC bill, and were held in Kathmandu, as well as in three districts (Banke, Bardiya and Dang) in the Mid-Western region (the most affected region during the conflict). The main objective of these consultations was to raise awareness among different actors 'about what the key issues are for establishing a credible and effective transitional justice process and to encourage informed discussion on the issues' (Cochran-Budhathoki and Worden 2007). These consultations provided an opportunity to bring together a number of relevant actors in one space. Even at this early stage participants reported that they were concerned about being sidelined during the TJ process in Nepal. I was informed that participants did not want to talk and to repeatedly tell their stories only to have promises broken again; they were informed the organisation would convey their messages but the organisation could not guarantee they would be heard.[31] Many participants felt alienated from the TJ process and were unaware of the scheduled Ministry of Peace and Reconstruction consultations in each of the five regions. I was informed that the feedback from the United States Institute of Peace workshops was not provided to government officials or other personnel.[32]

In 2007 TJ brokers ICTJ and Advocacy Forum undertook a quantitative and qualitative study entitled *Nepali Voices: Perceptions of Truth, Justice, Reconciliation, Reparations and the Transition in Nepal* (ICTJ and Advocacy Forum 2008). This was the first study of its kind in Nepal and reveals the opportunities that participation provides to enable victims to voice their needs. The study was intended 'to bring victims' voices to the forefront of the national debate and to ensure that transitional-justice mechanisms involve stakeholders, especially victims and their families' (ICTJ and Advocacy Forum 2008, 10–11). The objectives were to determine the opinions and expectations of the victims and their families on a range of TJ issues, such as truth-seeking, justice, reconciliation, accountability, reparations and human rights violations. The survey was designed by TJ experts and TJ brokers (mostly human rights representatives) from Kathmandu and abroad. Over 800 Nepali victims were surveyed. In addition to the survey, ten focus-group discussions were conducted, thematically categorised into child soldiers, disappearances, internally displaced persons and women victims of sexual violence. Separate discussions were held for marginalised communities, including women, *Janajatis* (indigenous groups), Dalits and *Madhesis*.

The newly established Ministry of Peace and Reconstruction conducted consultations regarding the draft bills on the TRC and the CIEDP. These were conducted in each of the five regions, with cluster meetings in Kathmandu (for women, *Janajatis* and children) and also expert group meetings. I was informed that the objectives of these consultations were to promote awareness among victims about the content and status of the draft bills, to allow victims the opportunity for their voices to be heard and their views considered in finalising the bills and to facilitate the production of a memo to Constituent Assembly members in the form of amendments to the bills.[33] Each consultation took approximately two days during which a film about truth commissions around the world, dubbed in Nepali, was shown and a TJ handbook was provided to participants (courtesy of the United States Institute of Peace) before participants were invited to share their views.[34]

In total, over 150 victims from around 55 districts in each of the five regions participated (IOM 2011a). According to OHCHR:

> [t]he participants were chosen to represent groups most affected by the conflict but which have been largely excluded from any consultation on how the state should properly address the consequences of the conflict. Participants were given an opportunity to share their experiences, identify the cause and consequences of the conflict and to explore possible responses in the post-conflict period. As such, the organisations were given the tools to make a meaningful contribution to a national process

> on transitional justice and to have their voices heard prior to the establishment of any mechanisms, such as a Commission on Disappearances or a Truth and Reconciliation Commission.
>
> (2008)

For each of these consultations, the Chief District Officer (CDO), who was supposed to be in consultation with political parties and civil society within the district, was responsible for determining which victims should be nominated in each district. In one district the day before one consultation the CDO was told that his draft participant list was not broad-based and inclusive. The CDO explained this was because he did not know any victims of the state and did not have an overview of which organisations to invite. Most invitations were distributed the day before the consultation. Although it was an invitation-only event, the consultations were effectively open to those who did not receive invitations; interestingly, some victims who heard about the consultation by word of mouth attended, which perhaps indicates that victims sought an opportunity to be heard.

According to a human rights worker involved in the consultations, victims had a variety of expectations. He explained:

> For some, with due respect to the victims, they thought the whole purpose of the TRC was to get reparations and compensation. They thought 'what do I get because I was a victim' which is not the norm but many victims didn't understand the idea of 'victim' and the philosophy of TRC. For them the war has ended; they say 'I suffered a lot, we have suffered a lot and then what is the state going to give us? What are the peace dividends?' For some they say 'we didn't fight for any reparations or whatever we fought for a cause so we don't need any reparations. There has to be justice, there has to be political transformation; society has to change.' There were some that said 'why did I lose my husband or father or daughter or son those people must be punished there cannot be just reconciliation they are murders.' … [T]here was everything on the table.[35]

Ultimately, the workshops were conducted for victims to examine the two draft bills that were before the Constituent Assembly. The latest draft TRC bill (including recommendations from other regional consultations) was distributed to participants at the workshop, and not prior, which no doubt impacted upon their ability to provide comments and recommendations. I was informed that the introductions to the workshops by the Ministry of Peace and Reconstruction representatives focused on the TRC bill and not on wider issues of TJ and the concept of truth commissions.[36] It was asserted that Constituent Assembly members were there so that they could reiterate the views discussed when attending future discussions in the Assembly. This resonates with McAdam, Tilly and Tarrow's conceptualisation of mediation where individuals act as privileged intermediaries (2001, 141).

The consultation process took over one year, which a respondent involved in the consultations said gave the politicians an excuse to delay further action (see Chapter 6).[37] These consultations were transcribed by The Asia Foundation (an INGO) and the transcriptions were handed over to Ministry of Peace and Reconstruction. The Ministry of Peace and Reconstruction did not circulate/share copies of these transcripts with other organisations involved in the consultations, including the National Human Rights Commission, OHCHR or victims' associations.[38] A number of suggestions from the consultations were included in the draft bills, which shows the benefits of participatory activities being incorporating into TJ. However, owing to the political requirements to legislate these TJ provisions, the bills also retained controversial provisions to which civil society, the international community and victims' groups were opposed.

Women's experiences

Another area that participatory activities have focused on is women's experiences.[39] TJ brokers (Advocacy Forum, ICTJ, UN Women and WOREC) conducted the following studies and consultations. In 2010 Advocacy Forum in collaboration with ICTJ published a pilot qualitative study entitled *Across The Lines: The Impact of Nepal's Conflict on Women.* The objective of this study was to investigate the impact of the armed conflict on women in Nepal with a specific objective of helping advocate for the inclusion of women's experiences, concerns and voices in the TJ process. This example is noteworthy as women are traditionally marginalised in Nepal. The project used various methods (e.g. in-depth interviews surveys, focus group discussions and informal sessions) and included women affected by the conflict and from different communities. The report states that:

> [t]he process listened to the voices of women, and sought to document their experiences and opinions on how the conflict affected their lives, how they coped with the situation at the time and after the conflict ended and to identify their present needs and demands.
>
> (Advocacy Forum and ICTJ 2010, 11–12)

Recommendations for the government included establishing mechanisms to ensure 'that victims of sexual crimes receive appropriate reparations and that women participate in the entire reparations process from the shaping of policies to implementation, monitoring and evaluation', 'that women's voices are heard and that women can participate in ongoing negotiations and policy debates' and for the media to advocate for women's participation in TRC and CIEDP (Advocacy Forum and ICTJ 2010, 102–103, 107).

WOREC has conducted a range of activities including an 'interactive program' entitled Peace building Process: Past, Present and Future, which is focused on UN Security Council Resolution 1325. At this event 'women affected by the conflict, [and] survivors of violence in [a] transitional period asked the questions, raised their voices and demanded accountability to ensure their rights from the government, political parties and other stakeholders' (WOREC 2014). In attendance was the Vice Speaker of Constitutional Assembly, NGO workers and human rights advocates. WOREC also hosted another event in 2011 when 'women directly affected by conflict shared their stories and demanded accountability from the top brass of the political parties' (WOREC 2014). Among those present was Chairperson of CPN-UML, Mr Jhal Nath Khanal, the Chairperson of CPN-Maoist Mr Puspa kamal Dahal, Mr Madheshi Morcha and Mr Upendra Yadav. While the political representatives committed to examine the issues raised and fulfil their demands, WOREC contends that no action has been taken.

A national consultation on women's perspectives on TJ was held on 21 September 2013 (WOREC 2014).[40] The consultation was hosted by two national Nepali NGOs (NAWHRD and WOREC). There was a wide range of participants including 'women affected by conflict, women human rights defenders and survivors of violence', 'representatives from the National Women [*sic*] Commission', the National Human Rights Commission, the Ministry of Women, Children and Social Welfare, the Ministry of Peace and Reconstruction, various UN agencies and donors to the UN Peace Trust Fund, political representatives and NGO workers (WOREC 2014). The objective of the consultation was '[t]o define Justice from women's perspective and draft a module addressing transitional justice issues from women's perspectives' (WOREC 2014). Part of the program covered the issues, 'What is justice for women?' 'What needs to be done for women to make [them] feel the justice?' 'What kind of environment is needed?' and how can justice for the victims of violence be ensured? (WOREC 2014). It was intended that a position paper based on surveys conducted with women be shared and discussed. The expected outcome was to develop a 'module' that addressed TJ from women's perspectives.

Relief and reparations

Another area that participation has addressed is relief and reparations. OHCHR and the International Organization for Migration (IOM) conducted strategic meetings and consultations with victims' groups, civil society, human rights organisations and government agencies. The first round of activities were part of the Ministry of Peace and Reconstruction TRC and CIEDP consultations (see above) where 'internationally established principles and best practices of reparations were shared and victims were invited to share their expectations of the reparations policy being developed' (IOM 2011a). In September 2011 OHCHR commenced regional consultations on the draft reparations policy with victims, civil society and district level government officials. The objectives of the consultations were 'to seek [the] input of conflict victims, government officials and civil society interlocutors on specific aspects of the draft reparations policy and to provide participants with conceptual clarity on different aspects of reparations measures and international best practices' (IOM 2011b). Victims were consulted about their expectations regarding an outreach strategy and implementation plan; a set of recommendations was provided to the government based on victims' feedback entitled *Outreach: Conflict Victim's Perceptions and Recommendations*. An outline for the framework on the reparation policy was also drafted after these regional consultations.

Also, an ICTJ study assessed victims' experiences with the Interim Relief Program (Carranza 2012). Through a close analysis of the implementation of the Interim Relief Program and the process of listening to the victims, the findings of this report were intended to inform a future reparations policy. Government representatives (including from the Ministry of Peace and Reconstruction) and Local Peace Committees, political parties, civil society and victims' organisations were involved in individual interviews, focus group discussions and workshops. Approximately 1200 people (including 257 'conflict affected persons') either shared information in group discussions or were directly interviewed. It was stated that the voices of victims helped to identify issues in relation to the Interim Relief Program and that additional elements were required to implement a reparations policy (Ministry of Peace and Reconstruction 2010).

Families of the disappeared

Participation was also employed in relation to families of the disappeared. Research on family associations of disappeared victims was initially conducted by Simon Robins, a former ICRC worker. The aim was to mobilise victims of these associations to influence policy and to provide support for victims in their communities. The survey was designed by Robins in conjunction with the family associations. The study found that victims' needs were primarily to know the truth about their relatives who had disappeared and for basic economic support; and while the respondents were in favour of justice, this was of relatively low priority (Robins 2011a, 160, 2011b, 86).[41] Another project entitled *From Victims to Actors: Mobilising Victims to Drive Transitional Justice Process* was carried out by Robins in collaboration with the National Network of Families of Missing and Disappeared, Nepal and three district associations of families of the disappeared, headed by Ram Bhandari[42] (Robins and Bhandari 2012). The principal aim of the project was twofold: 'to understand the challenges of mobilisation and to concretely advance it; and, to challenge a transitional justice process that has been entirely Kathmandu based and has marginalised victims' (Robins and Bhandari 2012). Semi-structured interviews and focus group discussions were conducted by members of victims' groups who also designed the interview questions. The study found the participants' priorities were (in decreasing order) livelihood, truth about the missing person and retributive justice. Families also reported that family associations were a source of information and advice about the TJ process and services available.

More recently ICTJ, partnered with UN Women, published a briefing paper on wives of the disappeared (Tyynela, Withers and Bajracharya 2013). Surveys were conducted with 462 women in 20 districts. Focus groups were conducted in 12 of the 20 districts. The researchers included victims or relatives of the disappeared. The aim of the research was to determine how wives of the disappeared were coping and the extent to which the Interim Relief Program addressed the challenges that these women face (Tyynela, Withers, and Bajracharya 2013, 1). The report notes that the truth about their husbands' disappearances and justice is prioritised; although the study does not define what justice in this context means (see Chapter 6). The report highlights the multifaceted nature of the hardship endured by wives of the disappeared in Nepal (e.g. legal and administrative obstacles, family pressure and limited food supplies).

Ex-combatants

Most of the studies on ex-combatants (see, for example, Martin Chautari 2013; Subedi 2014; Yadav 2016) have focused on the DDR process and/or female ex-combatants' experiences, but are not necessarily participatory activities. Robins and Bhandari adopted a similar participatory action approach in their study on ex-combatants; the results of which was published in a 2016 report entitled 'Poverty, Stigma and Alienation: Reintegration Challenges of Ex-Maoist Combatants in Nepal'. The study found:

> that the process of demobilising the PLA was one led by the political imperatives of the leaders of dominant political parties, rather than the interests of the nation or ex-combatants themselves. The greatest challenge to the process was and is the large gap between the expectations of ex-PLA and what they received on demobilisation. There remain a number of acute challenges in their process of political, social and economic reintegration, to the extent that 75% of these combatants-turned-civilians could foresee the future use of arms for political means if instructed so by their leadership.
>
> (2016)

The study also investigated the role of the ex-combatant association.

From the outline above it is evident that participation on a wide range of topics has occurred in Nepal. The majority of this participation has been in the form of consultations and surveys. Further analysis of these participatory activities is provided in Chapter 6, which provides details of the extent to which the activities impacted the TJ agenda.

Notes

1 Prior to the end of the conflict a commission to investigate disappearances investigated 36 cases of disappearance and clarified the whereabouts of 24 cases

(Fullard 2008, 9). Not long before the end of the conflict, in April 2006, the Neupane Committee investigated 776 cases, tracing the status of 174 disappeared persons.

2 However, the first formal commitment to establish mechanisms addressing human rights violations was contained in the Baluwatar agreement (8 November 2006).

3 This was first mentioned in the ceasefire Code of Conduct in 2006.

4 *Rabindra Prasad Dhakal on behalf of Rajendra Prasad Dhakal (Advocate) v Government of Nepal.* 2007, 3575. Nepal Supreme Court, 1 June 2007.

5 The proposed legislation was the Truth and Reconciliation Act and the Disappearances (Crime and Punishment) Act.

6 *Madhav Kumar Basnet et al., v the Government of Nepal.* 2014, 069-WS-0057. Nepal Supreme Court, 2 January 2014.

7 *Commission of Investigation of Disappeared Persons, Truth and Reconciliation Ordinance* (2013).

8 *Madhav Kumar Basnet et al., v the Government of Nepal.* 2014, 069-WS-0057. Nepal Supreme Court, 2 January 2014.

9 For example, the TJ Act provides that the NHRC chairperson or a member designated by the chairperson is to be part of the Recommendation Committee. However, the Committee was operating without the required NHRC person. The appointment of the NHRC person to the Recommendation Committee was delayed due to the government's failure to appoint new commissioners to the NHRC, which has had ongoing staffing issues. The terms of the NHRC chairperson and four commissioners expired on 16 September 2013. The Constitutional Council, chaired by the Prime Minister, recently forwarded its recommendations of commissioners to the NHRC and the nominees were endorsed by Parliamentary Hearing Special Committee on 17 October 2014. Also, a female Constituent Assembly member, Sapana Pradhan Malla, declined her nomination to the Recommendation Committee until the Act was amended to be 'victim-friendly' (The Himalayan Times 2014). Further, since the Recommendation Committee was chaired by former Chief Justice Om Bhakta Shrestha, a writ petition was filed pursuant to Article 106 (2) of the Interim Constitution, which forbids a former chief justice to be appointed to any government agency except to the NHRC (eKantipur 2014). Gyanendra Raj Aran, lawyer and chairperson of the Conflict Victims' National Society, raised concerns stating that the Recommendation Committee should have waited for the court's ruling before proceeding with its work (eKantipur 2014).

10 Order 069-WS-0057 (see Honorable Justice Kalyan Shrestha, Honorable Justice Girish Chandra La, and Honorable Justice Sushila Karki 2014).

11 Years later the country is still rebuilding and millions of people reportedly remain homeless.

12 Other relevant policy documents include Measures for Financial Support and Relief for Conflict Victims pursuant to cabinet decision, 25 April 2008; Guidelines for Providing Relief to Beneficiary of a Deceased Person pursuant to cabinet decision, 5 October 2008; and Guidelines for Providing Relief to the Beneficiary of a Disappeared Person pursuant to cabinet decision, 12 January 2009 (see ICTJ 2011a). See Chapter 6 for further details.

13 I acknowledge that there are more TJ actors (see Elster 2004; Theidon 2006; Shaw 2010), but for the purposes of this book I focus on four groups of actors.

14 There are other TJ expert organisations (e.g. the Institute of Justice and Reconciliation and the Centre for Justice and Reconciliation), some of which have a regional or continental focus.

15 Personal interview, 11 October 2012, Kathmandu.

16 Personal interview, 11 October 2012, Kathmandu.

17 There are approximately 40,000 NGOs in Nepal, 5,000 of which work in the field of human rights (UNDP 2010b, 68).
18 Personal interview, 11 September 2012, Rolpa.
19 These organisations include: FOHRID Human Rights and Democratic Forum, INHURED International, the Informal Sector Service Centre, Advocacy Forum and the National Human Rights Commission.
20 Personal interview, 20 September 2012, Kailali.
21 Personal interview, 20 September 2012, Kailali.
22 Personal interview, 5 March 2012, Kathmandu.
23 Personal interview, 2 March 2012, Kathmandu.
24 Personal interview, 2 March 2012, Kathmandu.
25 Although victims are predominately from marginalised caste and ethnic communities I did not actively raise issues of caste and ethnicity in my interviews; rather if victims raised these issues as part of their responses I followed them up in order to enable respondents to prescribe meaning to issues of caste and ethnicity on their own terms.
26 By local, I refer to individuals and organisations engaged in a range of micro-level relationships (see Baines 2007, 412) generally from the village to the district level in Nepal. I acknowledge that are intersections and overlaps between the local, national and international levels.
27 Personal interviews, 17 October 2012, Kathmandu.
28 Personal interview, 17 October 2012, Kathmandu.
29 I note that the following list is by no means exhaustive.
30 As it is difficult, if not impossible, to determine the genuine reasons why.
31 Personal interview, 11 October 2012, Kathmandu.
32 Personal interview, 11 October 2012, Kathmandu.
33 Personal communication, 4 January 2013.
34 The film was called *Confronting the Truth* and the publication was the *Transitional Justice: Information Handbook* (2008).
35 Personal interview, 11 October 2012, Kathmandu.
36 Personal communication, 21 November 2012.
37 Personal interview, 16 October 2012, Kathmandu.
38 Personal communication, 27 September 2012 and personal interview, 16 October 2012, Kathmandu.
39 Various organisations (such as Sankalpa Women's Alliance for Peace, Justice & Democracy, Advocacy Forum, ICTJ, United Nations Population Fund and UN Women) have conducted activities for women on TJ. These mainly included Training of Trainers programs and workshops.
40 The previous year WOREC Nepal, NAWHRD and APWLD jointly organised a national consultation entitled 'Women's Right in Nepal: Rhetoric and Reality, Challenges to Human Right, Peace, Democracy and Development,' on 21 September 2012.
41 Many of these findings were supported by the ICTJ study with wives of the disappeared (Tyynela, Withers and Bajracharya 2013).
42 Bhandari has regularly published opinion pieces in the English media in Nepal about TJ and the plight of families of the disappeared; he became the CVCP Chairperson and is now the General Secretary.

References

Adhikari, Aditya, Bhaskar Guatam, Surabhi Pudasaini, and Bhadra Sharma. 2014. 'Impunity and accountability in Nepal.' http://asiafoundation.org/resources/pdfs/NPimpunityandpoliticalaccountability.pdf.

Advocacy Forum. 'Who we are.' http://advocacyforum.org/about-us/index.php.
Advocacy Forum. 2012. 'SC directs government to vet officials.' Last modified 13 August 2012. http://advocacyforum.org/news/2012/08/sc-directs-government-to-vet-officials.php.
Advocacy Forum. 2014a. 'AF published a report on vetting in Nepal.' Last modified 11 July 2014. http://advocacyforum.org/news/2014/07/af-published-a-report-on-vetting-in-nepal.php.
Advocacy Forum. 2014b. 'Nepal: Transitional justice at crossroads.' www.advocacyforum.org/downloads/pdf/publications/tj/transitional-justice-at-crossroads-2014.pdf.
Advocacy Forum, and ICTJ. 2010. 'Across the lines: The impact of Nepal's conflict on women.' www.ictj.org/sites/default/files/ICTJ-Nepal-Across-Lines-2010-English.pdf.
Apland, Kara. 2012. 'The power and politics of transitional justice.' Last modified 16 January 2012. http://justiceinconflict.org/2012/01/16/the-power-and-politics-of-transitional-justice/.
Baines, Erin K. 2007. 'Innocent women and children: Gender, norms and the protection of civilians by R. Charli Carpenter.' *Perspectives on Politics* 5(2):401–403.
Balasco, Lauren Marie. 2013. 'The transitions of transitional justice: Mapping the waves from promise to practice.' *Journal of Human Rights* 12(2):198–216.
Bhandari, Ram Kumar. 2011. 'The role of victims' organisations in transition from conflict: Families of the disappeared in Nepal.' Master's Degree, Institute for Peace Research and Security Policy, University of Hamburg.
Bisset, Alison. 2014. 'Transitional justice in Nepal: The commission on investigation of Disappeared Persons, Truth and Reconciliation Act 2014.' www.biicl.org/documents/334_nepal_update_-_bisset.pdf?showdocument=1.
Boesenecker, Aaron P., and Leslie Vinjamuri. 2011. 'Lost in translation? Civil society, faith-based organizations and the negotiation of international norms.' *International Journal of Transitional Justice* 5(3):345–365.
Budhathoki, Shobhakar. 2014. 'Transitional justice in post-conflict societies and Nepal's efforts.' *INFORMAL* 34(1–2):4–11.
Business Standard. 2016. 'Former Nepal PM Deuba charged with human rights violation.' *Business Standard*. www.business-standard.com/article/news-ani/former-nepal-pm-deuba-charged-with-human-rights-violation-116061700591_1.html.
Cardenas, Sonia. 2004. *Adaptive states: The proliferation of national human rights institutions*. Boston, MA: Carr Center for Human Rights Policy, Harvard University.
Carranza, Ruben. 2012. 'Relief, reparations, and the root causes of conflict in Nepal.' www.ictj.org/sites/default/files/ICTJ-Nepal-Reparations-2012-English.pdf.
Cochran-Budhathoki, Karon, and Scott Worden. 2007. 'Transitional justice in Nepal: A look at the international experience of truth commissions.' www.usip.org/publications/2007/09/transitional-justice-nepal-look-international-experience-truth-commissions.
CVCP Nepal. 2014. 'Conflict victims common platform on transitional justice: Nepal.' www.facebook.com/pages/Conflict-Victims-Common-Platform-on-Transitional-Justice-Nepal/770718082976594?sk=info&tab=page_info.
Daly, Erin. 2008. 'Truth skepticism: An inquiry into the value of truth in times of transition.' *International Journal of Transitional Justice* 2(1):23–41.
eKantipur. 2014. 'Victims seek amendment in TRC formation.' Last modified 15 September 2014. www.ekantipur.com/2014/09/15/capital/victims-seek-amendment-in-trc-formation/395065.html.

Elster, Jon. 2004. *Closing the books: Transitional justice in historical perspective.* Cambridge: Cambridge University Press.

Farasat, Warisha, and Priscilla Hayner. 2009. *Negotiating peace in Nepal: Implications for justice.* IFP Mediation Cluster: Institute for Peacebuilding / International Centre for Transitional Justice. https://ictj.org/sites/default/files/ICTJ-IFP-Nepal-Negotiating-Peace-2009-English.pdf.

Fullard, Madeleine. 2008. *Disappearances in Nepal.* www.ictj.org/sites/default/files/ICTJ-Nepal-Disappearances-2008-English.pdf.

HRW. 2014. 'Nepal: Fix flawed truth, Reconciliation Act.' Last modified 8 July 2014. www.hrw.org/news/2014/07/08/nepal-fix-flawed-truth-reconciliation-act.

HRW. 2016. 'Nepal: 9-point deal undermines transitional justice.' Human Rights Watch. www.hrw.org/news/2016/05/12/nepal-9-point-deal-undermines-transitional-justice.

ICG. 2007. 'Nepal's constitutional process.' *Asia Report* No. 128 – 26 February 2007. https://d2071andvip0wj.cloudfront.net/128-nepal-s-constitutional-process.pdf.

ICG. 2009. 'Nepal's faltering peace process.' *Asia Report* No. 163 – 19 February 2009. https://d2071andvip0wj.cloudfront.net/163-nepal-s-faltering-peace-process.pdf.

ICJ. 2009. 'Disappearances in Nepal: Addressing the past, securing the future.' www.icj.org/IMG/revised_Briefing_paper_on_Nepal_Enforced_Disapp_-_FINAL_1_.pdf.

ICJ. 2014. *Alternative report of the international commission of jurists (ICJ) to the UN Human Rights Committee on the combined second, third and fourth periodic reports of Nepal under the international covenant on civil and political rights.* Edited by International Committee of Jurists. Geneva: United Nations Human Rights Committee.

ICJ. 2017. 'About.' www.icj.org/about/.

ICTJ. 2011a. 'From relief to reparations: Listening to the voices of victims.' www.ictj.org/sites/default/files/ICTJ-NPL-Relief-to-Reparations-Report-2011-English.pdf.

ICTJ. 2011b. *Trainers' manual on transitional justice.* Kathmandu: ICTJ.

ICTJ. 2015. 'Nepal.' www.ictj.org/our-work/regions-and-countries/nepal.

ICTJ, and Advocacy Forum. 2008. 'Nepali voices: Perceptions of truth, justice, reconciliation, reparations and the transition in Nepal.' www.ictj.org/sites/default/files/ICTJ-Nepal-Voices-Reconciliation-2008-English.pdf.

IOM. 2011a. *United Nations Peace Fund for Nepal (UNPFN) project status update for the period of April–June 2011.* www.nepal.iom.int/images/stories/Quarterly_update_April-June_2011.pdf.

IOM. 2011b. *United Nations Peace Fund for Nepal (UNPFN) project status update for the period of July–September 2011.* www.nepal.iom.int/images/stories/Quarterly_update_July-September_2011.pdf.

Kamat, Ram Kumar. 2016. 'Attorney General for addressing concerns about transitional justice.' *The Himalayan Times.* https://thehimalayantimes.com/nepal/attorney-general-addressing-concerns-transitional-justice/.

Kritz, Neil. ed. (1995). *Transitional Justice: How Emerging Democracies Reckon with Former Regimes (Vol. 1).* Washington, DC: USIP Press.

Marg, Shantiniketan. 2010. *Discrimination and irregularities: The painful tale of interim relief in Nepal.* http://advocacyforum.org/downloads/pdf/publications/Discriminations_and_Irregularities_A_painful_tale_of_Interim_Relief_in_Nepal.pdf.

Martin Chautari. 2013. 'Political risk and ex-combatants.' In *Policy brief.* Nepal: Martin Chautari. http://himalaya.socanth.cam.ac.uk/collections/journals/mcpb/pdf/MC_PolicyBrief_09_ENG.pdf.

McAdam, Doug, Sidney Tarrow, and Charles Tilly. 2009. 'Comparative perspectives on contentious politics.' In *Comparative politics: Rationality, culture, and structure: advancing theory in comparative politics*, edited by Mark Lichbach and Alan Zuckerman, 260–290. Cambridge: Cambridge University Press.

McAdam, Doug, Sydney G. Tarrow, and Charles Tilly. 2001. *Dynamics of contention*. Cambridge: Cambridge University Press.

Merry, Sally Engle. 2006. *Human rights and gender violence: Translating international law into local justice*. Chicago, IL: University of Chicago Press.

Ministry of Peace and Reconstruction. 2010. The challenges and success of the interim relief program and future reparations policy in Nepal Kathmandu, 15–16 November.

MPTF. 2011. Annual programme narrative progress report. http://mptf.undp.org/document/download/8962.

myRepublica. 2016. 'Oli, Dahal sign 9-pt deal.' *myRepublica*. http://admin.myrepublica.com/politics/story/41802/oli-dahal-sign-9-pt-deal.html.

myRepublica. 2017. 'House panel tells govt to amend TRC and CIEDP Act.' *myRepublica*. www.myrepublica.com/news/14707/.

Nagendra Adhikari, Kavre. 2016. 'Govt not cooperating with TRC: Spokesperson.' *The Kathmandu Post*. http://kathmandupost.ekantipur.com/news/2016-01-29/govt-not-cooperating-with-trc-spokesperson.html.

Nepal, Indu. 2016. 'Nepal's botched truth and reconciliation program.' *The Record*. www.recordnepal.com/wire/nepals-botched-truth-and-reconciliation-program/.

Nepal Monitor. 2011. 'Government relief efforts for Nepal conflict victims.' Last modified 19 July 2011. www.nepalmonitor.com/2011/07/government_relief_ef.html.

NepalNews. 2010. 'NHRC urges govt to proceed cases of HR violation through civil courts.' www.nepalnews.com/main/index.php/news-archive/19-general/3068-nhrc-urges-govt-to-proceedcasesof-hr-violation-through-civil-court.html.

OHCHR. 2008. 'Joint statement to the press: OHCHR-Nepal and NHRC conduct joint workshop on transitional justice with NGOs representing marginalised groups in the Far-Western Region.' http://nepal.ohchr.org/en/resources/Documents/English/pressreleases/Year%202008/OCT2008/2008_10_20_TJ%20workshop%20Dhangadhi_E.pdf

OHCHR. 2009. 'Press release: The United Nations launches a "Peace through Justice" project', 18 July.

OHCHR. 2013. 'OHCHR comments on the Nepal 'Commission on investigation of disappeared persons, truth and reconciliation ordinance – 2069(2013).' www.ohchr.org/Documents/Countries/NP/OHCHRComments_TRC_Ordinance.docx.

OHCHR. 2014. 'Special rapporteur on the promotion of truth, justice, reparation and guarantees of non-recurrence.' www.ohchr.org/EN/Issues/TruthJusticeReparation/Pages/Index.aspx.

OHCHR. 2016. 'Nepal: OHCHR position on UN support to the Commission on Investigation of Disappeared Persons and the Truth and Reconciliation Commission.' www.ohchr.org/Documents/Countries/NP/Nepal_UN%20osition_supportTRC_COIDP_Feb2016.pdf.

Orentlicher, Diane F. 2007. '"Settling accounts" revisited: Reconciling global norms with local agency.' *International Journal of Transitional Justice* 1(1):10–22.

Pandey, Lekhanath. 2016a. '18 types of reparation schemes proposed for war-era crimes.' *The Himalayan times*. https://thehimalayantimes.com/nepal/18-types-reparation-schemes-proposed-war-era-crimes/.

Pandey, Lekhanath. 2016b. 'Can't support CIEDP, TRC; Act faulty: United Nations.' *The Himalayan Times*. https://thehimalayantimes.com/nepal/cant-support-ciedp-trc-act-faulty-united-nations/.

Pandey, Lekhanath. 2016c. 'Govt fails to bring laws for operation of TRC and CIEDP.' *The Himalayan Times*. https://thehimalayantimes.com/nepal/govt-fails-bring-laws-operation-trc-ciedp/

Pandey, Lekhanath. 2016d. 'Internal dispute, govt apathy hit TRC.' *The Himalayan Times*, https://thehimalayantimes.com/nepal/internal-dispute-government-apathy-hit-trc-truth-and-reconciliation-commission/.

Pandey, Lekhanath. 2016e. 'Police seek details of conflict victims' complaints, denied.' *The Himalayan Times*. https://thehimalayantimes.com/nepal/police-seek-details-conflict-victims-complaints-denied/.

Parajuli, John Narayan. 2016. 'CIEDP takes plaints amid questions about process.' *The Kathmandu Post*. http://kathmandupost.ekantipur.com/news/2016-04-15/ciedp-takes-plaints-amid-questions-about-process.html.

Phuyal, Hari, and Shreejana Pokhrel. 2012. *Evaluation report*. The Peace through Justice Project, implemented by the Office of the High Commissioner for Human Rights – Nepal . http://mptf.undp.org/document/download/10993.

Rai, Dewan. 2016a. 'CIEDP publishes 2,800 names of conflict victims.' *The Kathmandu Post*. http://kathmandupost.ekantipur.com/news/2016-11-29/ciedp-publishes-28000-names-of-conflict-victims.html.

Rai, Dewan. 2016b. 'Govt employees reluctant to join truth commissions.' *The Kathmandu Post*. http://kathmandupost.ekantipur.com/news/2016-02-09/govt-employees-reluctant-to-join-truth-commissions.html.

Rai, Dewan. 2016c. 'Govt endorses regulations for TJ bodies.' *The Kathmandu Post*. http://kathmandupost.ekantipur.com/news/2016-02-17/govt-endorses-regulations-for-tj-bodies.html.

Ramji-Nogales, Jaya. 2010. 'Designing bespoke transitional justice: A pluralist process approach.' *Michigan Journal of International Law* 32(1):1–58.

Rausch, Colette. 2017. 'Reconciliation and transition justice in Nepal: A slow path.' Peace Brief. United Institute of Peace. www.usip.org/sites/default/files/PB227-Reconciliation-and-Transitional-Justice-in-Nepal-A-Slow-Path.pdf.

Redress. 2014. Submission to the Human Rights Committee ahead of its examination of Nepal's second periodic report under the international covenant on civil and political rights. www.redress.org/downloads/publications/AF%20REDRESS%20APT%20Nepal%20submission%20for%20website.pdf.

Robins, Simon. 2011a. 'Addressing the needs of families of the missing: A test of contemporary approaches to transitional justice.' PhD Post-war Recovery Studies, Department of Politics, University of York.

Robins, Simon. 2011b. 'Towards victim-centred transitional justice: Understanding the needs of families of the disappeared in postconflict Nepal.' *International Journal of Transitional Justice* 5(1):75–98.

Robins, Simon. 2012. 'Transitional justice as an elite discourse: Human rights practice where the global meets the local in post-conflict Nepal.' *Critical Asian Studies* 44 (1):3–30.

Robins, Simon, and Ram Kumar Bhandari. 2012. 'From victims to actors: Mobilising victims to drive transitional justice process.' http://nefad.files.wordpress.com/2012/06/nefad_from-victims-to-actors-research-report1.pdf.

Robins, Simon, Ram Kumar Bhandari, and Ex-PLA Research Group. 2016. *Poverty, stigma and alienation: Reintegration challenges of ex-Maoist combatants in Nepal: A participatory action research project with ex-PLA fighters in Nepal.* Berghof Foundation. www.berghof-foundation.org/fileadmin/redaktion/Publications/Grantees_Partners/Policy_brief_Ex_Maoist_Combatant_in_Nepal.pdf.

Rowen, Jamie. 2012. 'Mobilizing truth: Agenda setting in a transnational social movement.' *Law & Social Inquiry* 37(3):686–718.

Sapkota, Bishnu. 2017. 'Architecture of peace in Nepal.' In *Two steps forward, one step back: the Nepal peace process*, edited by Dr Alexander Ramsbotham and Deepak Thapa, 24–26, Issue 26, Conciliation Resources. www.c-r.org/downloads/Accord-26-Nepal-WEB_0.pdf.

Sharma, Mandira. 2017. 'Transitional justice in Nepal: Low priority, partial peace.' In *Two steps forward, one step back: the Nepal peace process*, edited by Dr Alexander Ramsbotham and Deepak Thapa, 32–36, Issue 26, Conciliation Resources. www.c-r.org/downloads/Accord-26-Nepal-WEB_0.pdf.

Shaw, Rosalind. 2010. 'Linking justice with reintegration? Ex-combatants and the Sierra Leone experiment.' In *Localizing transitional justice interventions and priorities after mass violence*, edited by Rosalind Shaw, Lars Waldorf and Pierre Hazan, 111–132. Stanford, CA: Stanford University Press.

Shrestha, Honorable Justice Kalyan, Honorable Justice Girish Chandra La, and Honorable Justice Sushila Karki. 2014. Order 069-WS-0057. Nepal: Supreme Court.

Sriram, Chandra Lekha. 2007. 'Justice as peace? Liberal peacebuilding and strategies of transitional justice.' *Global Society* 21(4):579–591.

Subedi, D. B. 2014. 'Dealing with ex-combatants in a negotiated peace process: Impacts of transitional politics on the disarmament, demobilization and reintegration programme in Nepal.' *Journal of Asian and African Studies* 49(6):672–689.

Subotic, Jelena. 2012. 'The Transformation of International Transitional Justice Advocacy.' *International Journal of Transitional Justice* 6:106–125.

Tarrow, Sydney G. 2005. *The new transnational activism.* New York: Cambridge University Press.

Teitel, Ruti. 2003. 'Transitional Justice genealogy.' *Harvard Human Rights Journal* 16 (Spring):69–93.

The Himalayan Times. 2014. 'Malla's status delays TRC panel's progress.' Last modified 25 July 2014. www.thehimalayantimes.com/fullNews.php?headline=Malla%27s++status+delays+TRC+panel%27s+progress&NewsID=422273.

The Himalayan Times. 2016. 'SC quashes writ against nine-point agreement.' *The Himalayan Times.* https://thehimalayantimes.com/kathmandu/sc-quashes-writ-nine-point-agreement/.

The Kathmandu Post. 2015a. 'CIEDP asks govt to criminalise enforced disappearances.' *The Kathmandu Post.* http://kathmandupost.ekantipur.com/news/2015-09-01/ciedp-asks-govt-to-criminalise-enforced-disapperances.html.

The Kathmandu Post. 2015b. 'Govt's disregard for court order upsets victims of conflict.' *The Kathmandu Post*, http://kathmandupost.ekantipur.com/printedition/news/2015-11-16/govts-disregard-for-court-order-upsets-victims-of-conflict.html.

Theidon, Kimberely. 2006. 'Justice in transition: The micropolitics of reconciliation in postwar Peru.' *Journal of Conflict Resolution* 50(3):433–457.

Tilly, Charles, and Sydney G. Tarrow. 2007. *Contentious politics.* Boulder, CO: Paradigm Publishers.

TRIAL. 2012. 'Briefing note on the recent political developments in Nepal leading to a lack of access to justice for victims of gross human rights violations and international humanitarian law.' http://ictj.org/sites/default/files/Briefing%20Note%20to%20the%20SR%20on%20TJ%2023%2008%202012.pdf.

TRIAL. 2014. 'Nepal.' Last modified 24 June 2014. www.trial-ch.org/en/activities/litigation/the-advocacy-center-trial-act/acts-cases/nepal.html.

Trial International, Redress, HimRights, Advocacy Forum, and Justice and Rights Institute-Nepal. 2017. 'Nepal: Extension of transitional justice mechanisms' mandate should just be a start.' https://trialinternational.org/latest-post/nepal-extension-of-transitional-justice-mechanisms-mandate-should-just-be-a-start/.

Triponel, Anna, and Stephen Pearson. 2010. 'What do you think should happen? Public participation in transitional justice.' *Pace International Law Review* 22 (Winter 2010):103–144.

Tyynela, John, Lucia Withers, and Prabina Bajracharya. 2013. 'Beyond relief: Addressing the rights and needs of Nepal's wives of the disappeared. '*ICTJ Briefing*. www.ictj.org/sites/default/files/ICTJ-Briefing-Nepal-WivesofDisappeared-2013.pdf.

UN. 2014. 'Victims common platform on transitional justice.' www.un.org.np/headlines/victims-common-platform-transitional-justice.

UN General Assembly. 2013. *Communications report of special procedures*. http://daccess-dds-ny.un.org/doc/UNDOC/GEN/G13/164/42/PDF/G1316442.pdf?OpenElement.

UNDP. 2010a. 'Access to justice project entitled 'Enhancing Access to Justice (A2J) through media campaign, settlement fairs and strengthening community mediation practices.' www.americanbar.org/content/dam/aba/images/dispute_resolution/publications/A2J_%20white_paper.pdf.

UNDP. 2010b. 'Outcome evaluation of UNDP Nepal Access to Justice and Human Rights 2001–2010.' 1–100. https://erc.undp.org/evaluation/documents/download/4507.

UNDP. 2014a. 'Enhancing access to justice for the consolidation of peace in Nepal (A2J).' www.np.undp.org/content/nepal/en/home/operations/projects/closed-projects/poverty-reduction1/a2j.html.

UNDP. 2014b. 'Transitional justice project: "Peace through justice" (UNPFN/E-2).' http://mptf.undp.org/factsheet/project/00072059.

UNRCO. 2014. *Monthly report: November 2014*. https://reliefweb.int/sites/reliefweb.int/files/resources/UN_RCO_Monthly_Report_November_2014.pdf.

Wagle, Rishikesh. 2015. 'An overview of the Supreme Court's jurisprudence on transitional justice.' *National Judicial Academy Law Journal* 9(1):17.

WHR. 2012a. 'About us.' http://whr.org.np/about-us/#.VG58YfmUd8F.

WHR. 2012b. 'Sustainable peace for human rights and justice (Pillar III).' http://whr.org.np/our-pillars/pillar-iii-raahat/#.VFv39mMjP3U.

WOREC. 2014. 'Transitional justice from women's perspectives.' www.worecnepal.org/event/others/transitional-justice-women%E2%80%99s-perspectives.

Yadav, Punam. 2016. *Social transformation in post-conflict Nepal: A gender perspective, routledge research on gender in Asia series*. Abingdon: Routledge.

Part III

6 The politics of transitional justice in Nepal

> There is a Nepali proverb "kale kale milera kham bhale" which means "You are black, I am also so let's celebrate together." Basically top level politicians from both sides say "You did terrible things I did terrible things so let's be friends."
>
> (Nepali human rights worker, Kathmandu, 11 October 2012)

Based on Part I and Part II of this book, Part III argues that TJ is both a product, and a producer, of politics.[1] Specifically, TJ operates in a politically charged context, draws people into the political sphere and pervades other seemingly non-political arenas. In this chapter I argue that despite the pervasiveness of politics of and around TJ, there has been inadequate attention paid to politics in TJ policy and practice at the national level and also at other levels. Using the action spectrum (developed in Chapter 2) and the actor typology (developed in Chapter 5), in this chapter I examine how actors engage with and mould TJ and the impact of this interaction on the trajectory of TJ in Nepal. Given the state-centric bent of TJ practices, 'politics' is frequently taken to mean national level politics; however, I stress that the local[2] is a prime site of political activity, contestation and negotiation. Thus, by 'politics' I refer to politics at the local, national and international levels and importantly, I include the understanding that politics occurs both vertically (between various levels) and horizontally (within organisations and between actors at the same level). In this chapter I also examine the ways other voices have been heeded and included in the TJ process in Nepal. I argue that participation can provide avenues for the voices of victims and other actors beyond the national level to be heard, albeit not without significant challenges.[3]

This chapter examines TJ's experts' influences on the adoption of TJ in Nepal and the subsequent developments. It then analyses the language of TJ, revealing how politicians in Nepal have employed notions of reconciliation and amnesty. It also explores examples of TJ brokerage, particularly by human rights organisations. Additionally, it examines the role of the Office of the High Commissioner for Human Rights and its relationship with other UN agencies as well as with other actors in Nepal. Finally, it critiques the various participatory activities.

Experts' influence on the transitional justice agenda

The Comprehensive Peace Agreement and subsequent political agreements appear to commit to pursuing TJ through a variety of measures. Notable is the two-commission structure: a Truth and Reconciliation Commission (TRC) and a Commission of Investigation on Enforced Disappeared Persons (CIEDP). The provision for the TRC in Nepal is perhaps unsurprising given that the inclusion of a truth commission in peace processes has effectively been normalised in TJ processes around the world (Tyynela 2014, 80) (see Chapter 2). However, Nepal was the first country to pursue a TJ agenda with both a TRC and CIEDP intended to run concurrently.

As discussed in Chapter 5, the initiative to establish a TRC in Nepal was fuelled by international experts in the peace negotiations. Two TJ experts played a key role: Hannes Siebert, a South African consultant contracted by USAID as part of the US's Nepal Transition to Peace Project, and Günther Baechler, a Swiss consultant involved in the task force established to deal with issues relating to the peace process, including TJ. The task force 'encouraged the creation not only of the Commission on Disappearances, advocated by the human rights community, but also of a Truth and Reconciliation Commission' (Farasat and Hayner 2009, 16). The details of how this transpired have largely been revealed by Farasat's and Hayner's interviews with political actors (2009).

Siebert was instrumental in the adoption of the South African Truth and Reconciliation Commission model in Nepal. Prior to his involvement there was only limited discussion on the adoption of a truth commission (Farasat and Hayner 2009, 20–21). Siebert initiated a number of visits by Nepali politicians to South Africa as well as by South African experts to Nepal. Other international TJ experiences (e.g. in Peru, Northern Ireland and South Korea) were raised as possible points of comparison but the South African experience maintained primacy.[4] Of particular note is that pursuant to the *Promotion of National Unity and Reconciliation Act* (1995), the South African TRC was composed for three committees: the committee on human rights violations, the committee on amnesty, and the committee on reparation and rehabilitation. The committee on amnesty could grant amnesty in exchange for testimony before the human rights committee if two conditions were met: the perpetrator fully disclosed the acts for which they were responsible during the apartheid era; and, they demonstrated that 'these acts were committed for political reasons' (Murphy 2017, 3–4). While over 7,000 people submitted amnesty applications, 'amnesty was granted to approximately 850 individuals' (Murphy 2017, 4). These amnesties are subject to debate. They raise questions about the nature of justice and accountability, and the compromises undertaken in TJ processes. Despite these questions, amnesties in this and other contexts continue.

The truth commission was recommended in Nepal despite there being little to no knowledge of, or support for it (see Farasat and Hayner 2009, 26).

Reiterating this point, a recent report on truth commissions by ICTJ and the Kofi Annan Foundation contends:

> The case of Nepal, indeed, presents a troubling situation in which a truth commission, originally without organic support from society, was included in a peace process mainly to satisfy the interests of powerful stakeholders interested in finding an alternative to criminal prosecutions, thus, opening an onerous and prolonged debate on the incompatibility between the international obligations of Nepal and amnesties for serious human rights violations.
>
> (Tyynela 2014, 84)

This reveals the power and influence that an individual, particularly a TJ expert, can yield.

The major negotiating political parties agreed to the two commission structure in the Comprehensive Peace Agreement in part because they believed differing TJ mechanisms would foster their interests. Discussions about the TRC were initially driven by the interests of the Nepali Congress, one of the major political parties in the government. They argued that the TRC was a long-term mechanism to address past violations, most of which they attributed to the Maoist rebels (Farasat and Hayner 2009, 20). Nepali Congress was against prosecutions as the Nepali Congress leader, Sher Bahadur Deuba, was Prime Minister when the state security forces committed many severe human rights and humanitarian law violations (Adhikari et al. 2014, 66). While the Maoists were reportedly reluctant to consider the TRC and focused their concerns on revealing disappearances carried out by the security forces (see Chapter 4). Over time it appears that both the Nepali Congress and the Maoists recognised specific advantages of the TRC as a means to ensure amnesty. Indeed:

> the South African Truth and Reconciliation Commission's *emphasis on reconciliation and its amnesty provisions* were attractive to Nepali actors, for whom the formation of a truth commission was a more attractive option than one that might allow criminal accountability for past violations.
>
> (Farasat and Hayner 2009, 21, my emphasis)

The domination of negotiations by political parties resulted in narrow agreements that largely preserved the parties' self-interests and hindered wider discussions about other TJ measures (see Farasat and Hayner 2009, 27). A Nepali political advisor explained to me that '[s]ometimes people took the TRC to mean TJ forgetting that the TRC was an instrument of TJ'.[5] This demonstrates the way the adoption of the truth commission narrowed the TJ agenda in Nepal. As the peace process unfolded, TJ experts and brokers struggled to keep human rights, particularly conflict-related violations, on the public agenda because they continued to direct advocacy at weak interim and coalition governments without political clout (see Rawski and Sharma 2012, 183). Ultimately, there was a lack of understanding and consideration of the political dynamics beyond Kathmandu both prior to and after the conflict. This has been confirmed by TJ brokers Fred Rawski (former Country Representative of the International Commission of Jurists) and Mandira Sharma (Director of Advocacy Forum), who explained that:

> [l]inking human rights initiatives so intimately to the CPA and progress in the peace process reinforced the tendency to see events through the eyes of the political elite and their short-term interests. The international community and much of the national intelligentsia misjudged the political climate by viewing developments through a Kathmandu-centred lens.
>
> (2012, 196)

Further, while creating commissions has been the standard response to most major human rights events in Nepal, they usually yielded little power and were prone to political influence (see Rawski and Sharma 2012, 199; Torné 2013, 72).[6] This was evident in the CIEDP's Chairman's comments in 2016: 'People think this commission is just like any other … They feel that the report of our work will never be made public and its suggestions will never be implemented' (Nepal 2016). So it is curious that a CIEDP and TRC were included in the peace agreement given the poor legacy of these human rights commissions. It is evident that negotiating parties were presented with 'a pre-existing list of options' without TJ experts considering whether it would have been better to revise existing domestic institutions or initiate new processes (Clark and Palmer 2012, 9).

More broadly the timeframe envisaged for TJ mechanisms was problematic because it discounted the social, political and economic realities in post-conflict Nepal. In particular, the Comprehensive Peace Agreement provided that the TRC should be established within six months, during a period when there were elections scheduled, constitution drafting was underway and there were heated discussions about the disarmament and integration of ex-combatants (see Chapter 5). This dilemma was encapsulated by a member of the Ministry of Peace and Reconstruction who believed that the government's priorities for the peace process were first the constitution then the management of Maoist ex-combatants and only then TJ.[7] Irrespective of these post-conflict priorities, the six-month time frame left little scope for participatory activities by numerous actors and provided an unrealistic timeframe for legislation to be drafted and enacted before the commission was to be established (see below).

The language of transitional justice

Despite the initial lack of awareness and understanding of TJ and its accompanying concepts (e.g. 'truth,' 'reconciliation' and 'forgiveness') and mechanisms (e.g.

truth commissions and amnesties), over time these key terms have been appropriated and, at times, contested to suit political agendas. In Nepal national politicians frequently speak about 'reconciliation' when it seems they are referring to 'settlement' or even 'amnesty.' This is particularly evident in national politicians' ongoing advocacy 'for a South Africa-style amnesty as part of a transitional justice process' (Rawski and Sharma 2012, 198). In fact, the language used for amnesty provisions in various draft TJ legislation was influenced by the legislation for the South African Truth and Reconciliation Commission (Tyynela 2014, 82). A male Nepali working at a foreign embassy explained that two key challenges the embassy faced were the different understandings of TJ among political parties and the contention that the TRC is equivalent to amnesty.[8] This was reiterated by a male Nepali who worked for an international organisation involved in the TJ process who told me that '[t]he Truth and Reconciliation Commission has become the Amnesty Commission'.[9] Despite this adherence to the South African model, many key foreign diplomats and donors continue to advocate for greater accountability. For instance, a foreign embassy official from a country that was a key donor in relation to TJ informed me that '[w]e would want accountability to go further than it did in South Africa.'[10]

The preference of successive governments and high-level politicians for a South African-style amnesty has led some observers to contend that the Nepali TRC would be a self-protecting rather than a truth-revealing mechanism. A male human rights worker, speaking about the Nepali Congress and the Maoists at the time when the Maoists were in government, shared the following about the parties' positions on TJ:

> It is mutual protection so that they can have best possible option. It is the result of historical necessity that they have come together ... [T]he Maoists know they won't be in power for long. The military and police also know without cooperating with the Maoists it will be difficult to get protection from the political leadership.[11]

The human rights worker told me this situation is encapsulated in a Nepali proverb '*kale kale milera kham bhale*' (mentioned in Chapter 1), which means in effect, 'You are black, I am also so let's celebrate together.'[12] That is, the top level politicians from both sides say, 'You did terrible things I did terrible things so let's be friends.' He conveyed that it is difficult to separate political issues from TJ because there has been a tacit agreement.[13] Thus, although politicians and other actors are following the script of TJ, the government's initiative of forming the commissions is *performative* with little to do with justice for victims (see Guatam 2013, 5).

The instrumentalisation of the TRC is further evident in the fact that previous drafts referred to the 'Truth, Justice and Reconciliation Commission'; whereas subsequently 'political parties insisted that the word "justice" be omitted' (Farasat and Hayner 2009, 19). This is consistent with Boesenecker and Vinjamuri's findings that 'elites adopt truth commissions and other accountability strategies as much for political cover as for any other reason, in order to give legitimacy to less human rights-friendly policies that enable more hard-headed bargaining to proceed' (2011, 349).

Politicians in Nepal have frequently sought to include dubious 'forgiveness' or 'reconciliation' provisions in TJ legislation. 'Reconciliation' has been translated as *melmilap*, which means to get along and become friends. The Minister for Peace and Reconstruction, also the Minister for Law, Justice and Parliamentary Affairs, claimed that the most recent TRC bill took a 'reconciliatory approach' (eKantipur 2014). Referring to contentious draft provisions for victims to forgive perpetrators, a victim and district leader of a victims' association explained the TJ model 'looks like a forgiveness commission not a disappearance commission'.[14] Also, a political and human rights advisor told me that the draft TRC and CIEDP bills did not become stronger after the consultations; rather the human rights element deteriorated while the emphasis on 'reconciliation' increased (see Chapter 7).[15] It could be contended that the consultations were instrumentalised to curb international pressure to pursue TJ, thereby contesting and resisting international prescriptions of TJ (discussed further below). The trajectory of the drafting of the TJ legislation also reveals the continual struggle to ensure amnesty provisions are included (see Chapter 5). The TJ Act also empowers the commissions to initiate a reconciliation process in the absence of an explicit request by the victim or perpetrator, which stands in stark contrast to the dominant thrust of reconciliatory measures prescribed by TJ advocates.

Thus, the government's position of 'reconciliation' and 'amnesty' is an example of how TJ has been contested in Nepal. This contestation is particularly significant because the meanings national politicians afford to key concepts such as reconciliation and justice do not conform to the global TJ norms or liberal peacebuilding model (see Rubli 2011, 4). In Nepal it is evident that these terms have been strategically employed. Although actors may be speaking with the same vocabulary of justice, truth, and reconciliation, the meanings they attribute to these terms may differ considerably and at times the meanings may even contradict. This trajectory also reveals that '[j]ust as leaders may climb on the justice wagon, they may also hijack it' (Grodsky 2009, 688; see also Subotic 2007, 20–21).

My findings concur with those of Rubli in Burundi and Gowing in Sri Lanka that the language of TJ can obscure a range of divergent political positions. For Rubli (2012, 9–10), the amorphous and vague definitions of TJ and its goals and concepts 'make the policies and concepts susceptible to misuse and manipulation' by powerful national, local or international actors. In Sri Lanka, the government initially rejected international and national calls to establish an international independent commission; however, eventually the Lessons Learnt and Reconciliation Commission was established as a home-grown national initiative to promote unity and reconciliation. Gowing explains:

> In failing to understand the way in which the language of transitional justice may act as a 'cloak' that conceals a wide variety of interests and political positions, we run the risk of conferring legitimacy upon responses (such as the LLRC [Lessons Learnt and Reconciliation Commission]) that deviate heavily in practice from the norms and ideals that they purport to be premised upon.
>
> (2013, 30)

These issues have arisen in other transitional contexts. In South Africa, Wilson found that political and religious elites appropriated 'reconciliation' to legitimise the post-conflict settlement and to underpin a meta-narrative for nation-building (Wilson 2001, 123–155; Bhuta 2005, 247). In Colombia, Uprimny and Saffon (2007) found that the government's use of TJ discourse as a rhetorical instrument served to mask ongoing impunity. However, although civil society adopted a different understanding of these terms and contested the government's standpoint, Diaz (2007) found that at a minimum the government's version of TJ gave civil society a framework to critique the meaning, requirements and ownership of TJ. As she explains:

> [T]ransitional justice discourse has become a key instrument – both for actors from above and actors from below – to advance their causes. At a political level, the Colombian experience suggests that transitional justice discourses may be used as a strategy of resistance by certain sectors of civil society and communities affected by violence. In particular, the deployment of the truth, justice, and reparations rights discourses has proven to be a powerful tool for such 'players from below' in their struggle against impunity.
>
> (Diaz 2007, 23)

Divergent understandings of TJ were also evident at the local level and among foreign governments. In my interviews recently trained trainers or civil society members were unsure of the meaning of TJ, often conflating it with general justice measures during the transitional period. A female Nepali TJ practitioner cited a time when 'reconciliation' was translated as 'friendship' and spoke about the idea of producing a Nepali TJ glossary.[16] Foreign governments have also actively contested aspects of the Nepali government's and political parties' versions of TJ, particularly in response to the government's repeated calls for blanket amnesties as well as appointments of individuals suspected of conflict-related human rights abuses (see Chapter 5). The most direct contestation of the government's approach to TJ was in January 2013, when the UK arrested Nepal Army Colonel Kumar Lama for charges of torture committed during the conflict.[17] Lama was accused of detaining and torturing two Maoist rebels at the Nepal Army barracks in Kapilvastu district in 2005. This was the first time a serving Nepali Army officer had been arrested in a foreign country for human rights violations under universal criminal jurisdiction. Members of the Accountability Watch Committee (see Chapter

5) who were involved in pushing for the arrest of the colonel, and securing the arrest of Maoist cadres accused of murdering a journalist, have stated that the colonel's arrest has resulted in incitements of violence against them (UN General Assembly 2013). There were calls for the government to repatriate Col Kumar Lama. In March 2016 the Parliamentary Committee for Social Justice and Human Rights directed the Defence Ministry and the Ministry of Foreign Affairs to contact the UK authorities to arrange for Lama's case to be heard by 'Nepal's transitional justice mechanisms for trial' (Rai 2015). Given that at the time Nepal had not criminalised torture nor signed the Extradition Treaty or Mutual Legal Assistance Agreement with the UK, these calls were unsuccessful. This incident demonstrates that international actors can contest the ways politicians and governments carry out TJ, which also brings to fore challenges to state sovereignty (see for example Rai 2016b).

The above examples indicate that the scope of TJ and its associated mechanisms, particularly the TRC, have been contested and resisted and at times used for purposes which are not in line with the global discourse of TJ. In particular, it is evident that with the leaning towards the South African model, successive governments and high-level politicians in Nepal have employed TJ framing, discourse and dominant mechanisms to fulfil various political interests. It also reveals that international and domestic pressure to embark upon TJ may not produce compliance but may even produce effects that impede their objectives (see Grodsky 2009, 688), which in turn may bolster other actors' resistance to and contestation of TJ.

Politicised brokerage

The leaders of many NGOs are affiliated with political parties in Nepal and these leaders' advocacy is sometimes influenced by their party affiliation and political ideology (see Rawski and Sharma 2012, 192).[18] In some of my interviews I was informed that most human rights NGOs are affiliated with one of the major political parties: the Communist Party of Nepal (Unified Maoist-Leninists). I was also told about instances when political parties have even formed NGOs to counter other NGOs;[19] in so doing they thereby contest the ideas and positions of the established NGOs. One example arose when a local partner organisation was sought for the TJ network in one district. A well-established local NGO working on TJ was challenged by a NGO that had been recently formed by a political party leader. This resulted in the former NGO having to partner with the new political NGO in the TJ network.[20] This example demonstrates that actors seek to find overt and sometimes covert ways to resist and contest TJ at the local and district levels. By forming and supporting NGOs (as well as victims' groups), political parties and NGOs are able to resist and contest TJ. Just as human rights advocates are able to capitalise upon social movements and the political opportunities they present, so too are political parties (see Snellinger 2007, 286). As Lawoti explains, 'the public space is open to anyone, including the powerful and the privileged, the elite can also use it to maintain their domination and privilege' (2007a, 18). Other forms of resistance include Local Peace Committee coordinators delaying and obstructing interim relief applications from non-party supporters and the deliberate inflation of the number of ex-combatants prior to the delivery of compensation packages to enable a greater proportion of these funds to be used by the Maoist party and/or distributed to disqualified combatants who were ineligible to receive compensation (see Chapters 5 and 7).

Victims, perpetrators and community members also engage with TJ in divergent ways to pursue their own agendas, which may in fact be distinct from the objectives of the law (see Wilson 2003, 382; Merry 1990). I was told that political parties sometimes exploited certain victims' associations. A prominent Nepali human rights advocate said a major challenge in Nepal was to bring together victims who were polarised by political links. For example, many victims of the Maoists would not let victims of the state join victims' groups and become involved in meetings.[21] Also, a prominent victims' leader told me that Conflict Victims' Society for Justice – Nepal, a victims' group supported by Advocacy Forum, was a political organisation. It was also felt that Advocacy Forum was displeased with the attempts to establish a national victims' council, fearing that it would challenge Advocacy Forum's prosecution agenda. I was informed that Conflict Victims' Society for Justice – Nepal did not recognise victims unaffiliated with the group, and its members were 'sophisticatedly groomed' and saw prosecution as the only option, a position that reflected Advocacy Forum's position. In relation to this he said, '[s]ee how ideas are transferred?'[22] Here it appears that TJ brokers, depending upon their agendas, both actively merge victims into groups and deliberately keep victims separated (see McAdam, Tarrow, and Tilly 2001, 142).

And yet over time victims with political differences have found common ground. A male Nepali human rights worker from a national organisation involved in the TJ consultations explained that victims have come to realise that both sides in the conflict were wrong and as a consequence, have come together.[23] He stated that there has been an increasing realisation that 'we are victims irrespective of the side and should unite; we are all victims and we have been forgotten and betrayed. It is this realisation that has united them. Even political party cadres are now identifying as victims'.[24] Of interest is that he credited this shift in position to the work of civil society. This is an example of identity shift in contentious politics where individuals who formerly saw themselves as occupying distinct roles or positions come together and realise a unified identity through coordinated action. This identity shift provides 'new collective answers to the questions "Who are you?" "Who are we?" and "Who are they?"' (Tilly and Tarrow 2007, 216). The feeling that perpetrators (or their relatives) were enemies has given way, for some, to a mutual feeling of betrayal and disappointment for being used or 'fooled' by high-level politicians who made promises (including the reasons for initiating the conflict and garnering involvement from civilians) but did not deliver.[25]

Using political opportunities and a combination of strategic (in)action and delays, has also shaped the trajectory of TJ in Nepal. For example, in the changing environment the government delayed finalising draft TJ bills, establishing various TJ mechanisms and conducting prosecutions. Politicians declared the TRC as the reason why criminal prosecutions have not occurred. The use of TJ is both a way to appease the international community and to circumvent other countries exercising universal jurisdiction. Thus, by adopting this 'thin' performative TJ repertoire the negotiating political parties have been able to side-step criminal prosecutions. It also helped to ensure that a more robust version of TJ, like that advocated by the national human rights agencies and donors, would be less likely in the long-term because TJ had been 'done'. It is here that Subotic's findings ring true that 'international issue-linkage fatigue allows other target states in future policy interventions to try to "wait it out," judging that international actors will get tired, distracted, and will move on to a new project' (2007, 243). In response to the government's ongoing delays and lack of compliance with Supreme Court rulings and commissions' requests to criminalise disappearances and torture, the CIEDP Chairman stated: 'We waited for the government to draft the act … When it did not draft even in almost a year, we decided to prepare it ourselves even if it was not in the mandate of the commission' (Rai 2016a); this is another example of contestation.

It can be seen that many victims' calls for prosecutions have changed as a result of the delays. In my interviews this was frequently attributed to the provision of interim relief and the passing of time.[26] A district coordinator of a human rights organisation felt that the politicians 'wanted to neutralise people by giving money'.[27] A Nepali human rights activist made the same point when he argued that 'the compensation money from the government was given with the intention to make victims silent so they do not raise the issue of the Truth and Reconciliation Commission or the Commission on Disappearances'.[28] A male victim, NGO worker and member of his Local Peace Committee explained:

> After the passing of time, most victims think in the same way: they want peace, no conflict and to forget the past because they don't want another conflict. But two to three years ago this was not the case; victims wanted punishment of perpetrators but gradually this shifted.[29]

In addition, a Nepali human rights worker involved in the Ministry of Peace and Reconstruction consultations explained to me that victims' positions had changed from anger to fatigue:

> [I]n the initial stage victims had this anger and animosity that they must get revenge. That anger somehow transformed into hope. They say 'this happened and what actually happened to us was unfair, unjust and I deserve to get this so I will get this as part of the peace process as per the

> TJ mechanisms and I will find a way to reconcile with myself'. That hope gradually turned into frustration and I think at this stage the frustration has transformed into fatigue; fatigue that nothing is going to happen.[30]

He attributed this fatigue and disillusionment to the loss of momentum by political actors and this resulted in people losing confidence (discussed further in Chapter 7). It was felt that whether or not a victim wanted prosecution depended on which victim was asked. Reportedly, this depended on the level of education of the victims' family, their relative wealth and their awareness about TJ mechanisms: the higher their level of education, the better their livelihood security, and the greater their knowledge of TJ mechanisms, the more likely the family was to seek prosecution.[31] In contrast, he asserted, those who were uneducated, poor and not well informed about TJ mechanisms often sought compensation and reparations.[32] Also, he explained alleged perpetrators offered money to victims to ensure they did not file their case.[33] To illustrate this point a Nepali human rights worker shared with me an example where a conflict-related rape case was withdrawn because the victim was given 50,000 NPR by the defendant. The worker explained that 'for them the bread and butter is more important than justice.'[34] Victims' needs and ideas of justice will be further explored in Chapter 7.

Thus, the role of TJ brokers has been significant in the trajectory of TJ in Nepal. While they have been attributed with helping to unite victims from both sides of the conflict they are also politicised and have actively contested TJ in Nepal at both the local and national levels.

The role of OHCHR

The UN Office of the High Commissioner for Human Rights (OHCHR) has played an integral role in shaping TJ in Nepal. During the conflict the OHCHR monitoring mission had one of the most robust mandates internationally. A retired UN worker in Nepal said that it did not make sense that Nepal had the largest OHCHR presence; she saw the size and mandate of OHCHR in Nepal during the conflict as evidence of the organisation's other agendas.[35]

'The UN is one'

The TJ agenda pursued by OHCHR did not always accord with the TJ approach advocated by other UN departments and agencies. A representative at a foreign embassy explained that '[t]here was tension within the UN. OHCHR was not well integrated'.[36] The disunity within the UN was particularly evident in an interview with two Nepali UN workers from different agencies. They spoke about the UN Development Programme's (UNDP) push to work within the existing legal system to address conflict issues, which was not a position actively pursued by OHCHR.[37] They also revealed that there was poor connectivity between the UNDP, OHCHR and UN Women on the Access to Justice project, which trained women to be paralegals. In terms of TJ I was informed that the UNDP was leaning towards being prepared so that if TJ mechanisms (i.e. the TRC and the CIEDP) did not materialise they would find ways to use the existing legal mechanisms as 'victims can't wait'.[38] The disunity and tension played out in an interview when one UN worker told me that there was disunity within the UN, while the other UN worker from another agency quickly informed me that 'the UN is one'.[39] In many of my interviews it was apparent that different UN agencies, as well as other actors, were using TJ and its associated mechanisms and projects to compete and advance their respective interests. This suggests there is competition between UN agencies in Nepal.

OHCHR's risk assessment at the beginning of its Peace through Justice project (see Chapter 5) identified five factors that had the potential to influence the success of the project. These factors included the commitment of the government and political actors to address impunity and the cooperation of government ministries (MPTF 2011, 7). In order to mitigate these perceived risks OHCHR, in conjunction with other actors, engaged in networking and advocacy (MPTF 2011, 7). Yet, surprisingly an evaluation report of the project explained that:

> the desired progress envisioned through the project has *somehow come to a halt due to the recent development on politics of appeasement, compromise and reluctance* among political actors in rendering justice to the victims thereby forming an ever complicated scenario
>
> (Phuyal and Pokhrel 2012, 3, my emphasis)

Also of note is that one 'lesson learned' was that there was a high chance of transforming the TRC and CIEDP bills into amnesty laws (Phuyal and Pokhrel 2012, 19). The project evaluators recommended OHCHR could have enhanced its political lobbying 'at the top brass leadership level and convinced them that only serious cases, perhaps limited in number, having emblematic importance will be prosecuted' (Phuyal and Pokhrel 2012, 21). Further, the envisaged political advisor for OHCHR was not hired (Phuyal and Pokhrel 2012, 21). These examples reveal that there was limited awareness of the way TJ and politics shape each other as well as a disjuncture between the rhetoric of an awareness of the politics of and around TJ compared to evidence of this in practice.

OHCHR and other actors were also overly optimistic regarding the timing of establishing TJ mechanisms. This was particularly evident in the establishment by OHCHR, in coordination with the MoPR, of the Transitional Justice Resource Centre in April 2011 (see Chapter 5). The centre was managed by World Vision Advocacy Forum (a Nepali NGO) and key donors of the Centre included OHCHR, the UN Development Fund, the UNDP, the Danish International Development Agency and the European Commission.

The Centre's key objective was to provide specialist information for the TRC and CIEDP; it also included a TJ library (mostly English but some limited Nepali material), computers with the OHCHR Transitional Justice Reference Archive[40] and meeting rooms/spaces where a total of nine fortnightly talks on TJ were held (TJRC 2012). This Centre was set up during a period when it looked increasingly unlikely that the commissions would be established.

I was surprised that the TJRC was mentioned only a few times in my interviews. When I visited the Centre what stood out for me was the large number of staff; I also noticed only one person who was using one of the two public computers. I was puzzled that the Centre seemed to be set up to serve educated people in, or with access to, Kathmandu. This clearly presents a number of obstacles for the majority of the conflict-affected persons who are poor and reside in rural areas. Despite this the Centre was deemed to be a success of the Justice through Peace project, being an establishment that 'promoted informed discourses around transitional justice' (Phuyal and Pokhrel 2012, 3). The project evaluators contend that the Centre provides space for civil society to explore international best practices and lessons for 'integration into discussion about options for Nepal' (MPTF 2011, 7). These examples reveal the lack of understanding and consideration of the political situation in Nepal by various actors and the tendency to believe that sooner is better than later with TJ mechanisms. It also reveals that the way TJ is conceived is removed from the everyday realities of victims (see Chapter 7).

The lack of understanding and consideration of the political situation was also evident in the way TJ implementers operated. I was surprised that during the hyper-politicised environment in the lead up to the Constitution deadline in May 2012, a male Nepali working at the Ministry of Peace and Reconstruction believed the TRC would be established within one month.[41] My findings resonate with Oomen's research in Rwanda. She observed that 'project officers and consultants involved in the initiatives in the legal field in post-genocide Rwanda almost always considered themselves to be technical advisors, and their programmes to be unrelated to Rwandan politics' (2005, 899). The strategy adopted by OHCHR in Nepal appears to have been contentious not only within the UN but also between a key Nepali organisation.

The National Human Rights Commission and donors

OHCHR's relationship with the National Human Rights Commission (NHRC) was particularly contentious. As discussed in Chapter 5, the NHRC is a government-sponsored body whose purpose is to protect and promote human rights and which is tasked with implementing a range of TJ-related activities. On a number of occasions I was told that OHCHR should have complemented the NHRC; however there was a sense that there was duplication and competition between the two organisations. A Nepali representative at a foreign ministry told me that:

> in 2005 it was a different context; OHCHR was more supportive of national institutions until its mandate expired. The desire to extend its mandate was for its own staff instead of strengthening partners … It was not really a friend of people in need.[42]

Also, a male Nepali worker at the NHRC told me that 'OHCHR is equivalent to NHRC … [W]hat is the difference with the UN being here? … OHCHR politically guided the [TJ] process'.[43] Some claim the NHRC saw OHCHR as a rival for international funding support and in 2009 when OHCHR's mandate came up for extension the NHRC opposed another extension unless OHCHR's mandate was reduced to a technical assistance role (Rawski and Sharma 2012, 193). A representative at a foreign embassy explained that while it was the task of OHCHR to capacity build the NHRC it was actually in competition, 'spoonfeeding rather than capacity building'.[44] This resonates with findings that in East Timor where '[m]entoring programmes quickly disintegrated when UN personnel entirely took over the tasks at hand, and East Timorese became "sick" of internationals coming in and conducting "workshops"' (Nagy 2008, 282). Because of the nature of OHCHR's work and its ability to provide more remuneration than the NHRC, many NHRC staff gradually sought and gained employment with OHCHR, which impacted the NHRC's ability to perform its tasks.[45] As Sajjad found, '[t]he contentious relationship was inevitably the result of both performing in the same space, indeed [performing] similar functions, developing partnerships with the same national and international actors for support and competing against each other to prove their own effectiveness' (2011, 366).

Highlighting the contentious aspects of TJ, a representative at a foreign embassy flagged the potential direct and indirect consequences if the UNDP was to take over the role of OHCHR upon OHCHR's departure.[46] The representative explained that if this happened it would impact the UNDP's work in other countries, not just in Nepal. They also questioned whether OHCHR was in fact working in cooperation with donors and other actors, saying 'they had gone too far'.[47] This was a view that was reiterated by other representatives at foreign embassies who felt OHCHR had operated in an antagonistic and politicised manner.[48] However, a few people did feel that there was complementarity between the two organisations but that there were differences in organisational leadership style and difficulty interpreting the organisations' similar mandates. I was also told that donors were putting pressure on OHCHR to release their conflict report because they wanted to see results for the three-year project they had funded.[49] So it appears as though project-cycles and time constraints partly influenced the pressure exerted on OHCHR by donors and in turn the strategies it employed.

It comes as little surprise then that the presence of OHCHR in Nepal became deeply contentious. In December 2011 the government did not renew OHCHR's mandate in Nepal and requested the office to complete its operations in the country. When I was at a social meeting it was offhandedly remarked that the OHCHR was being 'kicked out' of Nepal and I was quickly informed that it was the government who had chosen not to renew OHCHR's mandate.[50] In an interview approximately six months after OHCHR had officially declared the cessations of its operations in Nepal, I was told that OHCHR had a small presence of two experts in the UN Resident Coordinator office because 'the government doesn't want to see OHCHR'. This person went on to say, '[t]his way it [OHCHR] has less level of influence. It was more strategic for the UN Resident Coordinator office to take lead rather than OHCHR'.[51] Again this comment demonstrates the ways the UN, as well as other TJ actors, have sought to negotiate and contest TJ in Nepal.

The Nepal Conflict Report

Perhaps the most contentious element of OHCHR's work was *The Nepal Conflict Report* (to accompany the Transitional Justice Reference Archive). In October 2012 OHCHR released the report on Nepal's conflict along with the archived documents of conflict-related cases and incidents in Nepal between 1996 and 2006. OHCHR contends that the report is a contribution to the TJ process in Nepal with the aim of assisting the Government, the future TJ commissions, the NHRC and civil society 'to advance transitional justice, combat impunity and enable the conflict's many victims to obtain justice' (OHCHR 2012, 1). The report expressed a concern about the withdrawal of 'political' cases by successive governments and the proposals for broad amnesty provisions in the TRC. I was also told that civil society could use the report as a tool to advocate for TJ mechanisms and to validate the cases they had investigated; so in this way OHCHR was complementing what NGOs and the NHRC had done and the report would be a positive tool.[52]

The scope of the investigations for the report and the timing of the release of the report has been an issue of contestation between OHCHR, the government, donors and other TJ actors. The government has been highly resistant to the report claiming that OHCHR exceeded its mandate. In many of my interviews people believed OHCHR had delayed the report to secure a mandate extension and to coerce the government to act on TJ. The OHCHR project evaluators advised that the report should remain in the possession of OHCHR in Geneva 'and may be used nationally or internationally in case of need' and recommended that OHCHR '[r]efrain from disclosing and transferring the confidential document to [the] government unless it is fully convinced that the political climate is favourable to do so' (Phuyal and Pokhrel 2012, 12, 23). A Nepali contractor affiliated with OHCHR's work explained that the delay in releasing the report was partly bureaucratic (to get approval from headquarters in Geneva and internally) and partly political.[53] The following comment by an advisor in a foreign embassy, which was a key supporter of OHCHR, demonstrates the frustration donors experienced:

> We have urged OHCHR for one year to publish the report and give it to government and to the media … [T]he OHCHR report is substantial contribution by the UN … There are a lot of [TJ] issues that don't need the government to do it and the report could help … OHCHR didn't have proper political analysis, it didn't sufficiently take on board donors and likeminded actors, it was overly optimistic regarding mandate extension … [W]e were keen to see OHCHR field office successful, but OHCHR didn't do enough.[54]

Others explained that people within the NHRC thought that OHCHR did not want to share its report with the NHRC lest the NHRC provide it to the government.[55] A male Nepali NGO worker who advised the government on TJ matters explained that he did not think the OHCHR timing of the report release was important given that the TJ mechanisms probably would not use the report as a resource. He questioned the UN's lack of strategy/planning after they released the report. He also explained that it was unlikely that a TJ mechanism would be established in the short to medium term: 'Political stalling … even legislation takes years. It depends on the power dynamics. Establishing TJ mechanisms in one to two years would be difficult.'[56] Despite the initial buzz after the report was released, it appears the respondent's thoughts have come to fruition with little impact in the national political sphere, but this does not preclude the report from having utility in the future.

It is apparent that there has been negotiation and contestation both within the UN (namely between the UNDP and OHCHR) and between the UN and other actors (particularly the government and the NHRC). OHCHR's approach left little room for consideration of the dynamics at play in post-conflict Nepal. In fact, the sense I got in most interviews was that OHCHR's activities in the latter part of the organisation's time in Nepal had severely impacted its relationship with the government and some key donors. While it is unlikely that a large organisation such as the UN can pursue matters such as TJ in a uniform manner throughout its agencies, it was evident in my interviews that OHCHR's approach stood in marked contrast to the approaches of other UN agencies. Furthermore, it appeared that OHCHR and the NHRC competed more than they cooperated, posing problems for the NHRC, the partner that OHCHR was supposed to capacity build. This impacted the ability of the NHRC to conduct its activities in an already hostile environment.

Participatory activities: the inclusion of local voices

It is clear from the examples above that politicians and international actors have played key roles shaping the TJ process in Nepal. Ultimately, decisions were significantly influenced by various international actors and made by a very small group of top male leaders of the major political parties, and local voices, including victims', were not given primacy in the TJ agenda. The remainder of this chapter explores the ways local voices were sought for inclusion in the TJ process.

The influential role of Siebert (the South African consultant) and the inclusion of TJ provisions in the CPA meant that a prime opportunity to engender broader participation was missed. Specifically, the threshold question of whether TJ should be pursued, and if so, when and how it should be pursued, was missed. Of crucial importance are the following observations:

> A broader range of comparative experience on transitional justice and more wide-ranging consultation on the design of any mechanism might have overcome the dynamics by which the TRC emerged within a CPA narrowly based on the need to move forward in the peace process. Notably absent at this stage and in the discussions that preceded the draft TRC bill ... was a national debate among the various stakeholders regarding the scope and relevance of a TRC for Nepal.
>
> (Farasat and Hayner 2009, 21)

A lack of participation during negotiations and pathway-setting of the TJ agenda, particularly by a group of TJ experts and the political elite, sends the message that 'we know best' and ensures that from the outset TJ is not driven by victims or 'the community' (see Cleaver 2001, 46).

However, since the peace negotiation process a number of attempts to broaden participation have been made. These activities were undertaken by various actors (TJ experts, TJ brokers, TJ implementers and victims' groups), which in turn impacted the potential for these activities to impact the official, national TJ process (see Chapter 5 for details of these activities). These consultations took place within an historical legacy of exclusion of minorities and the disadvantaged, particularly those outside Kathmandu. Most of these attempts to promote participation involved victims and other actors who were for the first time being asked about their experiences and expectations and thereby being presented with opportunities for their voices to be heard.

The majority of these participatory activities were consultations. Many of those running the consultations appear to have made varying attempts to ensure that the participants were representative of different types of victims and geographies. There also appeared to be challenges to accessing both female and male victims' perspectives. I was informed that in some MoPR regional consultations it was sometimes quite difficult to ensure that there were male and female victims from both sides of the conflict.[57] One Nepali human rights worker whose organisation helped establish and support one victims' group explained that their organisation also encouraged uninvited victims (who were not part of victims' groups) to attend the consultations.[58] Again, this demonstrates the challenges of selecting various individuals or groups as being representative of the voices of victims and the fear that some people's interests will not be considered if they are not physically present.

The focus on consultations as one the main participatory activities is problematic. This because as regardless of the quality and positive impact of these consultative processes, the decision-making power remained in the hands of actors who were not victims or affected community members. As early as 2008 (soon after the Comprehensive Peace Agreement was signed), victims, having told their stories on many occasions and having been met with only broken promises, were frustrated and disillusioned.[59] Also calls in consultations (and beyond) against amnesties are set in contrast with repeated government attempts to include blanket amnesty provisions (see Chapter 5). Here, it appears as though some TJ implementers utilised the consultation process as a means to legitimise already-made decisions with little obligation to consider or incorporate participants' voices and recommendations (see Cornwall 2008, 270). This demonstrates the serious, perhaps even at times irreconcilable, tensions between the voices of victims and TJ implementers in Nepal (see Leebaw 2011; Fletcher, Weinstein, and Rowen 2009; Fletcher, Weinstein, and Rowen 2001). Also, the focus on the TRC at the Ministry of Peace and Reconstruction's consultations could have unduly influenced and circumscribed how participants articulated their needs and what participants anticipated the sponsors of the consultations or other actors were in favour of delivering (see Mosse 2001, 21). Here Kothari's (2001) performance metaphor rings true that participants may learn the roles of 'good' participants.

Another issue that was perhaps not as adequately addressed was how safe people felt expressing their voices in these spaces. Victims participated in both formal and invited spaces. These different types of spaces present different challenges for the organisers of consultations. Examining Gaventa's work on power in development, Hughes et al. assert:

> there also exists another continuum of power pertaining to the spaces of engagement where development actors are working. Types of spaces fall into three categories. *Formal institutional spaces* are spaces where bureaucrats, experts, and/ or elected representatives make decisions with little consultation or participation of those who their decision is meant to effect. *Invited spaces* are spaces defined and designed by authorities where citizens are invited to participate in. In turn, *claimed or created spaces* are spaces either claimed by less powerful actors, or created more autonomously by them.
>
> (2003, 7–8)

The Ministry of Peace and Reconstruction consultations are illustrative in this regard. At the MoPR consultations were a wide range of stakeholders including political leaders/representatives and army personnel, as well as civil society organisations and victims. A Nepali human rights worker involved in facilitating these consultations explained that while these consultations were perhaps structurally representative of victims and other actors, it was another matter whether or not victims actually felt safe to exercise their voice.[60] I heard about one consultation (conducted on human rights and the Constituent Assembly) where a victim who was usually quite articulate froze and was unable to speak. The facilitators were later informed that the participant's silence was due to the presence of an army major, which triggered a flashback for the victim. While this example did not occur during the Ministry of Peace and Reconstruction consultations, the respondent was adamant that this type of issue was replicated in those consultations and that the high prevalence of mental health issues has gone unaddressed in Nepal.[61] Hence, it is not just the existence of these consultative (invited) spaces that matters, but the *ways* they are constituted.

In a country where there are over 100 languages, the choice of language is also significant. Most consultations and surveys are conducted in Nepali or English, which limits (or even excludes) people not fluent in these languages. For example, most reports are only translated into English or Nepali and not into local ethnic languages such as Maithili, Bhojpuri, Tharu and Tamang. Participatory activities can be circumscribed by the language used but so too by those who choose and define key terms. However, this challenge can be minimised if there is greater attention provided to the meanings the participants prescribe (rather than the meaning prescribed by facilitators or the program designers and funders). This issue was raised by victims' group leader Ram Bhandari. He explains:

> NGOs, donors and political leaders use vague words such as peace, reconciliation, amnesty, impunity, reparation and transitional justice etc., but the victims and their families living in the countryside do not understand these terms or the politics behind them … All the buzzwords and top-down practices of transition in Nepal that exclude the victims' communities have created a sense of disillusionment and hopelessness that has done nothing but cause increased frustration and anger for the families of victims.
>
> (Bhandari 2011, 69)

As discussed in this chapter, the word for reconciliation in Nepali (*melmilap*) seems closer to friendship, which poses issues when different actors use it with differing and, at times, competing interests and agendas. These concerns are reflected in the following observations from a human rights worker involved in the Ministry of Peace and Reconstruction consultations. He said:

> [i]n the early stage the biggest challenge was at the victims' level the idea of TJ mechanisms, the TRC; there was a low level of understanding and awareness. They only knew what happened to them. But they had little idea what has happened to them amounts to what level of violations and crime and what they could then be entitled to for example as rights be it seeking truth, getting justice or reparations. They know what happened to them they were more focused on sharing their own suffering: 'this is what I have suffered and this amounts to this level of violations I am supposed to get it as my right.' This is still the biggest issue.[62]

Also, the ways in which knowledge is produced and shared is of key importance. For example, measuring the degree of participation of individuals at a consultation by the quantity or even perhaps the quality of verbal contributions may be contrary to local norms and practices (see Cleaver 2001, 44). Thus, key to any attempt to promote participation is the understanding of the local norms in relation to decision-making and representation. Questions also need to be asked about context and culture: what is the historical, political and social context within which these participants are entering this participatory space and what are the positions and power ascribed to the different participants by virtue of their birth, education, kinship and networks? (see Lawoti 2007a; Hailey 2001, 96). I would argue that consideration of the legacies of the nature of interactions – the levels of trust and the degree of capacity between individuals, the state and other actors and agencies – before these participatory activities commenced, was neglected (see Lawoti 2007a, b, 2009; Mohan 2001).

I do acknowledge that there are real challenges of expecting rural, remote and illiterate victims to be active participants in the creation and implementation of TJ processes (for further discussion see Chapter 7). Consider, for example, the manner in which information is organised and presented, which can privilege certain individuals or groups and enable them to articulate their concerns. Once again, this means that power is in 'the hands of the most articulate and politically adept' (Hailey 2001, 94). There may be practical and technical difficulties for participants (e.g. amending draft legislation). For example, I was informed that in many of the Ministry of Peace and Reconstruction consultations, participants were not provided with the legislation that they were then asked to comment on before the consultations.[63] Thus, while some practical problems (e.g. in terms of timing and logistics) can be overcome for some individuals (e.g. providing the relevant documentation in advance), capacity, technical and political issues remain. These issues do not render futile attempts to promote participation, but they do require consideration in each context.

Ultimately, although a number of actors conducted participatory activities, we must ask questions about who benefited from these activities as both a means and an end. Specifically they should ask: To what extent, if any, did participants have real power to shape decisions? What was the real and perceived likelihood of, or commitment to, implementing participants' recommendations? To what extent were participants informed of the legislative and other constraints that would impact the extent to which these recommendations could be heeded?; It is apparent that a limited number of participatory action research studies have *assisted in* empowering various individuals but, as Chapter 5 reveals, most of the recommendations from TJ consultations have not been heeded; again, demonstrating the difference between different types of participation, not all of which are meaningful.

This chapter has demonstrated that the disregard or lack of sensitivity to the significance of politics and the political function of TJ has impacted the

TJ process. Throughout the TJ trajectory, victims and other community members have had limited scope to articulate their interpretations of TJ, including being able to challenge the need for the TRC. Participatory activities have offered opportunities but also challenges for various TJ actors, particularly victims (see Selim 2014). In Chapter 7 I examine further what victims and affected community members seek in the wake of the conflict.

Notes

1 This resonates with Slater's view on contentious politics. He argues that contentious politics receives more attention as a product, rather than as a producer, of political phenomena and that greater attention should be given to the 'politics that contentious politics produces' (2010, 275).
2 I consider the 'local' to comprise the sub-state, the community and the individual; fundamentally it is a 'standpoint based in a particular locality but not bounded by it' (Shaw, Waldorf and Hazan 2010, 6).
3 There are numerous ways to identify victims' needs (e.g. targeting representatives and gatekeepers and through social movements). However, the dominant approach is to seek victims' voices through participation as generally practised in development.
4 Personal interview, 5 April 2012, Kathmandu.
5 Personal interview, 17 October 2012, Kathmandu.
6 For example, the Mallik and Rayamajhi Commissions were formed to investigate the suppression of the 1990 and 2006 People's Movements.
7 Personal interview, 4 April 2012, Kathmandu.
8 Personal interview, 5 April 2012, Kathmandu.
9 Personal interview, 29 February 2012, Kathmandu.
10 Personal interview, 5 October 2012, Kathmandu.
11 Personal interview, 11 October 2012, Kathmandu.
12 Personal interview, 11 October 2012, Kathmandu.
13 Personal interview, 11 October 2012, Kathmandu.
14 Personal interview, 29 September 2012, Morang.
15 Personal interview, 17 October 2012, Kathmandu.
16 Personal interview, 5 March 2012, Kathmandu.
17 The UK is a signatory to the UN Convention Against Torture and Lama was to be tried under Section 134 of the *Criminal Justice Act* (1988).
18 It is important to highlight that not all NGOs in Nepal have political affiliations and while individuals working in human rights NGOs may have personal political ideologies this does not mean they pursue these political interests as part of their human rights work.
19 Personal interview, 6 April 2012, Kathmandu.
20 Personal interview, 3 April 2012, Kathmandu.
21 Personal interview, 17 October 2012, Kathmandu.
22 Personal interview, 11 October 2012, Kathmandu.
23 Personal interview, 11 October 2012, Kathmandu.
24 Personal interview, 11 October 2012, Kathmandu.
25 Personal interview, 11 October 2012, Kathmandu.
26 Personal interview, 5 March 2012, Kathmandu.
27 Personal interview, 11 September 2012, Rolpa.
28 Personal interview, 11 September 2012, Rolpa.
29 Personal interview, 22 March 2012, Dang.
30 Personal interview, 11 October 2012, Kathmandu.

31 Personal interview, 11 October 2012, Kathmandu.
32 Personal interview, 11 October 2012, Kathmandu.
33 Personal interview, 11 October 2012, Kathmandu.
34 Personal interview, 11 October 2012, Kathmandu.
35 Meeting, 15 October 2012, Kathmandu. A reason that was often cited was that OHCHR wanted to remain in the region to monitor Tibet.
36 Personal interview, 5 October 2012, Kathmandu.
37 Personal interview, 13 March 2012, Kathmandu.
38 Personal interview, 13 March 2012, Kathmandu.
39 Personal interview, 13 March 2012, Kathmandu.
40 This was an electronic database of approximately 30,000 documents and cases that were relevant to the conflict.
41 Personal interview, 4 April 2012, Kathmandu.
42 Personal interview, 5 April 2012, Kathmandu.
43 Personal interview, 16 February 2012, Kathmandu.
44 Personal interview, 9 March 2012, Kathmandu.
45 Personal interview, 11 October 2012, Kathmandu.
46 Personal interview, 9 March 2012, Kathmandu. OHCHR was concerned that in its absence Nepal lacked 'a credible third party … to continue the institutional legacy' of the TJ process (Phuyal and Pokhrel 2012, 7).
47 Personal interview, 9 March 2012, Kathmandu.
48 Personal interviews, 5 April 2012 and 5 October 2012, Kathmandu.
49 Personal interview, 11 October 2012, Kathmandu.
50 Meeting, 29 March 2012, Kathmandu.
51 Personal interview, 13 March 2012, Kathmandu.
52 Personal interview, 11 October 2012, Kathmandu.
53 Personal interview, 29 February 2012, Kathmandu.
54 Personal interview, 5 October 2012, Kathmandu.
55 Personal interview, 11 October 2012, Kathmandu.
56 Personal interview, 11 October 2012, Kathmandu.
57 Personal interview, 11 October 2012, Kathmandu.
58 Personal interview, 17 October 2012, Kathmandu.
59 Personal interview, 11 October 2012, Kathmandu.
60 Personal interview, 11 October 2012, Kathmandu.
61 Personal interview, 11 October 2012, Kathmandu.
62 Personal interview, 11 October 2012, Kathmandu.
63 Personal communication, 4 January 2013.

References

Adhikari, Aditya, Bhaskar Guatam, Surabhi Pudasaini, and Bhadra Sharma. 2014. 'Impunity and accountability in Nepal.' http://asiafoundation.org/resources/pdfs/NPimpunityandpoliticalaccountability.pdf.

Bhandari, Ram Kumar. 2011. 'The role of victims' organisations in transition from conflict: Families of the disappeared in Nepal.' Master's Degree, Institute for Peace Research and Security Policy, University of Hamburg.

Bhuta, Nehal. 2005. 'Between liberal legal didactics and political manichaeism: The politics and law of the Iraqi special tribunal.' *Melbourne Journal of International Law* 6(2):245–272.

Boesenecker, Aaron P., and Leslie Vinjamuri. 2011. 'Lost in translation? Civil society, faith-based organizations and the negotiation of international norms.' *International Journal of Transitional Justice* 5(3):345–365.

Clark, Phil, and Nicola Palmer. 2012. 'Introduction: Challenging transitional justice.' In *Critical perspectives in transitional justice*, edited by Nicola Palmer, Phil Clark and Danielle Granville, 1–16. Portland, OR: Intersentia.

Cleaver, Frances. 2001. 'Institutions, agency and the limitations of participatory approaches to development.' In *Participation: The new tyranny?* edited by Bill Cooke and Uma Kothari, 36–55. New York: Zed Books.

Cornwall, Andrea. 2008. 'Unpacking 'participation': Models, meanings and practices.' *Community Development Journal* 43(3):269–283.

Diaz, Catalina. 2007. 'Colombia's bid for justice and peace. Study Workshop 5 – Lessons from negotiated justice options in South Africa and Colombia.' Building a Future on Peace and Justice, Nuremberg, 25–27 June.

eKantipur. 2014. 'Acharya: Reconciliation basis for TRC formation.' Last modified 15 April 2014. www.ekantipur.com/2014/04/15/top-story/acharya-reconciliation-basis-for-trc-formation/388278.html.

Farasat, Warisha, and Priscilla Hayner. 2009. *Negotiating peace in Nepal: Implications for justice*. Institute for Peacebuilding / International Centre for Transitional Justice. https://ictj.org/sites/default/files/ICTJ-IFP-Nepal-Negotiating-Peace-2009-English.pdf.

Fletcher, Laurel E., Harvey M. Weinstein, and Jamie Rowen. 2009. 'Context, timing and the dynamics of transitional justice: A historical perspective.' *Human Rights Quarterly* 31(1):163–220.

Gowing, Richard. 2013. *War by other means? An analysis of the contested terrain of transitional justice under the 'Victor's Peace' in Sri Lanka*. Development Studies Institute Working Papers Series. London: London School of Economics.

Grodsky, Brian. 2009. 'Re-ordering justice: Towards a new methodological approach to studying transitional justice.' *Journal of Peace Research* 46(6):819–837.

Guatam, Bijay Raj. 2013. 'Ensure justice for victim in Nepal remains a challenge.' *INFORMAL* 33(1):3–6.

Hailey, John. 2001. 'Beyond the formulaic: Process and practice in South Asian NGOs.' In *Participation: The new tyranny?* edited by Bill Cooke and Uma Kothari, 88–101. New York: Zed Books.

Hughes, Alexandra, Joanna Wheeler, Rosalind Eyben, and Patta Scott-Villiers. 2003. 'Rights and Power Workshop Report.' Accountability and Participation, Development Research Centre on Citizenship, Accountability and Participation, Rights and Power Workshop, 17—20 November 2003, Institute of Development Studies, Brighton.

Kothari, Uma. 2001. 'Participatory development: Power, knowledge and social control.' In *Participation: The new tyranny?* edited by Bill Cooke and Uma Kothari, 139–152. New York: Zed Books.

Lawoti, Mahendra. 2007a. 'Contentious politics in democratizing Nepal.' In *Contentious politics and democratization in Nepal*, edited by Mahendra Lawoti, 17–47. London: Sage.

Lawoti, Mahendra. 2007b. 'Democracy, domination and exclusionary constitutional-engineering process in Nepal, 1990.' In *Contentious politics and democratization in Nepal*, edited by Mahendra Lawoti, 48–72. London: Sage.

Lawoti, Mahendra. 2009. 'Dissecting inclusion, knowledge and power.' *The Kathmandu Post*, 3 April.

Leebaw, Bronwyn. 2011. *Judging state-sponsored violence, imagining political change*. New York: Cambridge University Press.

McAdam, Doug, Sydney G. Tarrow, and Charles Tilly. 2001. *Dynamics of contention*. Cambridge: Cambridge University Press.

Merry, Sally Engle. 1990. *Getting justice and getting even: Legal consciousness among working-class Americans.* Chicago, IL: University of Chicago Press.
Mohan, Giles. 2001. 'Beyond participation: Strategies for deeper empowerment.' In *Participation: The new tyranny?* edited by Bill Cooke and Uma Kothari, 153–167. New York: Zed Books.
Mosse, David. 2001. '"People's knowledge", participation and patronage: Operations and representations in rural development.' In *Participation: The new tyranny?* edited by Bill Cooke and Uma Kothari, 16–35. New York: Zed Books.
MPTF. 2011. 'Annual programme narrative progress report.' http://mptf.undp.org/document/download/9875.
Murphy, Colleen. 2017. *The conceptual foundations of transitional justice.* Cambridge: Cambridge University Press.
Nagy, Rosemary. 2008. 'Transitional Justice as global project: Critical reflections.' *Third World Quarterly* 29(2):275–289.
Nepal, Janak. 2016. 'CIEDP's ability to deliver restorative justice questioned.' *The Kathmandu Post*, http://kathmandupost.ekantipur.com/news/2016-04-10/ciedps-ability-to-deliver-restorative-justice-questioned.html.
OHCHR. 2012. *The Nepal conflict report.* www.ohchr.org/Documents/Countries/NP/OHCHR_Nepal_Conflict_Report2012.pdf.
Oomen, Barbara. 2005. 'Donor-driven justice and its discontents: The case of Rwanda.' *Development and Change* 36(5):887–910.
Phuyal, Hari, and Shreejana Pokhrel. 2012. '"Evaluation report." The Peace through Justice Project,' implemented by the Office of the High Commissioner for Human Rights – Nepal. http://mptf.undp.org/document/download/10993.
Rai, Dewan. 2015. 'Chances of Col Lama's release from UK 'slim'.' *The Kathmandu Post*, http://kathmandupost.ekantipur.com/printedition/news/2015-03-15/chances-of-col-lamas-release-from-uk-slim.html.
Rai, Dewan. 2016a. 'CIEDP bill will criminalise disappearances.' *The Kathmandu Post*, http://kathmandupost.ekantipur.com/news/2016-02-02/ciedp-bill-will-criminalise-disappearances.html.
Rai, Dewan. 2016b. 'Col Lama's acquittal: Setback for moment, but 'victory in long run''. *The Kathmandu Post*, http://kathmandupost.ekantipur.com/news/2016-09-08/col-lamas-acquittal-setback-for-moment-but-victory-in-long-run.html.
Rawski, Frederick, and Mandira Sharma. 2012. 'A comprehensive peace? Lessons from Human rights monitoring in Nepal.' In *Nepal in transition: From people's war to fragile peace*, edited by Sebastian von Einsiedel, David M. Malone and Suman Pradhan, 175–200. New Dehli: Cambridge University Press.
Rubli, Sandra. 2011. 'Knowing the truth – What for? The contested politics of transitional justice in Burundi.' *Journal für Entwicklungspolitik* 27(3):22–43.
Rubli, Sandra. 2012. *Transitional justice: Justice by bureaucratic means?* www.files.ethz.ch/isn/154626/WP4_2012.pdf.
Sajjad, Tazreena. 2011. 'Inconvenient justice: The struggle to 'close the books' in Afghanistan and Nepal.' Doctor of Philosophy, International Relations, American University.
Selim, Yvette. 2014. 'The opportunities and challenges of participation in transitional justice: Examples from Nepal.' *Journal of International Development* 29(8):1123–1148.
Shaw, Rosalind, Lars Waldorf, and Pierre Hazan, eds. 2010. *Localizing transitional justice interventions and priorities after mass violence.* Stanford, CA: Stanford University Press.

Slater, Dan. 2010. *Ordering power: Contentious politics and authoritarian Leviathans in Southeast Asia*. Cambridge: Cambridge University Press.

Snellinger, Amanda. 2007. 'Student movements in Nepal: Their parameters and their idealized forms.' In *Contentious politics and democratization in Nepal*, edited by Mahendra Lawoti, 273–295. London: Sage.

Subotic, Jelena. 2007. 'Hijacked justice: Domestic use of international norms.' Doctor of Philosophy, University of Wisconsin-Madison.

Tilly, Charles, and Sydney G. Tarrow. 2007. *Contentious politics*. Boulder, CO: Paradigm Publishers.

TJRC. 2012. 'Fortnightly talk programme.' http://tjrcnepal.org/resources-downloads/fortnightly-talk-programme/.

Torné, Carlos Fernández. 2013. *Transitional justice process in Nepal: The state of the art and questions and scenarios for the future in Nepal*. Barcelona: Institut Català Internacional per la Pau.

Tyynela, John. 2014. 'Can truth commissions strengthen peace processes?' \t "_blank"www.ictj.org/sites/default/files/ICTJ-Report-KAF-TruthCommPeace-2014.pdf.

UN General Assembly. 2013. 'Communications report of special procedures.' http://daccess-dds-ny.un.org/doc/UNDOC/GEN/G13/164/42/PDF/G1316442.pdf?OpenElement.

Uprimny, Rodrigo, and Maria Paula Saffon. 2007. 'Uses and abuses of transitional justice discourse in Colombia.' PRIO Policy Brief, 6. Oslo: PRIO. www.prio.org/Publications/Publication/?x=7253.

Wilson, Richard A. 2001. *The politics of truth and reconciliation in South Africa: Legitimizing the post-apartheid state*. New York: Cambridge University Press.

Wilson, Richard A. 2003. 'Anthropological studies of national reconciliation.' *Anthropological Theory* 3(3):367–387.

7 Victims in Nepal

> Victims should be treated equally not depending on their political party. We are all victims.
>
> (President of a women's organisation, Rolpa, 10 September 2012)

As Chapters 5 and 6 revealed, the TJ agenda has been largely circumscribed by TJ experts, brokers and implementers. Also evident is that actors, including victims, will engage in participation according to their own interests. Against this backdrop we must ask: Who are considered victims? Who determines whether someone is a victim? What implications, if any, does this determination have? And what do victims want? To answer these questions this chapter examines the voices and perspectives of victims, ex-combatants, NGO workers and other community members, among others. In line with the constructivist grounded theory approach, I have sought to enable respondents' 'accounts to retain a degree of visibility in the text' to show the connections between my data and analytical findings (Mills, Bonner, and Francis 2006, 6).

This chapter analyses the implications of the victim label and the victim/perpetrator binary in the context of Nepal (see Chapter 3). It also examines the role of victims' groups in Nepal. Following this, it examines TJ at the local level with a particular focus on Local Peace Committees. This chapter also analyses what victims want and what justice means to them, and finally, the ways people deal with the past.

This chapter presents four key arguments. First, TJ experts, implementers and brokers play a significant role in identifying and recognising victims in Nepal, yet this recognition does not always accord with the views of conflict-affected persons. Second, victims' understandings of TJ is predominately limited to an awareness of the Interim Relief Program with few being aware of the TJ mechanisms, namely the TRC, the CIEDP, reparations and prosecutions. Third, when victims in Nepal are asked what they want, they frequently raise everyday social and economic concerns.[1] Fourth, it is by appreciating everyday complexities and concerns that TJ can be made more relevant.

Victims and perpetrators

The people I met in Nepal applied the victim label in different ways. Few people in conflict-affected areas referred to themselves as victims in our conversations, but when I asked directly if they considered themselves to be victims many answered yes. However, at times people discounted or denied their victimisation. For example, I met with a male business owner in Rolpa, the Maoist heartland. He was threatened and displaced during the conflict but did not consider himself a victim. He explained this denial or rejection of victimisation was because the conflict indirectly affected many people.[2] A male human rights activist in Rolpa made a similar remark: 'Even though I was captured many times by the Maoists and the army captured and beat me … [I]magine if this happens to me, how about other people?'[3] I also met with a Maoist supporter in Rolpa who wrote and performed revolutionary songs and poems during the conflict. He was incarcerated for seven years for his involvement with the Maoists. He remembered the incidents of his victimisation, and his incarceration, 'like a dream'.[4] He also did not consider himself a victim.[5]

The self-prescription of the victim label was complicated if the person had had a political role in the conflict and suffered an incidence of victimisation. This is evident in the comment above by the Maoist supporter; it is also exemplified by the story of a Maoist Commissar. During his time in battle his wife was captured and raped by state forces and two days later she was killed and her body was dumped. On one level this man may be considered a perpetrator for having ordered the use of violence and for his involvement in the Maoist insurgency; on another level he may be considered a victim. He may also be considered both a perpetrator and a victim. He explained that sentimentally/emotionally he considered himself a victim but, because he fought for the nation, and even though his wife was murdered, he was not exactly a victim.[6] Under the Interim Relief Program (discussed below) he was eligible for compensation for the death of his wife. Whether this man is considered a perpetrator, victim or both depends on who is applying the label(s) and for what purpose(s).

Some individuals considered themselves to be martyrs and (freedom) fighters. At times these terms were employed in addition to the victim label; at other times it appeared as though these terms were considered to be mutually exclusive. In my interviews it was particularly Maoist combatants who referred to themselves as fighters, and victims' families who referred to killed or disappeared combatants as martyrs or fighters. A male Nepali human rights worker who interacted with different victims' groups explained that the Maoist party had a different understanding of who was a victim compared to other local actors and that this impacted on their level of cooperation with victims' groups. He explained:

> They [the Maoists] resisted the very idea of categorising in their words "their people" as victims because they wanted to elevate their people

> because they said they were fighting for a revolutionary cause so that they were either martyrs or fighters. This was glorifying their involvement in the war.[7]

This glorifying process was also mentioned by a former People's Liberation Army (PLA) coordinator who referred to martyrs, glory fighters and republican fighters. He explained:

> PLA members die a different type of death. Before going to fight in guerrilla warfare we discussed that we are glory fighters and we won't return. When we were about to be separated we would shake each other's hand and again when we return. The tragedy of war is that you can't shake the hand of those who died.[8]

Notably, when people were referred to as martyrs and victims it seemed that the victim label was employed in order to ensure the person and their family received state recognition and support. For example, in Dadeldhura I met a group of victims who were attending a meeting for conflict-affected persons conducted by their Local Peace Committee. Although the meeting was open to all victims in the area there were only men present. A male respondent whose sister had been murdered allowed another male respondent present to speak more extensively with me but he was adamant that I record his name. Also present at this meeting was the brother of a murdered female Maoist ex-combatant. He explained that his sister was killed during the conflict: 'My sister was a martyr. For martyrs the compensation is ten lakhs [1,000,000]. We have only been given three lakhs [300,000] so there's seven lakhs [700,000] remaining to be paid to us. We are waiting for this …'[9] Also, the Maoist Commissar considered ex-combatants to be victims and he expected the state to recognise ex-combatants as republican fighters and martyrs and to take responsibility for their families.[10] In contrast, the daughter of a murdered Nepali Congress member referred to victims from both sides, not just victims of the state, as martyrs.[11] She felt that the TJ commissions should first declare all victims as martyrs and the government should treat victims from both sides equally. She believed that victims should be provided with compensation and some type of memorialisation (e.g. a statue, building or bridge named after martyrs), reiterating that this should be for victims of both sides because if only victims from one side of the conflict are considered martyrs then the other side might destroy the memorial.[12] She also linked victimhood and martyrdom with state recognition and compensation.

Victimhood was also linked to TJ mechanisms, namely the TRC. In my interviews, of the limited number of respondents who were aware of the TRC, many explained that its key function was to determine 'real' or 'genuine' victims and to produce a list of these real victims. For example, in Dadeldhura I met the wife of a man who was accused of being a Maoist and was subsequently tortured by the army. She told me that '[i]f the Truth and Reconciliation

Commission will form, then my husband who was really affected will be identified. The Truth and Reconciliation Commission will not be politically influenced, it will be independent and then victims will be identified'.[13] In another district a male Nepali human rights worker spoke about the need for the government to make one agenda to identify who are real victims.[14] This was echoed by an assistant secretary of Local Peace Committee who saw the identification of real victims as one of the key mandates of Local Peace Committees.[15] Additionally, a female human rights worker speaking about her human rights organisation's work in providing legal assistance to women, noted her organisation needed to identify the real victims as some were fake.[16] The difficulties identifying 'real victims' are discussed further below.

These examples reinforce the idea that victimhood and support are intimately connected for conflict-affected people in Nepal. In particular, the notion of 'real' victims appeared to be connected to the idea that such people would be provided with reparations through the TRC (for those who were aware of the TRC). This was the case in South Africa with the Truth and Reconciliation Commission. Although the Khulumani Support Group (a victims' association in South Africa) allowed individuals to self-identify as victims or survivors given that this group was organised *within the context of* the South African TRC, the group's definition of victim corresponded with the definition adopted by the TRC (Rombouts 2002, 229). So it is evident that TJ mechanisms have the ability to directly and indirectly influence who is considered a victim, even before they are formed.

The understanding that 'real' victims would be given reparations appears to have influenced some people to adopt a particular script and repertoire. For example, a victims' group for relatives of the disappeared changed its name from Society of the Families of the Disappeared to the Society of Families of Citizens Disappeared by the State.[17] The change of name:

> specifically evoked the state's duties towards its citizens and highlighted disappearance as a crime committed by state forces, in line with the international legal definition of enforced disappearance. It de-emphasized political identities and emphasized civic identities of the disappeared. In this way, it was also political, performative and strategic.
>
> (Marsden 2011, 278–279)

Despite the individualised focus on victims, for some people in Nepal some victims' individual suffering was subsumed within a collective narrative of sacrifice. For example, a male respondent in Rolpa spoke about how the district had the most victims who were sacrificed.[18] When I spoke with the Maoist Commissar about how communities were impacted by the conflict, he told me that '[i]n Rolpa a total of 763 people sacrificed their life and 31 people are disappeared … We lost so many people. To make a great nation you must sacrifice many lives'.[19] The idea of sacrifice was also apparent when I asked him his thoughts about the impact of the conflict on widows whose loved ones were killed by the state security forces or the Maoists. He explained:

> Sometimes when we meet widows even as a man we become sentimental and we but try to convince them that their husbands sacrificed their lives for the party for Nepal. Even I lost my wife for the betterment of Nepal. Without sacrifice, without losing something we can't achieve anything.[20]

A female ex-combatant spoke about how the Maoist party persuaded them that 'their name would be bigger' if they died and the importance of 'courage and sacrifice'.[21]

Pertinent here is Marsden's research on the way victims' individual concerns became part of a broader narrative. She explains that those disappeared by the state hold 'symbolic power for the Maoists' revolutionary project and their ongoing struggle with the state' (2011, 272). She also reveals how families' efforts to search for their disappeared relatives were drawn into the Maoists' 'broader political projects' whereby 'the disappeared have been drawn into the ideology of sacrifice alongside the martyrs' (Marsden 2011, 273). She explains:

> The shifting strategy of the [Maoist] Party towards the disappeared had emphasized their identities as kin, as 'citizens' and then as 'warriors.' … [T]hese shifts have mirrored the changes in the Party's wider positioning, aims and strategies in the arena of Nepali politics: from underground insurgent group; to political partner in the interim government; to leading party in the coalition government … [and then] back into opposition.
>
> (Marsden 2011, 276)

These examples buttress Lecomte-Tilouine's (2010) findings that individual stories can become subsumed into an anonymous collective. It is evident that these broader political objectives constrain (and at times enable) the individual narratives and repertoires of victims.

Often, in my interviews there was an assumption – particularly by TJ brokers – that victims were 'innocent'. A male worker at a national human rights organisation explained that most victims were so innocent and that they did not know anything:

> They don't know how to explain it; they use sign language to express why, what's our fault, what did we do wrong by gesturing … [T]o know the truth it's their right. Our organisation's focus is not on combatants it is on innocent people.[22]

Notable in this quote is that combatants are not deemed to be innocent whereas victims are. Innocence was also raised by a widow whose husband was in the army and was killed in a Maoist attack on their barracks. She said, '[t]he army was tricked. The army was innocent, they said they were not fighting for internal matters, it was the Maoists that tricked them.'[23] In Rolpa a man who was harassed by both the army and the Maoists and then tortured and detained by the army explained that he was an innocent man who knew little about the Maoist insurgency.[24] The notion of innocence is pertinent as there may be 'moral limits' to what can be demanded of perpetrators by 'unreconciled victims' (see Lu 2002, 115). This is particularly relevant with regard to the reconciliation provisions in the TJ Act.

As discussed in Chapter 5, the TRC in Nepal gives victims the opportunity to reconcile with perpetrators. There are a number of provisions relating to reconciliation including:

- the Commission has the power '[t]o initiate reconciliation and get reconciled the perpetrator and the victim';
- '[r]econciliation may be made: (1) If a perpetrator or a victim files an application to the Commission for reconciliation, the Commission may reconcile mutually between them'; and,
- 'the Commission shall not recommend for action to the following perpetrators: (a) Who have reconciled with victims' (Articles 13[b], 22, 24[2a]).

These provisions could put pressure on victims to reconcile without victims providing their consent. This indicates the ways TJ mechanisms can lead to undesirable outcomes. Further, it appears as though perpetrators deemed to have reconciled will be immune from prosecution; illustrating the ways the TJ process has been employed to fulfil political interests.

I also found that ex-combatants complicated the victim/perpetrator binary in Nepal. As discussed above, a national human rights organisation did not include ex-combatants in their activities because the organisation's focus was on 'innocent people'.[25] In contrast, a female ex-combatant with whom I spoke considered herself to be a victim. She explained to me that initially she did not know much about the Maoist ideology, but then powerful men and political leaders had indoctrinated her. She became a PLA commander and described that in the PLA barracks there was equal work and no discrimination between males and females. In relation to victimhood she explained:

> Yes, I do consider myself a victim. We live in a paternalistic society so if men were victimised by conflict and lost energy and time to the PLA it would be different. The conflict didn't give a bright future. Generally the conflict and Nepali society hinders the progress of women. Sometimes I have the desire to do something, to work, but I can't as much as I'd like because society does not want women to move about freely in the society.[26]

Pertinent here is that she explains her victimhood in relation to gender. The majority of victims in Nepal were female (see Chapter 4) so the gendered aspect of victimhood has ramifications. This will be discussed further below.

In fact, for some respondents the 'real' victims are the ex-combatants. For example a male NGO worker stated the government is already giving relief to victims but the real victims are the ex-combatants.[27] He explained this was because combatants gave up so much to fight for ideals and principles to support the Maoists. He went on to say that now they are given a few hundred thousand rupees, which the Maoist party was taking from them (see Chapter 4).[28] He, and other people I spoke with, lamented the opportunities these combatants had lost because they had spent the prime of their lives fighting or in captivity.[29]

Not only are former combatants officially not considered victims, they were classified into qualified and disqualified combatants as part of the disarmament, demobilisation and reintegration process in Nepal (see Chapter 4). A former leader of the People's Liberation Army explained that the UNMIN had disqualified many fighters and that these fighters came out of the cantonments with no money.[30] Some of those who were given payments ('a golden handshake') gave up to 10 per cent of this money to disqualified combatants.[31] A female NGO worker in Rolpa felt that disqualified combatants were one type of victim because '[s]ociety does not accept them, nobody accepts them'.[32] She believed it was likely that they would join armed groups if the government did not respond to their needs. In a similar vein a former underground Maoist guerrilla explained that if the government did not engage these ex-combatants, then 'they will join the next cause'.[33] He explained Nepalis' frustration with the political situation using an analogy of a 'farmer who worked the whole day every day and then reaped nothing.'[34] For him, many had joined the Maoists and fought, yet little had been achieved.

An informal discussion with a male Nepali working for an international development organisation revealed the added complexity of the qualified/disqualified classification. He explained that while the word 'disqualified' in English is not a particularly problematic term, when translated into Nepali it means 'unfit' or 'not in use' (*ayōgya*), which he explained has much more devastating, personal and emasculating connotations.[35] This is particularly noteworthy given the patriarchal structure in Nepal and the related notions of masculinity. These feelings about combatants as victims were not always shared, however. A widower who was tortured and imprisoned explained:

> The combatants were ready to fight. But those that passed away in the fighting are not victims, they agree with state's or the Maoists' philosophy and were ready to fight. Even the army police get 7 lakhs [700,000 NPR]. How can they be conflict victims? We civilians, we are the real victims.[36]

Female combatants and also child soldiers complicated the simplistic notion of the innocent victim and the guilty perpetrator (see Chapter 3).[37] A female ex-combatant I met in Rolpa (discussed above) told me that before she decided to join the Maoist rebels she was active in university politics. During the conflict she married a fellow comrade and twice became pregnant. The first time she miscarried and during the second pregnancy she was forced to seek medical assistance in India. She felt that she was abandoned by the Maoist party and was dismayed that her husband was disqualified for payment to ex-combatants because he had left the cantonments to earn a living (at the time of the interview he was employed in the Middle East). She spoke with conviction, questioned discrimination against females in the community and certainly defied the stereotype of a passive victim and perhaps also that of a guilty perpetrator. This example demonstrates that the standard victim/perpetrator view obfuscates the complexity of the members of these categories. In fact, many conflict-affected people I met demonstrated agency, eschewing the stereotype of being a passive victim (discussed below).

Thus, it is clear that any approach that assumes a strict division between victims and perpetrators does not reflect everyday realities in Nepal. For many, the notion of victimhood appeared to be related to the notion of state support. Pertinent, however, are the consequences for conflict-affected persons who are unwilling to adopt the standard repertoires and represent themselves as 'victims' within the TJ paradigm.

While innocence is often equated with non-combatants, so that ex-combatants are usually excluded from discussions about victims, when the notion of suffering is used to ascertain victimhood then this distinction does not seem to hold (see Bouris 2007, 36). Going beyond the scope of standard definitions of victims, Elster argues that the notion of victimhood should be ascertained by considering forms of *suffering* (rather than harm). He provides a tripartite definition of suffering that includes: *personal* suffering ('harm to body, life or liberty,' which can take place both during and outside conflict situations); *material* suffering ('the loss of real or personal property'); and *intangible* suffering ('the loss or lack of opportunities') (2004, 127, 168; see also García-Godos 2008, 122–3).[38] In my interviews it was unsurprising that Elster's first two types of suffering (personal and material) were mentioned (respondents cited examples of disappeared relatives, torture or having their homes or personal belongings confiscated). But noteworthy were the indirect references to Elster's third type of suffering, the intangible. This suffering was usually mentioned by or in reference to ex-combatants who spent up to ten years fighting in the conflict and, for some, almost five years in cantonments. The key issue for them was the loss of salary and employment opportunities. Thus, the identification and categorisation of victims and perpetrators based on their innocence or the harm they experienced fails to reflect the complex realities in post-conflict Nepal.

Victims' groups

Despite the blurred line between victims and perpetrators, a number of victims' groups have evolved since the end of the conflict and have become 'newly-self-identified political actors' (see McAdam, Tarrow, and Tilly 2001,

7–8). As discussed in Chapter 5, some victims' groups have the institutional backing of specific organisations (e.g. the ICRC, Amnesty Nepal and the Berghof Foundation). These organisations have helped to make these victims' groups more visible, given them greater recognition and provided varying degrees of financial and technical support.[39] Ultimately, because various TJ actors find victims' groups that are attached to recognised organisations to be generally more accessible than unattached groups, over time, these attached groups have provided a meaningful voice for victims and have become a convenient way to invite victims to various meetings and workshops in Kathmandu and regional headquarters. In this way these groups have been 'certified', meaning that external authorities have validated these actors, including at times their performances and claims (McAdam, Tarrow, and Tilly 2001, 121).

Given the dominance of TJ experts, implementers and brokers in shaping the TJ trajectory (Chapter 6), these groups have the potential to play a key role in Nepal. A leader of a key victims' group said that their association was formed because political parties had not addressed their TJ commitments, and that if these commitments had been addressed, there would be no need to campaign because 'this sort of office [organisation] is working for transitional justice'.[40] He pointed to the mattress resting up against the wall saying that he worked and slept in his small office. More recently, the Conflict Victims Common Platform (CVCP) was launched (see Chapter 5). The Platform – which was formerly headed by Bhandari – 'is a loose network' of 13 victims' associations, supported by the UN (CVCPNepal 2014, see also UN 2014). CVCP is intended to help victims overcome internal divisions (e.g. the divisions among victims of the state and victims of the Maoists), to assist with reframing the TJ debate in Nepal 'by bringing victims' needs to the centre' and to '[s]upport efforts to formulate a common position and demands' (UN 2014; see also UNRCO 2014, 5). The organisation has made a number of suggestions and submissions with regard to TJ, including criminalisation of serious rights violations, disappearances and torture; the removal of a 35 day statute of limitation on for rape; and, the incorporation of victims' right to truth, justice and reparation in the constitution (see for example Rai 2015). In April 2016 CVCP's concerns were encapsulated in 21 point memorandum that was provided to the TJ Commissions and Parliament as well as the NHRC, the MoPR and the Ministry of Law Justice and Parliamentary Affairs (Himalayan News Service 2016).

Some members of these victims' groups reported a sense of empowerment (an outcome of participation, see Chapter 3) as a result of being involved in these groups. For example, a widow who started a tailoring business told me she was assisted by the organisation of which she is now the President.[41] Her entry in the workforce and her role as a leader of this group is an example of the social transformation women have encountered in post-conflict Nepal (see Yadav 2016). Another widow who travelled over 30 kilometres by bus to meet with me explained how she had raised her voice, entered the workforce and taken on the causes of other female victims and that this had helped her to work through her trauma.[42] This transformation, particularly the increase in people's belief that they can make a difference, shows the opportunities that participatory approaches in TJ provide. There has also been a reported sense of unity among victims as a result of the efforts of civil society and these victims' groups (discussed further below). A select number of victims' groups are gaining direct contact with donors and are featured in the media. It will be interesting to see how TJ brokers will react to this shift in power relations and if this direct contact will remain.

Additionally, these victims' groups are one of the few avenues that enable victims to come together in Nepal. This is particularly significant given the unaddressed high level of mental health issues in Nepal. For example, a brother of a disappeared victim said that since his sister had returned home she spoke very little and was depressed. He explained she was disappeared when she was 12 years old and that she was deeply mentally disturbed because of the fighting she witnessed.[43] A male Nepali human rights worker who frequently met with victims and was involved in TJ consultations lamented that of the 65 psychologists and psychiatrists in Nepal, most were in Kathmandu which posed problems for rural victims.[44]

Although victims' groups have advantages, my research revealed these groups are not without problems and limitations. It is apparent that victims and indeed victims' groups have provided leverage for other actors to pursue their agendas. For example, one respondent explained that Conflict Victims' Society For Justice – Nepal, supported by Advocacy Forum, favoured accountability measures (namely prosecutions) because this is what Advocacy Forum advocates for. Another respondent reiterated this point saying that you can predict what a victims' group would ask for based on the position of the organisation that supports them.[45] One TJ broker, a national human rights organisation that provides support to these victims' groups, acknowledged that there was a tendency for this to happen but also noted that the organisation tries to support other victims' groups when possible and that the affiliated victims' group does not always agree with the organisation.[46]

Bringing together diverse individuals poses the problem that members are viewed as a homogenised group. This is particularly the case when victims' groups are composed of victims with varied experiences and backgrounds so that there is the potential for different voices within these groups to become conflated and obscured within the generic category 'the victims' (see Chambers and Guijt 2011, 112). Victims within these groups may have divergent or conflicting interests and expectations. Perhaps participants do not express other/additional interests because they have no confidence that they can be achieved (see Chambers and Guijt 2011, 118). For example, victims may self-censor because in Nepal there is a lack of basic social services for victims and non-victims alike. There is a danger that divergent voices both within and between victims' groups are muted to ensure that at least some voices are heard.

Also relevant are the impacts of class disparities and differing political goals within particular victims' groups. A Nepali NGO worker told me that there are internal divisions within victims' groups according to class and power.[47] One respondent noted that the priorities of some families of soldiers in one victims' group had changed because they had already been compensated and other victims within the group became concerned that this would impact the priorities of the victims' group in general.[48] Also significant are the findings that the concerns of members of the Society for the Families of the Disappeared 'have sometimes come into tension with the political strategy' of the Maoist party in relation to the disappeared (Marsden 2011, 275).

There are also issues regarding unity. Several victims' groups I met with spoke about the need to present a united front in order to have their voices heard by the government and donors. Related to this a human rights worker stated that the disunity among victims was one of the key challenges working in TJ. An example of this was noted above in that victims of the state who were affiliated with the Maoist party in the early post-conflict stage were strongly discouraged by the party from becoming part of victims' groups and getting involved in meetings to which victims and victims' groups had been invited.[49] This tendency for victims of the state and victims of the Maoists to remain apart was, however, gradually overcome. I was informed on a number of occasions that this was because both groups of victims were brought to see that they had the same pain and often had the same needs and wants.[50] A wife of the disappeared encapsulates this feeling in the following comment: 'Our sorrow is the same if we are a victim of the government or the Maoists. It's all the same sadness and sorrow.'[51]

Other issues have arisen. With funding and institutional support provided to some of these victims groups, the impression I got was that victims' groups were gradually becoming pitted against one another. It also seemed that donor support of victims' groups was potentially sapping the energy of the victims' movement and leading to 'projectisation' (see Cornwall 2007, 476). It is unclear the extent to which victims are aware of and/or participate in these more official groups (see Robins and Bhandari 2012). It is also unclear whether these groups consult with their members, or the ways financial, communication and geographical constraints limit the ability of groups to represent their members. Furthermore, it is unclear whether some self-designated victims' group leaders actually represent the views of their members.

There is also the issue of gender representation. Usually, across the spectrum of victims' associations (those aligned with political parties or human rights organisations or self-mobilised), the leaders are men (Marsden 2011, 278), despite the fact that a large proportion of victims are women. For example, a study of family associations of the disappeared found that representation was an issue for women, and people from lower castes (Robins and Bhandari 2012, 7, 9). Obstacles to the equitable participation of people from these groups are exacerbated by the fact that many of these people have had fewer education and professional opportunities than men from dominant ethnic, caste or religious groups. One leader of a district TJ network told me on numerous occasions that as a male, educated professional he had to do the work for other members of the TJ network because they were illiterate and uneducated.[52]

Thus, these victims' groups are not immune from unequal power relations and may, in fact, become microsites of exclusion, particularly for the poor, women and other disadvantaged groups. Also, over time there is the danger that some leaders (and participants) will become more involved than others such that the participation of other victims becomes nominal. Worse still, participation could potentially be co-opted from below as well as from above (see White 1996). However, despite these challenges these victims' groups are one of the few avenues through which victims have been able to articulate their concerns. Although the risk of homogenising victims' voices needs to be recognised, this unity has the potential to be a starting point for grassroots reconciliation and other activities. This potential is perhaps of even greater significance for remote rural people, because even though the TRC has finally been established, its reach beyond the capital and district headquarters is limited, highlighting the need for complementary (and perhaps alternative) national and local TJ processes (see Robins and Bhandari 2012, 35). Notwithstanding the challenges posed by the representation of victims and the formation of victims' groups in contexts where not everyone can participate, I contend it is preferable that representation, though imperfect, comes from self-organisation. This was reiterated by many of the people I spoke with in Nepal.[53] It is through these self-organised groups that what is conceived to be possible can be expanded, in part addressing the current preoccupation of a TJ toolkit composed of state-centric mechanisms (see Gaventa and Cornwall 2006). This will be discussed further in Chapter 8.

The Interim Relief Program

In light of these understandings of victims and perpetrators above, this section examines the official recognition of victims since the end of the conflict. As discussed in Chapter 5, the CPA mentioned the provision of relief and rehabilitation for people 'victimized and displaced as a result of conflict' (Article 5.2.4; see also Article 7.1.3). Initially it was unclear whether relief through the Interim Relief Program constituted the provision of relief pursuant to the CPA. This was clarified by the MoPR, which explained the relief was 'interim' and that the TRC and CIEDP would provide wider reparations, including compensation (Marg 2010, 2–3). In addition to the CPA, the Interim Constitution provides that the government is responsible for: relief, recognition and rehabilitation of victims (or the relatives of victims) who were injured, disabled or killed during the conflict; relief for families of the disappeared pursuant the CIEDP; and, compensation for private and public property damaged during the conflict (Article 33[p], [q], [r]; Marg 2010, 10).

The Interim Relief Program was governed by a number of policy guidelines.[54] The first was the Measures for financial support and relief for conflict victims (the Measures) that was approved on 25 April 2008. Other relevant policy documents include two separate guidelines that provide details for families of the deceased and families of the disappeared: the guidelines for providing relief to the beneficiary of a deceased person (approved on 5 October 2008) and the guidelines for providing relief to the beneficiary of a disappeared person (approved on 12 January 2009). These guidelines referred to victims as 'conflict-affected persons'. The categories of conflict-affected persons were: wives or next of kin of those killed or those disappeared; people abducted, disabled or injured during the conflict; and people whose property was lost or destroyed (ICTJ 2011a, 8). However, in December 2009 the Measures, which referred to 'conflict victims' in its title, was repealed and replaced by the Procedure for relief, compensation and financial support for *citizens* (my emphasis).

Pursuant to the Citizens Relief, Compensation and Economic Assistance Procedure, 'conflict victims' are regarded 'as those who depended on individuals killed in conflict, those who lost their body parts during conflict, those who were displaced, those who disappeared and their families, those abducted by the conflicting parties and those suffering damage to lives and property' (Nepal Monitor 2011).[55] Relief was provided in the form of monetary assistance, education scholarships, medical treatment and skills development training.

The Interim Relief Program was advertised in newspapers and through Local Peace Committees mainly in district headquarters and in some Village Development Committees[56] (ICTJ 2011a, 2). In some districts the program was advertised using local FM radio; although the frequency and duration of these advertisements are unclear (Marg 2010, 21). Relief provided was based on the applicant's loss. Proof of the applicant's relationship with the victim was required, including two photographs and, if relevant, a death certificate (Advocacy Forum 2010, 11). Applicants with property damage or loss were required to provide proof of ownership.

The process to obtain relief was complex. There were different processes for interim relief according to the type of victim the applicant was classified as, pursuant to the guidelines (see above) and the relief provisions sought. Usually the applications were to be lodged to the District Administration Office headed by the Chief District Officer who was responsible for certifying individuals as beneficiaries (ICTJ 2011a, 8). The applicant was also required to obtain a recommendation from their Village Development Committee. There were a number of relevant government ministries and bodies involved; for example, the MoPR was responsible for the relief for widows and the next of kin of those deceased through the District Administration Office, while the District Development Committee and the District Education office were responsible for healthcare and scholarships (ICTJ 2011a, 8). These government authorities often lacked the resources and funds to process claims; this was exacerbated by the lack of cooperation between various ministry officials (ICTJ 2011a, 8; Marg 2010, 18).

The implementation of the Interim Relief Program reveals the disjunctures between the local realities in Nepal and the practice of TJ. As discussed in Chapter 4, the majority of the victims in Nepal are from marginalised, rural, poor communities. In light of Nepal's poverty and geography, one concern is the way victims were notified about the Interim Relief Program. Many victims are illiterate or semi-illiterate and live in remote rural areas. A male member of a Local Peace Committee and academic explained victims were given little information about the Local Peace Committee or the support they could receive. He observed that victims who did come to the Local Peace Committee were politically linked.[57] For many illiterate or uneducated victims – especially women – completing the Interim Relief application was difficult, if not, impossible. In one district the money allocated for widows was returned because there were no claims made, despite the presence of widows in the district (Carranza 2012, 19). In many of my interviews widows and wives of the disappeared spoke of the need for brothers-in-law to assist with their applications, as they were unable to complete the applications themselves. This was further complicated by strained relationships between in-laws and widows or wives of the disappeared (discussed below).

The government contends that victims of rape and sexual violence were excluded as eligible victims in the Interim Relief Program because they could receive compensation through the criminal justice system or from the perpetrator (ICTJ 2011a, 13). However, the criminal justice system has prohibitive time limits: victims of conflict-related sexual assault and rape had to register their complaint to the police within 24 hours of the incident and applications to the court had to be filed within 35 days, while torture victims had up to six months. For victims of sexual assault and torture, registering the crime was often impractical or impossible, given the distances to police stations or medical facilities, and there were social, political and economic consequences for reporting such incidents (see, for example, Marg 2010). Furthermore, police perpetrated conflict-related crimes so this would have impacted people's willingness to report conflict-related incidents to the police. The gravity of this exclusion is encapsulated in Figure 7.1 below, which shows that incidents of torture were highest during the conflict.[58]

While torture, sexual assault and rape victims were excluded from the Interim Relief Program, victims who suffered property loss or destruction were included (Advocacy Forum 2010, 12–14; Carranza 2012). Given that torture victims were excluded from the Interim Relief Program they had to seek compensation through the courts pursuant to the *Torture Compensation Act* (1996), which entitled victims to a maximum of 100,000 NPR. However the courts rarely award compensation (Marg 2010, 13). Notably, any victims of the Maoists (or other armed opposition groups) were not eligible to apply for compensation under this Act (Marg 2010, 13). The second avenue available for victims of torture was to file a complaint with the NHRC. There have been over 3,000 complaints filed with the NHRC; however, compensation was only provided in seven of these cases (Marg 2010, 13; ICTJ 2011a, 15).

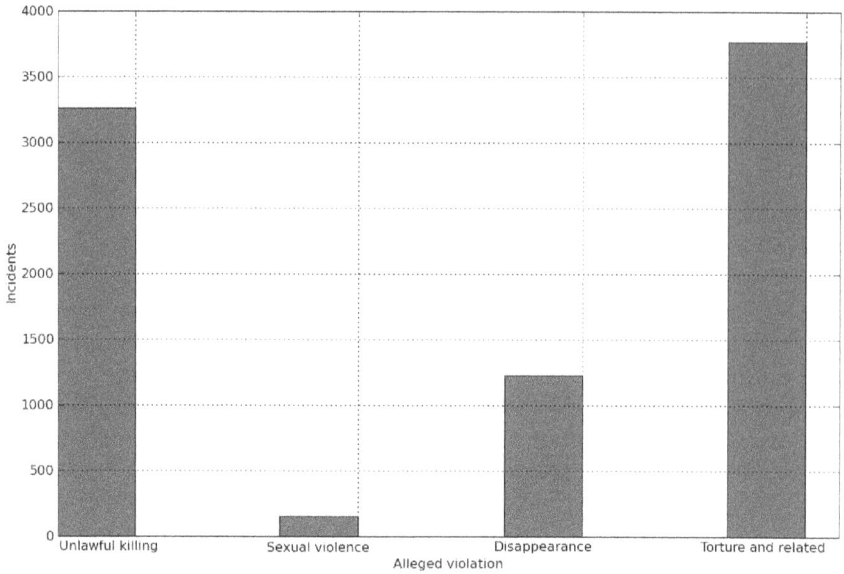

Figure 7.1 Recorded incidents by alleged serious violation (1996–2006)
Source: From *The Nepal Conflict Report*, by OHCHR. ©2012 United Nations. Reprinted with the permission of the United Nations.

While officially people who were tortured were not deemed to be victims under the Interim Relief Program, this distinction did not hold on the ground. The wife of a man who was tortured by the army on his way to do an exam told me that the Local Peace Committee did not recommend his name for compensation.[59] She lamented that real victims did not get compensation but those with political influence did (see below). The implications of this aspect of the Interim Relief Program are highlighted by the following example. In Rolpa, one of the most conflict-affected districts in Nepal, I met with a man who told me that the Royal Nepalese Army became suspicious of him because of his comings and goings as he walked between work and home past the army barracks.[60] He told me he was a 'simple man' and not involved in politics; however, he was ordered to the army barracks and questioned on several occasions; this raised Maoist suspicions. One day he was taken in by the Royal Nepalese Army for questioning and was beaten and tortured and upon his release – over 32 days later – he was told he must become an informant for the army. He plunged into a spiral of alcoholism and depression; he told me he decided that if he was drunk this would deter both the Maoists and the army from questioning him. Not long after this his wife was killed by a landmine, which he believed was planted by the army to prevent the People's Liberation Army from entering the area. Under the Interim Relief

Program he was considered a victim and eligible for relief because he was a widower, not because he was tortured. He explained:

> I myself am a victim and a widower so that's why there should be classification of victims and parameters applied to determine who are the most victimised and who are least victimised and on this basis provide [medical] treatment, compensation and guarantee employment for orphans.[61]

Again, the impact of the way the Interim Relief Program included and excluded people is apparent.

The provision of relief to those with property damage was also problematic. Approximately 80 per cent of the population in Nepal live in rural areas and depend on subsistence farming for their livelihood; however, most farmers do not own their land or property (IFAD 2013). Providing relief to those with property generally benefits those who are wealthier. This is demonstrated by the fact that frequently claims for property loss or destruction have been made or supported by politicians, parliamentarians and ministers (Carranza 2012, 27), who comprise the wealthy and privileged in Nepal.

In some cases the Interim Relief Program provided disparate relief to relatives of victims in similar situations. While up to three children of a deceased victim were entitled to an education stipend, children of those disappeared were not eligible (Marg 2010, 16). The guidelines were broadened to include children of the disappeared; however, many government representatives were unaware of the amendments to the guidelines that broadened the eligibility of scholarships to include children of the disappeared (ICTJ 2011a, 2). Also, the first set of guidelines for the Interim Relief Program provided 100,000 NPR to the family of deceased persons and only 25,000 NPR to the family of disappeared persons. To overcome this disparity wives of the disappeared have deliberately declared their husbands dead (not missing) (Tyynela, Withers, and Bajracharya 2013, 12). Whether a family reported their relative as deceased or missing had a significant impact on victims' everyday lives because of various religious and cultural customs (see below) (see also Robins 2012). For example, in Nepal if the wife of a disappeared husband chose to falsely declare him dead in order to receive the higher amount of relief, then as a widow she must no longer wear red *tikka*, clothing or bangles associated with being married but must wear white (*bidhuwa*) for the rest of her life and she cannot participate in religious ceremonies as it is considered bad luck (*asuv*). Reflecting upon the stories I heard from widows in Nepal reminded me of the work of Veena Das, who when writing about Punjabi widows in Delhi, India, explained that the:

> performance of gendered identity of widowhood has the force of a compulsory social ritual ... A widow, especially a young childless widow, understands her vulnerability, for she must incorporate in her behaviour the culturally held belief that she is inauspicious.
>
> (2007, 68)

It is clear that the complexities of the inclusion and exclusion of victims in formal TJ processes create a perverse reality emphasising the need to embrace the everyday realities that individuals face in Nepal. Also apparent are way individuals sought to challenge established repertoires.

The Interim Relief Program's scope of beneficiaries is also of concern. Nepal has a relatively conservative patriarchal structure where the male is deemed the breadwinner who is responsible for his immediate family (spouse and children) as well as parents and other siblings (*gharmuli*). The Interim Relief Program did not provide relief for parents but did provide relief for spouses. This not only caused livelihood challenges but also frequently caused family disputes; again demonstrating the clash between the local realities and the practice of TJ. In a group interview I conducted with relatives of police who were killed in the Terai, an elderly mother whose police officer son was killed during the conflict explained it was only her and her husband in the home. Her husband was ill, there was no one with earning capacity in the home and they had no one take care of them. The lack of financial support thus had a great impact on their lives.

In some cases the lack of provision for other family members had flow-on effects for widows, particularly those who remained in the homes of their in-laws. It is customary in Nepal for wives to move to their in-laws' homes when they get married (*bihe hunu* or *ghar janu*). Many widows I interviewed spoke about strained (in some cases life-threatening) relations with their in-laws due to economic and social-cultural factors. I was told that in most cases the widow and her children are considered a financial burden, a bad omen (*asuv*) and are often blamed for the passing of their husband. One widow from Rolpa told me that her brother-in-law had tried to strangle her and threatened her, saying 'I will kill you'. [62] Her mother-in-law told her that she had better take her children and go to her maternal house, but the widow refused to leave because she was concerned that if she did she would not secure her children's inheritance of the paternal property. There were other similar stories of physical, emotional and verbal abuse, yet owing to social, cultural and financial reasons many widows feel compelled to remain in their in-laws' homes.

My interviews revealed that the lack of attention to everyday lives in many instances led to women becoming revictimised when relief was received. In fact, these women frequently encountered challenges at the family level and beyond. A widow and NGO worker explained:

> No one listens to their [the widows'] voice. At the Village Development Committee level they are always shunned. After the government gives them compensation packages, when their in-laws find out, they face problems. The brother-in-law tries to rape them if they don't give them the money or some women are murdered in some situations. Society blames widows and is suspicious about their activities. It's not easy for widows – there is a lot of harassment unless they hand over all of the money [relief].[63]

Pertinent here are Nagy's comments regarding female victims: 'When "truth" is structured around *extraordinary* violence, women predominantly bear witness on behalf of deceased partners, children and grandchildren, that is, as indirect or secondary victims. Consequently women's stories of violence and suffering do not fully emerge' (2008, 286).

The inclusion of property damage as category for relief reveals the Interim Relief Program focused on repairing the *financial loss* rather than addressing harm (Carranza 2012, 16; see also the discussion about Elster above). As the ICTJ found, this impacts 'the capacity of victims to provide income to sustain their needs; the violations have affected their health, their opportunity to access education, and their ability to provide a better future for themselves' (2011a 19). This focus on financial harm also has gender implications.

The gender implications are particularly evident in the way the guidelines dealt with widows who remarried. While the guidelines neglected to mention remarriage of widowers, they stated that a remarried widow or wife of disappeared person would be ineligible for relief because she had a new breadwinner (Procedure for Relief, Compensation and Financial Support for Citizens 2066; Carranza 2012, 15). In Nepal it is more acceptable for widowers to remarry. As I discussed in Chapter 1, two widowers I interviewed had remarried within a year or so of their wives passing; whereas none of the widows I interviewed had remarried. When I asked these widowers if they felt that the community treated them in the same way they treated widows, they answered yes. One widower felt that 'the grievances are the same, they lost their husband, I lost my wife.'[64] However, it was only widows who reported extreme experiences of social ostracism. For example, a widow who had started a small business after her husband passed away explained that when she went to Kathmandu for various TJ workshops, people in her community often said she was 'a loose woman'.[65] She sensed people speaking badly about her and that many avoided interacting with her. She felt that people resented that she used the interim relief money to build a home for herself.[66] And yet despite these stories of ostracisation, there were many examples of widows and wives of the disappeared who saw their victimhood as an opportunity to become an agent for social change (discussed above).

The impact of the criteria for determining the eligibility for relief of conflict-affected people had implications beyond the Interim Relief Program. As discussed in Chapter 5, during the conflict there were various compensation and rehabilitation programs that also categorised and excluded conflict-affected people. For example, widows of armed forces personnel who died during the conflict were provided with financial support from both the Ministry of Defense and the Ministry of Home Affairs. This support overlapped with the general Ministry of Peace and Reconstruction provisions for conflict widows (Adhikari et al. 2014, 24–25). In fact '[t]hese categories emerged out of specific projects, each concerned with a bounded social group. In practice, there were a number of overlaps, as social categories cannot be cleanly demarcated' (Adhikari et al. 2014, 25). While many people did receive relief, others (particularly families of victims in the security forces) have received relief twice or more under different categories (Advocacy Forum 2010, 7). In one compensation scheme the category for an 'internally displaced person' excluded those displaced by the security forces and only included those displaced by Maoists (Advocacy Forum 2010, 9).

As has been discussed, while the Interim Relief Program is not a reparations program, the selection of victims, the scope of who is determined to be a victim and the treatment of victims reveal a focus on financial loss, not harm. Further, the Interim Relief Program did not sufficiently take into account the nature of Nepali society and the everyday realities that victims face. Evident in the Program is the abstraction of the extraordinary violence of the conflict from everyday violence and complexities, including the ways victims understand and experience victimisation. The demands made in relation to evidence and proof put those who are marginalised at a disadvantage with very real ramifications for people's day-to-day lives. Few victims were satisfied with the Interim Relief Program, with most explaining that it did not address their needs and rights (Carranza 2012, 18–19). The difficulty is that victims wanted immediate relief in the form of a lump sum *as well as* long-term support, particularly with respect to employment and education opportunities (see above). This reveals the challenges in TJ processes.

Although the Interim Relief Program had many components that addressed victims' everyday concerns (e.g. health, education and livelihood training) to various extents, the way the program was designed and its political weaknesses (particularly the requirement for recommendations from Local Peace Committees) meant that victims encountered numerous challenges applying for and obtaining assistance. This was particularly the case for victims who were illiterate, lived in remote places and/or were without political affiliations. This will be discussed in the next section.

The role of Local Peace Committees

Local Peace Committees have had varied abilities to shape and challenge ideas about who is deemed to be a victim and the level of support victims receive. As discussed in Chapter 5, the terms of reference of the Committees required a range of non-political representatives – including four victims – to be part of the Committee. This provided opportunities for traditionally marginalised individuals – often denied voice in institutional spaces – to be involved in TJ-related decision-making, a key component of meaningful participatory approaches. However, frequently the four victims represented political parties in the locality and decisions were ultimately made by the Committee coordinator along party lines (see ICTJ 2011a, 9). Despite their broad mandate the majority of Local Peace Committees narrowly focused their activities on reviewing victims' applications for interim relief. This is demonstrated in the comment that: 'The Local Peace Committee is a compensation committee.'[67] The Local Peace Committee facilitated and verified victims' applications. On the basis of recommendations from the Local Peace Committee, the Chief District Officer in the District Administration Office would decide whether to approve an application then refer it to the Ministry of Peace and Reconstruction for consideration (for further details see ICTJ 2011a).

There were numerous examples of the Local Peace Committees influencing applications for interim relief. A member of a TJ network in Dhanghadi explained that 'Local Peace Committees are divided into political groups. They also have conflicts but their name is peace committee'.[68] My findings concur with a study by the ICTJ which found 'that victims who are not affiliated with a political party do not get the same level of support from LPCs as those with affiliations' (2011a, 9). In one incident 'an LPC member told a victim, "Sorry, we can't do anything for you because you are not a member of our party"' (ICTJ 2011a, 9).

Pertinent too is that victims and affected community members often linked interim relief and justice more broadly with access to wealth and politics. A widow who commenced working for the first time when her husband was murdered during the conflict told me that 'justice is for the rich only'.[69] This was echoed by a Nepali human rights NGO worker in Rolpa who felt that 'if anyone is clever with access to political organisation they get compensation, but poor people with little access get little. The compensation is distributed randomly. Power leads to more'.[70] A male Local Peace Committee coordinator in Kailali observed that when political parties elect the coordinator, that person only raises the problems of their own supporters and cadres.[71] He told me as he was not officially connected to a political party he believed he was chosen as a coordinator of the Local Peace Committee because of the political party friction within his Local Peace Committee. Interestingly, he believed that civil society is composed of people who have influence with political parties. Also, the daughter of a murdered Nepali Congress member noticed that 'Maoist leaders treated victims differently.'[72] She believed that, '[v]ictims should be treated equally not depending on political party. We are all victims'.[73] This politicisation was also evident within a TJ network. A NGO worker explained that despite being part of the TJ Network, he was often excluded from events pertaining to TJ while political party members were invited. These views correspond with Snellinger's explanation that in Nepal:

> mobilization of external groups is contentious. Networking and relying on one's filial, professional and political contacts is a part of everyday life to such a degree that it is often difficult to distinguish between those types of networks. Politics in Nepal relies on culturally entrenched systems of patronage.
>
> (2007, 283–284)

On many occasions respondents/victims attributed receiving interim relief to the political party leading the coalition government at the time. The daughter of the murdered Nepali Congress member said she received her compensation from the Maoists.[74] A widow and NGO worker explained that she did not know anything about her husband's murder and the location of his body. She explained '[w]hen the UML was in government they provided compensation'.[75] A male victim whom I met at a Local Peace Committee workshop in the Far-Western region, who explained his family had received relief for his sister's murder, shared a similar position. He told me his brother is a Maoist supporter so the party helped them to get compensation because Prachandra (the Maoist party leader) was in power at that time.[76] Another example was a male Nepali Congress member who was attacked by Maoists during the conflict. I asked him whether he had received support from the government. He explained that he had because the Nepali Congress was in government at the time of the incident.[77] Further, he told me a key challenge for victims when trying to get justice was the party in power. He lamented, '[n]ow the government is Maoist they never listen to our voice if people are from other parties.'[78] So for many, particularly victims, relief is deeply politicised.

In my meetings with Local Peace Committees and local TJ actors I was told about numerous fake claims for interim relief. There are a number of possible ways to interpret these actions of making fake claims, for which the continuum of actions on the spectrum assists (see Chapter 2). But above all these actions may suggest agency and a desire to survive. The daughter of a murdered Nepali Congress member, who was a member of her Local Peace Committee, reported that people were falsely claiming everyday accidents in order to access interim relief funds.[79] This resonates with Kerkvliet's research where he found that people from lower classes in the Philippines 'individually and collectively do things outside the state's sanctions and controls that contradict official plans and prescriptions and throw monkey wrenches into the state's ability to implement programs' (1995, 399). These points demonstrate that individuals and political parties engaged in contestation and resistance with respect to the Interim Relief Program.

By examining the Interim Relief Program and the actions surrounding it we can identify the different ways TJ actors, particularly TJ implementers, identified and recognised victims. Ultimately, Local Peace Committees were sites of political manoeuvring, contestation and resistance. Relief was provided to those deemed eligible and who were able to negotiate the various logistical, family and political challenges outlined above. It is clear that there is considerable complexity involved in applying and accepting the label victim. This will be discussed further in Chapter 8.

Relief and justice

What do victims want?

Against this background this section discusses the perspectives of victims and other community members after the conflict. In my interviews victims frequently discussed the need for long-term survival particularly with reference to compensation, education, health and skills development/livelihoods training. For example, a wife of one of the disappeared felt that there should be greater skilled-based training and education for her children.[80] A widow expressed that every victim has their own problems and that it would be good to have compensation but that people were losing faith in the government day by day.[81] A number of Local Peace Committee members from various districts explained that victims asked for compensation, incoming generating schemes and employment.[82] This was reiterated by a Local Peace Committee Assistant Secretary who informed me that victims were concerned the compensation would run out and that their children needed scholarships so they could secure work and have life security.[83] Similarly, a victim whose father was murdered, and who was a member of her Local Peace Committee and President of a women's organisation, believed that rather than give compensation it was better for the government to provide employment and education.[84] These concerns were reiterated by a number of NGO workers involved in TJ networks and programs.[85]

In my interviews the importance of compensation for female victims was also emphasised.[86] Female victims with children often spoke about the need to provide long-term security, particularly education, for their children. A widow explained that compensation was only part of what victims wanted and that they sought the provision of education.[87] Similarly, a widow with a son and a daughter explained that despite being threatened by her in-laws and at times being unable to afford to eat, she only thought of her children's future and how they could be self-sufficient.[88]

For families of the disappeared knowing the truth about their loved ones' whereabouts was also crucial. However, this desire was often in conjunction with their everyday concerns. A male worker at a women's organisation explained that families of disappeared victims say they need:

> First, victims' livelihood because their breadwinner disappeared, second, there is the religious and cultural need of Hindu rituals for burial. Third, the dilemma is that they want to know truth if their loved one is either dead or alive and in what condition and fourth, justice demands: property rights, birth certification and death certification.[89]

In a similar vein, a male leader of a victims' group, whose family member was disappeared, explained that the relatives of people murdered or disappeared first want to know what happened, second they want perpetrators and victims to be part of a legal process in order for the family to feel justice, and third they want the victim's family to receive compensation including security of life.[90]

It is clear that long-term security was a common concern for different types of victims; however, it was also apparent that the lack of social provisions by the state has implications for how TJ is conceived in Nepal. A female NGO worker recognised the resource challenges in Nepal:

> It's not easy for our government to give money continually to victims; a little amount is acceptable. The government should reconcile people in society, provide jobs and create opportunities and give training for people to earn money.[91]

An ex-combatant who wanted the state to recognise combatants as victims also echoed these views. She said:

> We would be happy if government delivered justice to us. It must guarantee children's education and health insurance. We are not seeking money but to provide security to our family … How do you ensure it's possible for a family to survive? You sustain them; giving money makes them dependent.[92]

In a similar vein an injured male policeman who was a victims' representative in his Local Peace Committee believed that victims need relief for the rest of their lives but that even at the present time the government was unable to provide sufficient economic packages. Although some women and children were helped, he felt that this was not the case for victims' parents. He explained he was physically and mentally injured and depressed and that he had lost his power to work. He complained that he had done well for his country but there was no respect. This echoes the findings of Stanko and Hobdell (1993) that revealed that male victims of ordinary crime who were unable to take care of their families and themselves reported a sense of vulnerability, which could be connected to the notion of masculinity. Widowers are fewer in Nepal and overall have been researched less. According to Elias (1990), this lack of research of male victims in general is because they are rarely seen as victims, with more sympathetic responses afforded to children, women and the elderly (see also Spalek 2006, 85). In Nepal this could also be due to the fact that it is socially acceptable for males to remarry, so that many widowers who remarried may no longer identify themselves as such (see discussion about widows and widowers above).

Other community members also echoed these victims' views about the need for long-term survival and everyday needs. A female villager from the Mid-Western region who was forced by Maoist insurgents to march and do labour and who had her house searched by army personnel, explained that '[t]he government never guaranteed life, health and education of children. The government has done little'.[93] Also, a male academic who was a member of his Local Peace Committee emphasised the everyday needs of victims: 'Justice leads to social justice and equal access of opportunity. Support of state services and the day-to-day problems of security, citizenship and education.'[94] In a similar vein the President of a district Nepal Bar Association and former President of a conservative political party stated that the key TJ goals should be the identification of the disappeared, education and employment.[95] For him the government should remember why the conflict happened (injustice, poverty, marginalisation and oppression) and address these issues.[96] Again emphasising the need for a long-term solution, a principal of a school in Rolpa explained that '[t]he Government should provide facilities and support to victims. There should be a permanent type of solution …'[97] Similarly, an Assistant Secretary of a Local Peace Committee said the compensation 'will finish but children need scholarships for full education then to get good job, secure their life and have proper life security.'[98] A male human rights advocate gave a more extensive response about what the government should do to address what happened during the conflict:

> What is done is done. Now we have to build a Truth and Reconciliation Commission and a Commission on Disappearances. Through these commissions we can find out who are the victims and how they were victimised … People do not respect those who were tortured and sexually assaulted. The perpetrators who did this should be identified and prosecuted and the victims should be compensated. There should also be a memorialisation park, a record of the incidents, a charity in the name of those who died and assistance for the education, employment and health of the victims' families and their children. We have to respect those who died for sake of the common good.[99]

His response encompasses truth-finding, reparations and memorialisation as well as the provision of education, employment and health. His response encapsulates the position of TJ experts, brokers *and* victims but this was the exception, not the norm.

Indeed my findings in terms of people's awareness about TJ were exemplified by the following comment made by a male NGO worker who fled to district headquarters during the conflict:

> People have very little or no knowledge about TJ. It is only people in headquarters, Kathmandu and bigger cities and those that studied it that know about TJ. The general awareness is very low. For rural people the law is what the major three political parties decide.[100]

This comment echoes the thoughts of a Nepali human rights worker who has regularly met with victims of the conflict: 'To illiterate people TJ means nothing to them.'[101] He told me buzzwords like 'sustainable peace' and 'prosperous Nepal' do not mean a thing to 'common people'.[102] Interestingly, for a Local Peace Committee coordinator, the government's fixation on a TRC and CIEDP model was probably to demonstrate to the international community that Nepal was 'doing a fair job'.[103] Again revealing the performative nature/aspect of TJ, even for actors whose interests seemingly do not accord with TJ norms.

My findings confirm the findings of various studies with victims in Nepal. See Chapter 5 for a detailed discussion of the various participatory activities.

While until recently there was a dearth of analysis of the voices of victims and affected community members, when people were asked what justice means to them their answer involves (but is not limited to) forms of justice and injustice that affect their everyday lives.

For example, as discussed in Chapter 5, ICTJ and Advocacy Forum undertook a quantitative and qualitative study entitled *Nepali Voices: Perceptions of Truth, Justice, Reconciliation, Reparations and the Transition in Nepal* (2008). Most of the victims surveyed stated that their most urgent concerns and needs were of an economic and social nature. Notably, these findings sit in contrast to the predominant push for legal accountability by key TJ brokers. The survey demonstrates how victims' prioritisation of social and economic issues challenges the dominant understanding of TJ (see Robins 2012). However, Pasipanodya (2008, 387) is deeply critical of how victims were defined in this study, which included household participants of any family that had 'suffer[ed] one or more of the following four categories of human rights violations: disappearance, extrajudicial killing, torture, and rape' (ICTJ and Advocacy Forum 2008, 10). She explains that '[a]s a consequence of this limited view of victims, males are overrepresented in the survey, making up four in five of victims surveyed.' (Pasipanodya 2008, 387). This provides a limited view of what victims need. Again, the significance of the victim label and category formation is evident.

Despite victims' calls for the state and various actors to address their everyday needs, the priorities of organisations operating in the TJ space (e.g. pursuing TJ mechanisms such as prosecutions or the TRC) have frequently remained dominant. The *ICTJ Trainer's Manual on Transitional Justice* (2011b), used to train selected participants in Nepal is indicative of these issues (see Chapter 5). While participants were asked if there are any other strategies that should also be included as part of TJ, the focus of the training was to explain the common TJ strategies: truth-seeking, reparations, prosecution and institutional reform. For example in the truth-seeking section of the manual the purpose is '[t]o understand how truth-seeking relates to the historical record, justice, and closure for harms of the past' (ICTJ 2011b, 26). There is an optional 'Point of View' exercise (ICTJ 2011b, 27).[104] This activity is followed by a presentation on truth-seeking. Information covered includes:

- What is truth-seeking?
- Why is truth important?
- What type of truth-seeking body is most commonly tasked with finding out the truth?
- What are the potential benefits of a truth-seeking body?
- How do these truth-seeking bodies ensure victims' right to truth?

(ICTJ 2011b, 28–29)

This training was structured in such a way as to leave little scope for participants to question if truth-seeking is important and indeed whether truth-seeking can be harmful. It also did not provide scope for participants to conceive of additional or other mechanisms that might contribute to the process of truth-seeking, assuming this is what participants want. Accordingly, the ICTJ training provided limited scope to derive a context-specific Nepali approach to TJ.

It is apparent that at times TJ experts, brokers and implementers seek to pursue another agenda even when victims voice different needs. Victims voiced their need for long-term security; however, this poses difficulties for Nepal, a post-conflict state that is fragmented and is now undergoing post-earthquake reconstruction. This reality points to the need to manage the expectations not only of TJ proponents but also of conflict-affected people.

Conceptions of justice

In my interviews I also asked respondents what justice meant to them. Respondents framed justice as a time of equal rights and opportunities; their responses reflected their everyday concerns. A widow explained justice was 'to own rights'.[105] She had been asked to become the President of a women's victims' group but she declined because of her family responsibilities. When I asked her about the challenges she faced getting justice she explained that these included having to take care of two children and getting a certificate to obtain compensation (interim relief). Although she did not actively follow politics she believed that the (then yet to be promulgated) constitution must include references to people's suffering and grievances.

For a Maoist Commissar, justice was conceived as a time of no discrimination. He told me: 'In my opinion there will be justice if there will be similar chances, no discrimination between have and have nots. If all have equal income generating then this is justice.'[106] A similar position was held by a male NGO worker: 'For victims, all violations of human rights must be traced out clearly. In other words, justice means no discrimination and everyone treated equally.'[107] A widower who was tortured explained that justice has two components: 'First, to identify the perpetrators who did the crimes and second, respect from the state to provide rights that can be enjoyed equally by all.'[108] When I asked a widow what was needed to feel like she had justice, she explained: 'Mostly my rights, if something happens to get my rights … [I]f I receive my rights there is justice, if I lose my rights there is no justice.'[109] When I probed what she meant by rights she explained compensation, land rights and her husband's property. These conversations reveal that respondents, including some victims, articulated justice in terms of rights.[110]

However, justice was also deemed to be for people who were from upper classes or who had political connections. A business owner in the Maoist heartland in Rolpa said that 'we talk about justice or the unjust but the downtrodden never get justice'.[111] He hoped that the new constitution would bring 'justice for the high and low class, even the simple man'.[112] The President of a district Nepal Bar Association and former President of a conservative political party explained that justice should mean equality for all; that is it should apply to victims of both sides. For him, justice included political rights like equal employment for all and compensation to help victims forget their sorrow.[113] For a male Nepali NGO worker who was harassed by the Maoists and fled to his district headquarters, justice included a 'fearless life for people' with peace and no threats.[114] Another Nepali NGO worker who was involved in TJ consultations said that '[m]ost people who participated said we want justice and to know but at the same time we need help to survive to send children to school; not money but education, health and access to employment'.[115] Further, he explained:

> Human rights lawyers love jargon of justice and prosecution but when it is real victims speaking it is a different issue … Justice part not totally gone. They feel hopeless but they still want justice. When you look at the class of the victim the upper and middle class have reasonable support already. The lower class care more about economic support; their difficulties are day-to-day survival. Victims have tried to get justice for seven years.[116]

Thus, not only were economic and social concerns the cause of the initial conflict (see Chapter 4), these issues are also integral to what victims want to see addressed in the wake of the conflict.[117] However, these meanings of justice, which emphasise people's experiences of inequality and hardship, do not accord with the ways TJ is implemented. Although victims are essentially constructed because of the human rights violations committed against them (Humphrey 2005), TJ has relied on a narrow paradigm of what constitutes human rights violations. As I have argued elsewhere, the focus has been on examining civil and political rights violations without adequately or systematically addressing economic, social and cultural rights violations (Selim 2012; Selim and Murithi 2011; see also Arbour 2006; Pasipanodya 2008).[118] This failure is despite the fact that economic, social and cultural rights violations are often the causes of conflict and political turmoil. This means that there are differences between what TJ experts, implementers and brokers and victims deem to matter in a post-conflict environment, including what they consider constitutes justice. Notice too that absent from what people said they wanted were the goals of the dominant TJ paradigm such as reconciliation, healing and forgiveness. This will be explored below.

Ways of dealing with the past

While I am wary of essentialising Hindu and Buddhist perspectives, it is apparent that people's religious understandings potentially impacted a range of issues related to victimisation. This included people's attitudes about why harm occurred, who/what was responsible, punishment and peace. This should come as little surprise given that religion has played and continues to play a major role in Nepal; however, given the top-down approach in which the TJ process was shaped in Nepal (Chapter 6), it seems unlikely that these factors were considered.

Nepal is the first country with a Hindu majority population to undergo the process of TJ. The population is predominately Hindu (81.3%) with Buddhism being the second largest religion (9%) (Central Bureau of Statistics 2012, 4). Hinduism in its liberal form incorporates Buddhism (Bista 2001, 30). While most people identify as Hindu, there are pervasive Buddhist influences in most aspects of Nepali culture; in fact, '"Buddhism" as practised is diverse, often Hinduised, and ethnic and regional in character' (King 2014, 363; see also Smith 2009, 19). Many social and religious practices are commonly observed by both Buddhists and Hindus. During my time in Nepal the lack of difference between Buddhism and Hinduism was often articulated in the phrase 'same same'.

Muslim (4.4%), Christian (1.4%) and other religious groups are also present in Nepal (Central Bureau of Statistics 2012, 4). These faiths have also been imported and practised in similarly hybrid forms. The indigenous people of Nepal (*Janajatis*) were traditionally Buddhist or animist but over time have been 'Hinduised' and although many of the indigenous peoples of Nepal now consider themselves to be Hindu, they continue to practise certain non-Hindu traditions (Robins 2011, 106; Allen 1997; see also Chapter 4). Notably key to the indigenous movements in Nepal has been the rejection of Hinduism. The Maoists' platform, although never completely free of religious influences, was attractive to many indigenous and minority groups because it promised a secular future.

Hinduism has played a major role in shaping the state (see Chapter 4). Despite the relatively marginal status of Buddhism in Nepal compared with Hinduism, the role it played is also relevant. As King explains 'the state employs Buddhist symbolism and a strong normative discourse regarding Buddhist pacifism as part of the processes of nation building' (2014, 373). Nepal is the birthplace of Buddha and this location has been developed into a 'peace zone' (Owen 2014, 46). Also noteworthy is that 'Buddhism is being used by political and religious leaders at a national level to emphasise the peaceful nature and future of a nation recovering from a decade long civil war' (Owen 2014, 46).

For some of the TJ brokers I met who were involved in the TJ process, Hinduism and Buddhism were often compared with Christianity and Ubuntu,[119] which formed the basis of the South African Truth and Reconciliation Commission. Two Nepali human rights advocates spoke about the inappropriateness of adopting the South African forgiveness model in Nepal, explaining that 'Ubuntu comes from South Africa but we have a Buddhist culture and we also have that the enemy should be terminated. It's called the revenge of Mahābhārata. So we can't borrow from Ubuntu.'[120] Also various Nepali NGO workers and human rights advocates told me that the notions of 'forgiveness' and 'reconciliation' were not culturally or contextually appropriate in Nepal, compared with the predominately Christian contexts of South Africa. One human rights advocate who was involved in the TJ process in Nepal since early discussions explained:

> The expert [Siebert] was from South Africa but South Africa doesn't fit in Nepali context especially the amnesty part. Forgiveness in Hinduism does not exist that much in daily practice (compared to Christian society). There is a need to rethink reconciliation, forgiveness and amnesty.[121]

Yet, despite the relatively commonplace sentiment among respondents that Christian notions of forgiveness and Ubuntu have no place in Nepal, analysis of Hindu and Buddhist scriptures reveals there is reference to notions such as forgiveness.

Forgiveness

When I asked people about whether perpetrators should be pardoned, many respondents explained their response in relation to forgiveness saying that for the smaller incidents there should be forgiveness but 'higher crimes' or 'systematic violations' should not be forgiven but prosecuted. For a Nepali worker whose organisation was part of the TJ network in his district, victims and perpetrators did not think about forgiveness with the conflict having ended many years ago. He explained that 'the main thing people want is peace, they don't want to disturb each other'.[122] A female victim and a leader of a women's NGO relayed that some women were disturbed by the conflict and did not want to forgive.[123]

The notion of forgiveness (*ksama* or *ksamata*) is present in Hinduism; although it is difficult to ascertain 'a theological basis' for forgiveness given the number of viewpoints and traditions in Hinduism (Rye et al. 2000). For example, forgiveness is listed as one of the divine qualities along with other qualities such as compassion (*karuna*) and non-violence (*ahimsa*) in *Bhagabhadra Gita* (the *Gita*), which is considered the universal scripture of Hinduism (Hunter 2007, 36; see also Rye et al. 2000, 38). The *Gita* is part of the *Mahabharata.*[124] The *Mahabharata* and the *Ramayana* are considered the two Sanskrit epics in Hinduism (Lochtefeld 2002, 399; see also von Brück 2004). These epics 'have a quasi-scriptural status: incidents and personalities from them are widely cited as authoritative exemplars of correct behavior' (Hunter 2007, 36). Both epics include 'extended discussions of forgiveness and revenge' (Hunter 2007, 36). It has been noted that at least one version of the *Mahabharata* was entitled 'Revenge' (Gandhi 2000, xxviii). Explaining the relationship between the two epics Lochtefeld states that:

> If the *Ramayana* can be characterized as the tale of the "good" family, in which the brothers cooperate to support and preserve their family, the

> *Mahabharata* describes the "bad" family, in which hard-heartedness and lust for power in an extended royal family ultimately cause its *destruction.*
> (2002, 399)

Forgiveness, karma ('the law of cause and effect') and anger appear to be related in Hinduism. Within Hinduism 'one's actions (karma) determine one's future lives' (Smith 2009, 24). Rye et al. explain that because of karma 'individuals face [the] consequences of their actions in subsequent reincarnations. Therefore, one can presume that lack of forgiveness, negative feelings, and unresolved, seething anger can only spill over into future births' (2000, 29). Notions of 'the good, or spiritually beneficial' (*sreyas*), tolerance or forbearance (*titiksha*), non-violence (*ahimsa*) and sin (*pape*) also provide insight into forgiveness (Hunter 2007, 37; see also Rye et al. 2000, 29–30). S*reyas* means that 'sometimes it will be best to face hardship and make tough decisions, although painful in the short-term, because they lead us onwards and upwards' and pertinently this benefits the individual's life as well as the community (Hunter 2007, 37). While forbearance means that whatever occurs the individual should not feel resentment or anger (Hunter 2007, 37). Again this relates to karma as:

> an "enemy" is in fact only the instrument of a process which we ourselves initiated, and for which we are responsible. If I had not created a problem for myself because of some past action, I would not now be experiencing a difficulty. To a devout believer in this theory, taking revenge on an "enemy" means to shoot the messenger and ignore the message.
> (Hunter 2007, 37)

Ultimately, the notions of non-violence (*ahimsa*), forgiveness (*kshama*) and peace (*shanti*) are included in key Hindu scriptures and texts demonstrating 'the error in hate, anger, and violence, and the advantages of consensus, compassion, and justice' (Coward and Smith 2004, 49). Particularly pertinent with respect to retributive justice is the notion that:

> those who accept the law of karma and reincarnation may be relatively willing to let go of longing for retribution: they feel that the perpetrator will inevitably receive a comeback for their deeds, so it is almost irrelevant to go out of one's way to try to inflict some kind of punishment or revenge.
> (Hunter 2007, 37; see also Keethaponcalan 2014; Rambachan 2003; Flood 2008)

So it is apparent that forgiveness is relevant to Hinduism 'even if less explicitly so than within the Christian tradition' (Hunter 2007, 1). What is more, these notions appear to in some ways impact the ways victims deal with the past.

Fatalism was also raised by some of my respondents. For example, when a Nepali human rights worker observed the changes in victims' emotions (from anger to hope to fatigue and disillusionment, prompted by the passing of time and the provision of relief) he explained this disillusionment and fatalistic attitude had connections with Hinduism:

> There is a deep-rooted fatalistic aspect of victimhood philosophy in Hindu text that 'what happened, happened, there was a good reason for it, that is why I have to accept it and move on'. It is in the Gita philosophical text that what will happen will happen for good … So you have no control of what will happen but you have control of what you decide to do.[125]

Also responding to a question about justice a female ex-combatant said that 'fatalistic women curse fate rather than the system'.[126]

Fatalism is a philosophical position, of the *Ajivika* school of thought of Hinduism, which holds that all things are preordained 'by an impersonal deity (*niyati*)' (Lochtefeld 2002, 226). It is the notion that 'all actions and effects are beyond individual will and what is fated to happen is bound to happen irrespective of one's motivation' (Soundara Rajan 2001, 60). Interestingly, Elder explains that there are in fact:

> close parallels between the Gita's teaching that man must act according to his duty but that the results of those actions are in God's hands … and the Christian belief that somehow "all things work together for a good to those who love God".
>
> (1966, 231)

Peace and justice

At times Buddhism was raised in my interviews, particularly in relation to what peace meant to them. A widow posited that 'Nepal is the birthplace of Buddha and he is recognised as a peace advocate'.[127] Pertinent here are Dennis' findings about the ways the claim 'Buddha was born in Nepal' has been 'leveraged for divergent political purposes', which illuminates 'the larger debates over secularism and Nepali national identity' (Dennis 2017, 177). Also, a male victim and NGO worker explained that '[n]ot everyone is born as Buddha. If there is some injustice, people are physically and mentally disturbed and this leads to conflict'.[128]

Buddhism is a religion and philosophy concerned with overcoming suffering (*dukkha*) (Tanabe 2014, 124; see also Cathwell and Kawanawi 2009).[129] The Four Noble Truths (*catur-aryasatya*) doctrine, 'Buddha's first and foundational teaching,' form the core of every school of Buddhism (Tanabe 2014, 126). The first and second noble truths cover the causes of violence, conflict and suffering while the third and fourth 'prescribe the cure for this unpleasant way of living' and 'how to promote a peaceful way of living' (Der-lan Yeh

2006, 97). The dependent origination (*pratītyasamutpāda*) provides that all of existence (including insentient beings) is interconnected (Der-lan Yeh 2006, 92). The interconnectedness of all existence combined with the root of violence being in the mind 'implies that suffering of others is like one's own and the violence committed by others is like the violence one commits oneself' (Der-lan Yeh 2006, 91; Hertog 2010, 93; see also Deegalle 2003; UNDV 2009). According to Tanabe:

> the cause of violence of any kind lies in our own minds and so making a critical analysis of the nature of one's mind or the principles of epistemic function allows us to deepen internal dynamics of violence: knowing, first of all, reality as a mind-construct, critically reflecting how mind turns into the root cause of suffering and contemplating and enacting the way to resolve it constitute the core of Buddhism.
>
> (2014, 125)

Rather than focus on the harm done, Buddhism holds it is important to examine the entire event in context along with the causes and conditions of it occurring (Der-lan Yeh 2006, 97). Pertinently, Buddhism provides that emotions such as anger can lead to an individual forgetting the interdependent nature of existence, for all individuals contribute directly or indirectly to violence (Der-lan Yeh 2006, 106). It is through this realisation that all individuals are involved in the 'web of violence' that dichotomies of 'us' versus 'them' or the 'good guys' versus the 'bad guys' is weakened in individuals' minds and this 'allows them to face the adversary with a more inclusive, understanding attitude' (Der-lan Yeh 2006, 106). These ideas could have relevance to understanding the victim/perpetrator dichotomy in Nepal (discussed further in Chapter 8).

Buddhism also emphasises peace (Omer 2012, 19). Pichler (2014, 85) persuasively argues that there are links with Buddhism and restorative justice where the focus on healing and repair (rather than punishment) is linked to Buddhist concepts of karma and non-violence. More broadly for many scholars and practitioners, Buddhist philosophy and practices 'are largely synonymous with peacebuilding and conflict transformation principles' (Owen 2014, 44; see also Der-lan Yeh 2006, 91; Schmidt-Leukel 2004).

However, there is debate whether there is a clear conception of justice in Buddhism. According to von Brück (2009, 159–160), Buddhism's attitude to justice can be identified in the following precepts: the achievement of mental balance, the overcoming of mental defilements (*kleshas*) (e.g. ego) and the recognition of the co-dependent origination of all sentient beings. For Tilakaratne, issues of justice are articulated through various concepts (e.g. *dhamma*) and can be derived from the foundational Buddhist idea that 'all human beings are equal' (2006, 4, 7). Pertinently for Tilakaratne, the 'Buddhist theory of punishment is not retributive but reformative' (2006, 5). The concept of karma, which emphasises the existence of cosmic justice, may account in part for the reason why Buddhism lacks a clear concept of justice

(Tilakaratne 2006, 9–10, 20). These issues require further empirical research to ascertain ways to provide more context specific understandings and approaches to TJ in Nepal an indeed other Hindu and Buddhist contexts.

Revenge and moving on

It was also difficult to discern whether people (victims and affected community members) sought to move on or to seek punishment, or both. I was frequently surprised by what I took to be the detached manner in which victims relayed tragic and horrific personal experiences. In many instances people spoke about the extraordinary and unfamiliar as ordinary and familiar. In many interviews people explained that what is done is done and that their main concern is their long-term livelihood. This sentiment is exemplified in the following remarks, which were relayed to me to explain how people have learnt to cope with the legacy of the conflict:

> In just one case one family were completely destroyed and devastated. We visited them in 2006, in 2008 and again in 2011 and their level of understanding, their attitude to conflict and their own victimhood had drastically changed. In this family there were three brothers. The eldest brother was a teacher who the Maoists killed. Then the other two brothers were implicated in the killing and were accused of being Maoists and then they were disappeared and later found to have been killed … All three widows live in the same village, in the same community, use the same community forest, use the same public water tap and their house is connected. You can imagine how they could have faced this situation but now they are gradually talking to each other, sharing their pain and extending cooperation and they are members of the same family. It's amazing, you see? Gradually, these victims are now seeing their enemy somewhere else, not those in the neighbourhood. Otherwise in the past they used to say 'this was the guy behind the killing of my husband or disappearing my husband or my son' now they are seeing that because of all those instigators [party leaders and politicians] we are now being played.[130]

Remarks such as these gave me the impression that in many respects victims found ways to get on with life. Indeed 'the performance of everyday life' became a means of enduring situations of insecurity and poverty, of the victims compartmentalising the conflict's 'legacies into manageable moments rather than being engulfed by them' and rebuilding relationships (Prieto 2012, 528; Shaw and Waldorf 2010, 20; Theidon 2014, 9). These ways of moving are 'a far cry from justice in any international meaning of the term' (Nee and Uvin 2010, 181).

While some victims have found a pragmatic resolution to their difficulties, others have remained angry and sought punishment and revenge. A Nepali human rights worker told me that victims were very emotional when they spoke at the Ministry of Peace and Reconstruction consultations (discussed in

Chapter 5). He told me that there were often quite heated discussions and that 'victims have this anger when they speak'.[131] A victims' group leader explained that in his group there were divergent priorities, with some wanting to return the 300,000 NPR (relief) they received and to exact revenge.[132] Also, a worker at a women's group conveyed that family members of victims were saying that if there was no justice then there would be war again.[133] A man who was beaten and assaulted during the conflict was not sure if he would fight or be violent if the perpetrator(s) were identified and apologised.[134]

Along with anger notions of bitterness were raised. A business owner in Rolpa said that there was 'bitterness inside the heart'.[135] And a female villager in a mid-western district stated: 'In my village both sides – army and Maoists – were killer and killed. Generally, people do not openly talk. People have bitterness inside their hearts.'[136] A daughter of a murdered Nepali Congress member also identified this bitterness. For her, reconciliation occurs in the periphery in villages so there is a need to bring TJ programs to villages.[137] This view resonates with Gready's (2005, 8–9) articulation of 'embedded justice' (see Chapter 3).

At times both positions were held simultaneously. That is, people sought punishment and revenge while expressing their desire to move on. What is more, these emotions and positions are not static. When I asked a widow how would she feel if she were given the choice to pardon her husband's murderer she responded: 'Who are ready to excuse their beloved's killer? What's gone is gone. I used to think about carrying a long knife to kill my husband's killer but gradually that idea faded away.'[138] A male NGO worker from Rolpa articulated a similar sentiment: 'What is done is done. Now we have to build the Truth and Reconciliation Commission and the Commission on Disappearances. Through these commissions we can find victims and find out how people were victimised …'[139]

While I was ignorant of it at the time my initial standpoint – which compared people who wanted revenge with those who wanted to move on – over-simplified the ways people dealt with the past. Also, I assumed forgiveness was a 'counterpoint' to revenge. Yet, as Jeffery states, 'forgiveness does not always adhere to [a] set of neat and tidy analytical distinctions' (2011, 79, 80). Perhaps the line is less clearly demarcated. Further, the practice of forgiveness at the interpersonal and communal level is not necessarily dependent on that what occurs at the state level (Jeffery 2011, 91). Through my research regarding Hinduism and Buddhism I have been able to nuance this 'either-or' position (see Finnström 2010, 15). And it is here that the challenges lie for TJ experts, brokers and implementers: it takes time to identify and work through predicaments such as these and it requires a deep engagement with people's everyday realities. In the final chapter of this book I provide further analysis regarding the issues raised in this chapter.

Notes

1 This builds upon my previous research see Selim and Murithi 2011 and Selim 2012.

2 Personal interview, 12 September 2012, Rolpa.
3 Personal interview, 11 September 2012, Rolpa.
4 Personal interview, 10 September 2012, Rolpa.
5 Personal interview, 10 September 2012, Rolpa.
6 Personal interview, 9 September 2012, Rolpa.
7 Personal interview, 11 October 2012, Kathmandu.
8 Personal interview, 9 September 2012, Rolpa.
9 Personal interview, 21 September 2012, Dadeldhura.
10 Personal interview, 9 September 2012, Rolpa.
11 Personal interview, 12 September 2012, Rolpa.
12 Personal interview, 12 September 2012, Rolpa.
13 Personal interview, 21 September 2012, Dadeldhura.
14 Personal interview, 20 September 2012, Dhanghadi.
15 Personal interview, 29 September 2012, Morang.
16 Personal interview, 1 October 2012, Ilam.
17 Bhandari (2011, 44) refers to this group as the Society of Families of Those Disappeared by the State and the Society of the Families of Warriors Disappeared by the State.
18 Personal interview, 11 September 2012, Rolpa.
19 Personal interview, 9 September 2012, Rolpa.
20 Personal interview, 9 September 2012, Rolpa.
21 Personal interview, 8 September 2012, Rolpa.
22 Personal interview, 20 September 2012, Kailali.
23 Personal interview, 12 September 2012, Rolpa.
24 Personal interview, 11 September 2012, Rolpa.
25 Personal interview, 20 September 2012, Kailali.
26 Personal interview, 8 September 2012, Rolpa.
27 Personal interview, 14 March 2012, Bara.
28 There were reports that qualified combatants were forced to hand over a portion of their payments to the Maoist party and that these payments were supposedly passed on to disqualified combatants.
29 This was reiterated by two male human rights workers. Personal interview, 11 October 2012, Kathmandu.
30 Personal interview, 9 September 2012, Rolpa.
31 Personal interview, 9 September 2012, Rolpa.
32 Personal interview, 19 September 2012, Kailali.
33 Personal interview, 9 September 2012, Rolpa.
34 Personal interview, 9 September 2012, Rolpa.
35 Personal interview, 11 September 2012, Rolpa.
36 Personal interview, 11 September 2012, Rolpa.
37 Although female combatants and child soldiers fought in the conflict, they are usually considered to be victims, often being defined as innocent, faultless and blameless due to a perceived lack of agency (see McEvoy and McConnachie 2012, 533–534).
38 As part of the 'Mass victimization and restorative justice' research project in Bosnia and Herzegovina, a self-administered quantitative survey examined the issue of suffering. Respondents were asked about their perceived suffering in three categories (physical, material and psychological) in two time periods (during and after the war) (Parmentier, Rauschenbach, and Weitekamp 2014, 45 and 48).
39 Personal interview, 16 October 2012, Kathmandu.
40 Personal interview, 5 April 2012, Kathmandu.
41 Personal interview, 8 September 2012, Rolpa.
42 Personal interview, 16 March 2012, Bara.

43 Personal interview, 21 September 2012, Daldeldhura.
44 Personal interview, 11 October 2012, Kathmandu.
45 Personal interview, 16 October 2012, Kathmandu.
46 Personal interview, 17 October 2012, Kathmandu.
47 Personal interview, 11 October 2012, Kathmandu.
48 Personal interview, 17 October 2012, Kathmandu.
49 Personal interview, 17 October 2012, Kathmandu.
50 Personal interviews, 7 March and 17 October 2012, Kathmandu.
51 Personal interview, 8 September 2012, Rolpa.
52 Personal interview, 23 March 2012, Kathmandu.
53 Personal interview, 21 September 2012, Dadeldhura and 29 September 2012, Morang.
54 It was difficult to ascertain the trajectory of events, guidelines and efforts. In addition to my fieldwork data I was greatly assisted by a number of NGO reports (see for example ICTJ 2011a; Carranza 2012; Marg 2010; Advocacy Forum and ICTJ 2010).
55 Other relevant policy documents include Measures for Financial Support and Relief for Conflict Victims pursuant to cabinet decision, 25 April 2008; Guidelines for Providing Relief to Beneficiary of a Deceased Person pursuant to cabinet decision, 5 October 2008; and Guidelines for Providing Relief to the Beneficiary of a Disappeared Person pursuant to cabinet decision, 12 January 2009 (see ICTJ 2011a). See Chapter 6 for further details.
56 Village Development Committees are government grassroots-level structures tasked with information sharing.
57 Personal interview, 1 October 2012, Ilam.
58 Incidents were derived from OHCHR's reporting along with national and international NGOs.
59 Personal interview, 21 September 2012, Dadeldhura.
60 Personal interview, 11 September 2012, Rolpa.
61 Personal interview, 11 September 2012, Rolpa.
62 Personal interview, 12 September 2012, Rolpa.
63 Personal interview, 20 September 2012, Kailali.
64 Personal interview, 9 September 2012, Rolpa.
65 Personal interview, 8 September 2012, Rolpa.
66 Personal interview, 8 September 2012, Rolpa.
67 Personal interview, 17 October 2012, Kathmandu.
68 Personal interview, 20 September 2012, Kailali.
69 Personal interview, 16 March 2012, Bara.
70 Personal interview, 11 September 2012, Rolpa.
71 Personal interview, 20 September 2012, Kailali.
72 Personal interview, 12 September 2012, Rolpa.
73 Personal interview, 12 September 2012, Rolpa.
74 Personal interview, 12 September 2012, Rolpa.
75 Personal interview, 20 September 2012, Kailali.
76 Personal interview, 20 September 2012, Kailali.
77 Personal interview, 20 September 2012, Kailali.
78 Personal interview, 20 September 2012, Kailali.
79 Personal interview, 12 September 2012, Rolpa.
80 Personal interview, 8 September 2012, Rolpa.
81 Personal interview, 16 March 2012, Bara.
82 Personal interviews, 1 October 2012, Ilam and 25 March 2012, Dang.
83 Personal interview, 29 September 2012, Morang.
84 Personal interview, 12 September 2012, Rolpa.

85 Personal interviews, 11 September 2012, Rolpa and 18 March and 25 March 2012, Dang.
86 Personal interview, 20 September 2012, Kailali.
87 Personal interview, 16 March 2012, Bara.
88 Personal interview, 12 September 2012, Rolpa.
89 Personal interview, 29 September 2012, Morang.
90 Personal interview, 29 September 2012, Morang.
91 Personal interview, 19 September 2012, Kailali.
92 Personal interview, 9 September 2012, Rolpa.
93 Personal interview, 9 September 2012, Rolpa.
94 Personal interview, 1 October 2012, Ilam.
95 Personal interview, 12 September 2012, Rolpa.
96 Personal interview, 12 September 2012, Rolpa.
97 Personal interview, 12 September 2012, Rolpa.
98 Personal interview, 22 March 2012, Dang.
99 Personal interview, 11 September 2012, Rolpa.
100 Personal interview, 2 March 2012, Dang.
101 Personal interview, 11 October 2012, Kathmandu.
102 Personal interview, 11 October 2012, Kathmandu.
103 Personal interview, 20 September 2012, Kailali.
104 This exercise required one person to stand in the centre and three people (observers) to stand in front and to both sides of this person. Three other observers are asked to leave the room. The first set of observers in the room is invited to report what they can see of the person in centre. The second set of observers is invited to return to the room and to also report what they can see. Debriefing questions for this activity included: 'Do any of the three observers have a complete perspective on the volunteer's face from where they stand?' and 'How can we get accurate descriptions of events that took place in the past?'
105 Personal interview, 12 September 2012, Rolpa.
106 Personal interview, 9 September 2012, Rolpa.
107 Personal interview, 11 September 2012, Rolpa.
108 Personal interview, 11 September 2012, Rolpa.
109 Personal interview, 22 September 2012, Kailali.
110 These findings are in contrast to Robin's research, which critiques transitional justice and human rights discourse more broadly as an elite discourse (see Chapter 3).
111 Personal interview, 10 September 2012, Rolpa.
112 Personal interview, 10 September 2012, Rolpa.
113 Personal interview, 12 September 2012, Rolpa.
114 Personal interview, 22 March 2012, Dang.
115 Personal interview, 10 October 2012, Kathmandu.
116 Personal interview, 10 October 2012, Kathmandu.
117 As discussed in Chapter 4, several studies have concluded that the primary causes of the Nepali conflict were economic and social grievances, including landlessness; poverty; uneven development; structural, identity-based exclusion; and inequality (see, for example, Pasipanodya 2008; Do and Iyer 2010).
118 While the Universal Declaration of Human Rights makes no distinction between these sets of human rights, over time there has been a tendency to separate and prioritise civil and political rights over economic, social and cultural rights.
119 Personal interviews, 11 October 2012, Kathmandu.
120 Personal interview, 11 October 2012, Kathmandu.
121 Personal interview, 11 October 2012, Kathmandu.
122 Personal interview, 21 September 2012, Dadeldhura.
123 Personal interview, 20 September 2012, Kailali.

124 The power battle between two Royal factions is at the heart of the *Mahabharata* (Lochtefeld 2002, 207–208). In this epic tale there are two students: Drona, who is poor and unable to feed his family and Drupada, who becomes King of Panchala. Drona approaches Drupada for alms but when Drupada refuses his request Drona vows revenge. Drona goes on to teach the art of war and demands half of Drupada's kingdom in return; ultimately, Drona acquires half of Drupada's kingdom, leading to Drupada to vow revenge on Drona.
125 Personal interview, 11 October 2012, Kathmandu.
126 Personal interview, 11 September 2012, Rolpa.
127 Personal interview, 16 March 2012, Bara.
128 Personal interview, 22 March 2012, Dang.
129 For further details about Buddhist concepts of suffering see Tilakaratne (2008).
130 Personal interview, 11 October 2012, Kathmandu.
131 Personal interview, 11 October 2012, Kathmandu.
132 Personal interview, 19 October 2012, Kathmandu.
133 Personal interview, 29 September 2012, Morang.
134 Personal interview, 20 September 2012, Kailali.
135 Personal interview, 10 September 2012, Rolpa.
136 Personal interview, 10 September 2012, Rolpa.
137 Personal interview, 12 September 2012, Rolpa.
138 Personal interview, 12 September 2012, Rolpa.
139 Personal interview, 11 September 2012, Rolpa.

References

Adhikari, Aditya, Bhaskar Guatam, Surabhi Pudasaini, and Bhadra Sharma. 2014. 'Impunity and accountability in Nepal.' http://asiafoundation.org/resources/pdfs/NPimpunityandpoliticalaccountability.pdf.

Advocacy Forum. 2010. 'Review of implementation of the recommendations made by the UN after its visit to Nepal in December 2004.' http://nepalconflictreport.ohchr.org/files/docs/2010-09-00_document_af_eng.pdf.

Advocacy Forum, and ICTJ. 2010. Across the lines: The impact of Nepal's conflict on women. www.ictj.org/sites/default/files/ICTJ-Nepal-Across-Lines-2010-English.pdf.

Allen, N. J. 1997. 'Hinduization: The experience of the Thulung Rai.' In *Nationalism and ethnicity in a Hindu kingdom: The politics and culture of contemporary Nepal*, edited by David N. Gellner, Joanna Pfaff-Czarnecka and John Whelpton, 303–324. London: Routledge.

Arbour, Louise. 2006. 'Economic and social justice for societies in transition.' Annual Lecture of Transitional Justice, New York University School of Law, 25 October 2006.

Bhandari, Ram Kumar. 2011. 'The role of victims' organisations in transition from conflict: Families of the disappeared in Nepal.' Master's Degree, Institute for Peace Research and Security Policy, University of Hamburg.

Bista, Dor Bahadur. 2001. *Fatalism and development: Nepal's struggle for modernization*. Hyderabad: Orient Longman Limited.

Bouris, Erica. 2007. *Complex political victims*. Herndon: Kumarian Press.

Carranza, Ruben. 2012. *Relief, reparations, and the root causes of conflict in Nepal*. www.ictj.org/sites/default/files/ICTJ-Nepal-Reparations-2012-English.pdf.

Cathwell, Cathy, and Hiroko Kawanawi. 2009. 'Buddhism.' In *Religions in the modern world: Traditions and transformations*, edited by Linda Woodhead, Hiroko Kawanawi and Christopher Partridge, 41–69. London: Routledge.

Central Bureau of Statistics. 2012. *National population and housing census, 2011*. Kathmandu: National Bureau of Statistics.

Chambers, Robert, and Irene Guijt. 2011. 'PRA five years later.' In *The participation reader*, edited by Andrea Cornwall, 109–121. London: Zed Books.

Cornwall, Andrea. 2007. 'Buzzwords and fuzzwords: Deconstructing development discourse.' *Development in Practice* 17(4–5):471–484.

Coward, Harold, and Gordon Smith, eds. 2004. *Religion and peacebuilding*. Albany, NY: State University of New York Press.

CVCPNepal. 2014. 'Conflict victims common platform on transitional justice: Nepal.' Accessed 9 January 2015. www.facebook.com/pages/Conflict-Victims-Common-Platform-on-Transitional-Justice-Nepal/770718082976594?sk=info&tab=page_info.

Das, Veena. 2007. *Life and words: Violence and the descent into the ordinary*. Berkeley: University of California Press.

Deegalle, Mahinda. 2003. 'Is violence justified in Theravada Buddhism?' *Ecumenical Review* 55(2):115–121.

Dennis, Dannah. 2017. 'Mediating claims to Buddha's birthplace and Nepali national identity.' In *Media as politics in South Asia*, edited by Sahana Udupa and Stephen D. McDowell. London: Routledge.

Der-lan Yeh, Theresa. 2006. 'The way to peace: A Buddhist perspective.' *International Journal of Peace Studies* 11(1):91–112.

Do, Quy-Toan, and Lakshmi Iyer. 2010. 'Geography, poverty and conflict in Nepal.' *Journal of Peace Research* 47(6):735–748.

Elder, Joseph W. 1966. 'Fatalism in India: A comparison between Hindus and Muslims.' *Anthropological Quarterly* 39(3):227–243.

Elias, Robert 1990. 'Which victim movement: The politics of victim policy.' In *Victims of crime: Problems, policies and programs*, edited by Arthur J. Lurigio, Wesley G. Skogan and Robert C. Davis, 226–250. Newbury Park: Sage.

Elster, Jon. 2004. *Closing the Books: Transitional justice in historical perspective*. Cambridge: Cambridge University Press.

Finnström, Sverker. 2010. 'Reconciliation grown bitter? War, retribution, and ritual action in Northern Uganda.' In *Localizing transitional justice interventions and priorities after mass violence*, edited by Rosalind Shaw, Lars Waldorf and Pierre Hazan, 135–156. Stanford, CA: Stanford University Press.

Flood, Gavin. 2008. 'Reconciliation, peace and justice in Hinduism.' In *Conflict and reconciliation: The contribution of religions*, edited by John W. Bowker, 58–88. Toronto: The Key Publishing House Inc.

Gandhi, Rajmohan. 2000. *Revenge reconciliation: Understanding south Asian history*. New Delhi: Penguin Books.

García-Godos, Jemima. 2008. 'Victim reparations in transitional justice – what is at stake and why.' *Nordic Journal of Human Rights* 26(2):111–130.

Gaventa, John, and Andrea Cornwall. 2006. 'Challenging the boundaries of the possible: participation, knowledge and power.' *IDS bulletin* 37(6):122–128.

Gready, Paul. 2005. 'Analysis: Reconceptualising transitional justice: embedded and distanced justice.' *Conflict, Security & Development* 5(1):3–21.

Hertog, Katrien. 2010. *The complex reality of religious peacebuilding: Conceptual contributions and critical analysis*. Plymouth: Lexington Books.

Himalayan News Service. 2016. 'Conflict victims demand fair play.' *The Himalayan Times*, https://thehimalayantimes.com/kathmandu/conflict-victims-demand-justice/.

Humphrey, Michael. 2005. 'Reconciliation and the therapeutic state.' *Journal of Intercultural Studies* 26(3):203–220.

Hunter, Alan. 2007. 'Forgiveness: Hindu and western perspectives.' *Journal of Hindu-Christian Studies* 20(11):1–8.

ICTJ. 2011a. From relief to reparations: Listening to the voices of victims. www.ictj.org/sites/default/files/ICTJ-NPL-Relief-to-Reparations-Report-2011-English.pdf.

ICTJ. 2011b. *Trainers' manual on transitional justice*. Kathmandu: ICTJ.

ICTJ, and Advocacy Forum. 2008. Nepali voices: Perceptions of truth, justice, reconciliation, reparations and the transition in Nepal. www.ictj.org/sites/default/files/ICTJ-Nepal-Voices-Reconciliation-2008-English.pdf.

IFAD. 2013. *Enabling poor rural people to overcome poverty in Nepal*. www.ifad.org/en/web/knowledge/asset/39429831.

Jeffery, Renee. 2011. 'Forgiveness, amnesty, and justice: The case of the Lord's resistance Army in northern Uganda.' *Cooperation and Conflict* 46(1):78–95.

Keethaponcalan, S. I. 2014. 'Hinduism: War, peace, and peace and conflict studies.' In *Peace on earth: The role of religion in peace and conflict studies*, edited by Thomas Matyók, Maureen Flaherty, Hamdesa Tuso, Jessica Senehi and Sean Byrne, 287–302. New York: Lexington Books.

Kerkvliet, Benedict Tria. 1995. 'Village-state relations in Vietnam: The effect of everyday politics on decollectivization.' *The Journal of Asia Studies* 54(2):396–418.

King, Anna. 2014. 'Peacebuilding and post-conflict theory recovery in Nepal: A Buddhist case study.' Buddhist perspective towards achieving the UN Millennium Development Goals, Ninh Binh Province, Vietnam, 7–11 May.

Lecomte-Tilouine, M. 2010. 'Martyrs and living martyrs of the People's war in Nepal.' *South Asia Multidisciplinary Academic Journal* 4:2–19.

Lochtefeld, James G. 2002. *The illustrated encyclopedia of Hinduism*. New York: The Rosen Publishing Group, Inc.

Lu, Catherine. 2002. 'Human wrongs and the tragedy of victimhood.' *Ethics and International Affairs* 16(2):109–117.

Marg, Shantiniketan. 2010. *Discrimination and irregularities: The painful tale of interim relief in Nepal*. http://advocacyforum.org/downloads/pdf/publications/Discriminations_and_Irregularities_A_painful_tale_of_Interim_Relief_in_Nepal.pdf.

Marsden, R. 2011. 'The politics of loss in the people's war and its aftermath: The disappeared as kin, citizens and warriors.' *Studies in Nepali History and Society* 16 (2):271–295.

McAdam, Doug, Sydney G. Tarrow, and Charles Tilly. 2001. *Dynamics of contention*. Cambridge: Cambridge University Press.

McEvoy, Kieran, and Kristen McConnachie. 2012. 'Victimology in transitional justice: Victimhood, innocence and hierarchy.' *European Journal of Criminology* 9 (5):527–538.

Mills, Jane, Ann Bonner, and Karen Francis. 2006. 'The Development of Constructivist Grounded Theory.' *International Journal of Qualitative Methods* 5(1):25–35.

Nagy, Rosemary. 2008. 'Transitional justice as global project: Critical reflections.' *Third World Quarterly* 29(2):275–289.

Nee, Ann, and Peter Uvin. 2010. 'Silence and dialogue: Burundians' alternatives to transitional justice.' In *Localizing transitional justice interventions and priorities after mass violence*, edited by Rosalind Shaw, Lars Waldorf and Pierre Hazan, 157–182. Stanford, CA: Stanford University Press.

Nepal Monitor. 2011. 'Government relief efforts for Nepal conflict victims.' Last modified 19 July 2011. www.nepalmonitor.com/2011/07/government_relief_ef.html.

Omer, Atalia. 2012. 'Religious peacebuilding: The exotic, the good, and the theatrical.' *Practical Matters* 5:1–31.

Owen, Mark. 2014. 'Devising a methodological framework for analysing the potential of Buddhist peacebuilding.' Buddhist perspective towards achieving the UN Millennium Development Goals, Ninh Binh Province, Vietnam, 7–11 May.

Parmentier, Stephan, Mina Rauschenbach, and Elmar Weitekamp. 2014. 'Repairing the harm of victims after violent conflict: Empirical findings from Serbia.' *International Review of Victimology* 20:85–99.

Pasipanodya, Tafadzwa. 2008. 'A deeper justice: economic and social justice as transitional justice in Nepal.' *International Journal of Transitional Justice* 2:378–397.

Pichler, Carina. 2014. 'Peace through peaceful means: A Buddhist perspective on restorative justice.' Buddhist perspective towards achieving the UN Millennium Development Goals, Ninh Binh Province, Vietnam, 7–11 May.

Prieto, Juan Diego. 2012. 'Together after war while the war goes on: Victims, ex-combatants and communities in three Colombian cities.' *International Journal of Transitional Justice* 6:525–546.

Rai, Dewan. 2015. 'Conflict victims want provision of retrospective law.' *The Kathmandu Post.* http://kathmandupost.ekantipur.com/printedition/news/2015-07-20/conflict-victims-want-provision-of-retrospective-law.html.

Rambachan, Anantanand. 2003. 'The co-existence of violence and non-violence in Hinduism.' *Ecumenical Review* 55(2):115–121.

Robins, Simon. 2011. 'Addressing the needs of families of the Missing: A test of contemporary approaches to transitional justice.' PhD Post-war Recovery Studies, Department of Politics, University of York.

Robins, Simon. 2012. 'Transitional justice as an elite discourse: Human rights practice where the global meets the local in post-conflict Nepal.' *Critical Asian Studies* 44 (1):3–30.

Robins, Simon, and Ram Kumar Bhandari. 2012. 'From victims to actors: Mobilising victims to drive transitional justice process.' http://nefad.files.wordpress.com/2012/06/nefad_from-victims-to-actors-summary-and-plan-of-action-eng.pdf.

Rombouts, Heidy. 2002. 'Importance and difficulties of victim-based research in post-conflict societies.' *European Journal of Crime, Criminal Law and Criminal Justice* 10 (2–3):216–232.

Rye, Mark S., Kenneth I. Pargament, M. Amir Ali, Guy L. Beck, Elliot N. Dorff, Charles Hallisey, Vasudha Narayanan, and James G. Williams. 2000. 'Religious perspectives on forgiveness.' In *Forgiveness: Theory, research, and practice*, edited by Michael E. McCullough, Kenneth I. Pargament and Carl E. Thorsen, 17–40. New York: The Guilford Press.

Schmidt-Leukel, Perry. 2004. 'War and peace in Buddhism.' In *War and peace in world religions*, edited by Perry Schmidt-Leukel, 33–56. London: SCM Press.

Selim, Yvette. 2012. 'Transitions: creating space to address injustice after conflict or political turmoil.' *openDemocracy*, Last modified 12 February 2012. www.opendemocracy.net/opensecurity/yvette-selim/transitions-creating-space-to-address-injustice-after-conflict-or-politica.

Selim, Yvette, and Tim Murithi. 2011. 'Transitional justice and development: Partners for sustainable peace in Africa?' *Journal of Peacebuilding and Development* 6(2):58–72.

Shaw, Rosalind, and Lars Waldorf. 2010. 'Introduction: Localizing transitional justice.' In *Localizing transitional justice interventions and priorities after mass violence*, edited by Rosalind Shaw, Lars Waldorf and Pierre Hazan, 3–26. Stanford, CA: Stanford University Press.

Smith, David. 2009. 'Hinduism.' In *Religion in the modern world: Traditions and transformations*, edited by Linda Woodhead, Hiroko Kawanawi and Christopher Partridge, 41–69. London: Routledge.

Snellinger, Amanda. 2007. 'Student movements in Nepal: Their parameters and their idealized forms.' In *Contentious politics and democratization in Nepal*, edited by Mahendra Lawoti, 273–295. London: Sage.

Soundara Rajan, K. V. 2001. *Concise classified dictionary of Hinduism*. Vol. 5. New Delhi: Concept Publishing Company.

Spalek, Basia. 2006. *Crime Victims: theory, policy and practice*. New York: Palgrave Macmillan.

Stanko, Elizabeth, and Kathy Hobdell. 1993. 'Assault on men.' *The British Journal of Criminology* 33(3):400–540.

Tanabe, Juichiro. 2014. 'Buddhism and non-violent world: Examining a Buddhist contribution to promoting the principle of non-violence and a culture of peace.' *In Factis Pax* 8(2):122–149.

Theidon, Kimberely. 2014. '"How was your trip?" Self-care for researchers working and writing on violence.' *DSD Working Papers on Research Security*, edited by Enrique Desmond Arias. http://webarchive.ssrc.org/working-papers/DSD_ResearchSecurity_02_Theidon.pdf.

Tilakaratne, Asanga. 2006. 'Justice, kamma and dhamma: Does kamma in Buddhism make justice redundant.' 2nd International Conference of Sri Lanka Association for Buddhist Studies, 17–19 November, The University of Peradeniya.

Tilakaratne, Asanga. 2008. 'Suffering and liberation in Theravada Buddhism.' *International Journal of Buddhist Thought and Culture* 10:87–103.

Tyynela, John, Lucia Withers, and Prabina Bajracharya. 2013. *Beyond relief: Addressing the Rights and Needs of Nepal's Wives of the Disappeared*. ICTJ Briefing. www.ictj.org/sites/default/files/ICTJ-Briefing-Nepal-WivesofDisappeared-2013.pdf.

UN. 2014. 'Victims common platform on transitional justice.' www.un.org.np/headlines/victims-common-platform-transitional-justice.

UNDV. 2009. 'Buddhist approach to political conflict and peace development.' The International Buddhist Conference on the United Nations Day of Vesak Celebrations, Mahachulalongkornrajavidyalaya University, 4–6 May.

UNRCO. 2014. *Monthly report: November 2014*. https://reliefweb.int/sites/reliefweb.int/files/resources/UN_RCO_Monthly_Report_November_2014.pdf.

von Brück, Michael. 2004. 'War and peace in Hinduism.' In *War and peace in world religions*, edited by Perry Schmidt-Leukel, 11–32. London: SCM Press.

von Brück, Michael. 2009. 'An ethics of justice in Buddhism seen in a cross-cultural context.' *Journal of Oriental Studies* 19:158–165.

White, Sarah. 1996. 'Depoliticising the development: The uses and abuses of participation.' *Development in Practice* 6(1):6–15.

Yadav, Punam. 2016. *Social transformation in post-conflict Nepal: A gender perspective, Routledge research on gender in Asia series*. Oxon: Routledge.

8 Rethinking transitional justice

> People have very little or no knowledge about transitional justice. It is only people in headquarters, Kathmandu and bigger cities and those that studied it … The general awareness is very low. For rural people the law is what the major three political parties decide.
>
> (Male Nepali NGO worker, Rolpa, 2 March 2012)

In this final chapter, I summarise and expound upon the book's main arguments, drawing in particular on the analysis in Chapters 6 and 7. I also outline the book's contributions to the literature on TJ and highlight points that may be significant for other post-conflict contexts. As the first book to provide a single case study on TJ in Nepal this book makes major theoretical and empirical contributions to: TJ research in Nepal[1] and the Asia-Pacific[2] more broadly; the politics versus justice binary; the concept of victimhood; and, the literature on participatory approaches in development.

The politics of and around transitional justice

Transitional Justice in Nepal: Interest, Victims and Agency provides an in-depth analysis of the historical and political context which led to the Maoist insurgency in Nepal. The book outlines the causes of the conflict and the ways the conflict has shaped the political and social landscape in post-conflict Nepal. Using key TJ debates[3] as the point of departure, it also outlines the historical developments of TJ and in so doing provides a backdrop to how TJ arose in Nepal. The book draws upon interviews with a diverse range of stakeholders, including victims, ex-combatants, community members, political representatives, human rights advocates, journalists, representatives from diplomatic missions, international organisations and the donor community. These interviews revealed stakeholders' viewpoints, knowledge, attitudes and preferences about TJ and other post-conflict issues in Nepal, and informed the actor typology, which identifies different types of TJ actors (TJ experts, TJ brokers, TJ implementers and victims), their relationships with one another and the levels in which they operate (Chapter 5), making a significant empirical contribution to the research in Nepal and to TJ more broadly.

The book provides a detailed account of the TJ process in Nepal. In particular, this book explores the actions of, and relationships and processes between, actors in the name of TJ. It illustrates that for the majority of the post-conflict period various actors, including human rights organisations, victims' groups and donors, have described the TJ process in Nepal as stagnant or 'still-born'. This book has argued that, in essence, this assessment conflates the progress of TJ with a lack of (national level) political will. It also discounts the multitude of layers of action both *within* organisations (e.g. the UN) and *between* actors (victims' groups, the government of Nepal, human rights agencies and foreign governments). Rather than being stagnant, instead Chapters 6 and 7 reveal that the TJ process in Nepal is dynamic and highly contested by a range of actors. In Nepal actors frequently seek to advance their interests and make claims utilising the processes, mechanisms and language of TJ; however, it is difficult to identify and appreciate these political actions through a standard lens. I argue that when a broader lens/notion of politics is utilised it reveals the nature and extent of these political activities.

To analyse the politics of and around TJ in Nepal I put TJ in dialogue with resistance literature and contentious politics literature to derive an action spectrum (Chapter 2). The action spectrum can be used in Nepal and other post-conflict contexts to understand how actors engage with, mould and impact the trajectory of TJ. The spectrum also assists in identifying the range of actions (e.g. contestation, negotiation and resistance) and in turn helps to make visible the different understandings of justice. This broader notion reveals the political nature and dynamics of and around TJ in Nepal and beyond. This theoretical contribution also adds to the ongoing debate about politics versus justice.

This book reveals the difficulties TJ implementers, experts and brokers encounter when dealing with national and local politics. While these actors acknowledge to varying extents the need to understand the domestic context, it is clear that in practice they are still grappling with 'the politics at play' (see Menocal 2014, 11). In particular, this book argues that an understanding of Nepali politics, particularly before the conflict and at the local level, could have assisted with the design and implementation of distributing relief to victims. This research also reveals TJ can also be used as an instrument to frustrate or advance the goals of organisations, political parties and other actors; however, the extent to which this is recognised and addressed by TJ actors is limited. Moreover, there is a disjunction between actors who pursue TJ in an apolitical or minimally politicised manner and actors who use political avenues to adapt or circumvent the dominant TJ approach.

These findings are pertinent in other post-conflict contexts. While there has been a modest push for scholars and practitioners to recognise the politics of TJ, there has been limited guidance on how to do so. As this book demonstrates TJ is a particular form and vision of politics and as a political project TJ introduces and catalyses new political dynamics in post-conflict countries; accordingly, I advocate for greater consideration of actors' interests and local politics – the politics that predate, were impacted by and emerge after the conflict – and, in turn, both the actors' and politics' impact on TJ.

Based on my research in Nepal I advocate for a context-specific approach to TJ. This requires letting these dynamics play out to enable a different conceptualisation and operationalisation of TJ in *each* context. Doing so may mean that TJ will be caught up with actors, ideas and practices that may be normatively undesirable for some TJ actors; this may be the case particularly for TJ experts when political parties and other national actors seem to 'hijack' TJ. However, as this book has demonstrated, holding steadfastly to an imported model is also undesirable since many people have little awareness of the TJ process or do not seek the key TJ mechanisms, namely the Truth and Reconciliation Commission and the Commission of Investigation on Enforced Disappeared Persons. Clearly compromise is required.

Timing, peace agreements and truth commissions

There needs to be a greater recognition that prescriptive TJ measures in peace agreements have the potential to *impede* TJ's ability to be context-specific and victim-centric. The TJ structure in Nepal, as initially set out in the TJ provisions in the Comprehensive Peace Agreement, has been difficult to adapt to reflect the voices and needs of victims. Despite having good intentions, TJ experts and TJ implementers do not adequately address this predicament. This finding raises the question of whether TJ provisions, particularly provisions for a truth commission, should be included in peace agreements at all. TJ provisions in peace agreements rarely have scope for victims' and other actors' voices to be incorporated, although participatory approaches offer ways to ensure that these actors' voices are included in future consultations and negotiations (van Zyl 2005, 224–225). Calls by the UN Special Rapporteur on the promotion of Truth, Justice, Reparation and Guarantees of Non-Recurrence for the international community to critically examine trends in the practice of truth commissions are a welcome change (see de Greiff 2013). So too is the 2014 report by the ICTJ and the Kofi Annan Foundation, which signals a refreshing departure from previous policy reports on truth commissions (Tyynela 2014). The report heeds the challenges of international organisations making decisions in a context 'where ideal formulas are displaced by imperfect realities' and the ongoing difficulties to ensure victims' rights are not sacrificed (Tyynela 2014, vii).

While I am not discounting the value of commitments to address the legacy of the conflict, I call for caution to ensure that the TJ trajectory is not prematurely circumscribed, particularly by TJ experts or negotiating parties, which frequently include leaders implicated in the violence. I acknowledge that it may be undesirable that TJ should exclude these actors but the prominence they are given needs to be countered by the inclusion of other voices. This is where participatory approaches can offer ways for victims and affected community members to have a say in shaping TJ for their context.

Participation

This book also contributes to the literature on participatory approaches in development and TJ. I demonstrate how participatory approaches have been employed in Nepal in relation to TJ (Chapter 5) and I critique these approaches and highlight the challenges and opportunities of employing participation in TJ (Chapter 6). This book demonstrates that despite the range of issues covered and actors included in the various participation activities in the TJ process, barring some of the participatory action research work carried out, it is unclear to what extent the rhetoric of participation has impacted the practice of TJ in Nepal. Participatory activities have predominantly taken the form of surveys and consultations, which have provided greater insight into what victims seek from the TJ process. Victims voiced their need for long-term security, health provision, education and livelihood skills training. Although these attempts to broaden participation do have benefits there seems to be a naïve presumption that they will feed into the TJ process and the policies and programming of TJ implementers and brokers (see White 1996). As I have demonstrated, this is not always the case.

I argue that meaningful attempts to broaden participation in TJ should go beyond consultations and information-sharing to ensure that victims are partners and decisions-makers (Selim 2014). These attempts should take part at *every stage* of the TJ process, from asking whether communities want TJ and if so, what form it should take and how it should be implemented (see Lundy and McGovern 2008). If this occurs there is the potential for victims and affected community members to play a key role in designing and shaping various TJ processes.

Victims and everyday realities

I contribute to the emerging literature on everyday lives and TJ by engaging with anthropological literature and victimology literature and drawing upon my understanding of everyday realities in Nepal. Focusing on victims and their everyday lives, this book has demonstrated that the recognition and categorisation of certain victims in Nepal has a range of implications. I reveal that not only were economic and social concerns the cause of the conflict, but they are issues that are also integral to what victims want to see addressed in its wake (Chapter 7). In addition, I highlight that the goals of the dominant TJ paradigm, such as reconciliation were largely absent from what conflict-affected people said they want. Using the actor typology I highlight that in Nepal everyday issues that victims and community members deem to matter in the wake of conflict do not always accord with the approaches adopted by TJ experts, brokers and implementers.

Additionally, the meanings people ascribed to justice were also intimately related to people's everyday lives, particularly their socioeconomic concerns. My interviews also revealed that victimhood and state support were intimately connected for conflict-affected people in Nepal. This also included martyrs and freedom fighters who linked martyrdom with state recognition and compensation. While the term victim was often used in relation to state support, it did not seem to be used frequently in everyday life. Furthermore, for those who did employ these terms, their notion of who was a victim and who was a perpetrator was neither static nor uniform. In fact, some people who were perceived to be perpetrators are now considered victims, with some people now considering members of the political elite – those who made key decisions during the conflict, including giving orders to soldiers and combatants, and are now leading the country – to be the perpetrators. During my interviews there were mixed degrees of hope that these individuals would ever be held accountable.

Awareness of everyday realities in post-conflict settings is critical. My research revealed that for some the conflict was extraordinary; for others, however, the conflict was but one of many experiences of violence and injustice in their everyday lives. There are incompatibilities between the local political, cultural and social particularities and the dominant TJ paradigm (see Sanford and Lincoln 2010, 78). Yet, when these local particularities and TJ paradigms do differ, as has been the case in Nepal, frequently TJ experts, brokers and implementers insist that the TJ norms are indispensable. Negotiating between what Merry calls 'the generalizing strategies of transitional actors and the particularistic techniques of activists working within local contexts … is a key human rights problem' (2006, 103). It is embracing a 'thicker' and more contextualised understanding of TJ that TJ will be able to be more effective on the ground (McEvoy 2007).

Victims, perpetrators and ex-combatants

Drawing upon my interviews with conflict-affected people and other individuals, I disrupt the victim/perpetrator binary revealing that often those deemed to be ex-combatants or perpetrators consider themselves to be victims. This book demonstrates that whether someone is considered a perpetrator, victim or both in Nepal depends on who is applying the label(s) and for what purpose(s). Determining who the 'real' victims were was often connected to the TJ process, for those who were aware of it. Again, the notion of a real victim seemed connected to the state support, through reparations, that are expected to be recommended by the commissions.

The reality of post-conflict Nepal (as with many other post-conflict countries) is complex and the range of human rights violations and violators cannot be simply subsumed into the categories of victims and perpetrators. This was particularly the case with regard to the Interim Relief Program, where a number of people who would be considered to be victims pursuant to TJ norms (e.g. victims of torture or rape) were officially excluded from the program for reported pragmatic reasons, despite considering themselves to be victims.

Ex-combatants also complicated the victim/perpetrator binary. For some respondents these were the 'real' victims, with some explaining that it was the combatants who had been fooled by the Maoist leaders to fight for their cause and then they were abandoned in cantonments once the leadership had reached a political settlement. Female ex-combatants and child soldiers who participated in the conflict further complicate the notion of the innocent and passive victim or the guilty perpetrator; they demonstrate that the standard victim/perpetrator view belies the complex nature of the members of these categories in Nepal. This reveals that the categories utilised by various TJ actors often do not accord with the lived realities on the ground.

In this book I advocate for a rethink of the identification and categorisation of victims and perpetrators based on their innocence or the harm done. I propose that considerations of the notion of suffering may better reflect the realities in Nepal. This has implications for victims in general but also for ex-combatants. By relocating the focus then the complicated space that ex-combatants occupy in Nepal can more adequately be considered. This goes well beyond the scope of standard definitions of victims, but in so doing more readily reflects the complex realities in post-conflict Nepal.

The complex identities of individuals in post-conflict environments have implications for the ways external actors engage with TJ in Nepal and other post-conflict contexts. These pertain to who victims are, but also to what they need and want. This raises a number of issues for TJ practitioners, including the language used in TJ processes, the mechanisms implemented and, indeed, the focus of these mechanisms. People's understandings about justice and their wants and needs after the conflict reveal that there are differences between what TJ experts, implementers and brokers, and victims deem to matter in a post-conflict environment. For example, the emphasis on socioeconomic concerns in Nepal demonstrates the need for TJ practitioners to pay greater attention to addressing violations of economic, social and cultural rights (Selim 2012; Selim and Murithi 2011). Additionally, with the work of the commissions now underway it would be useful to consider if there are conflict affected persons who are unwilling to adopt the standard repertoires and represent themselves as 'victims'.

Other issues also arise. For example, what happens when various communities have found their own ways of moving on, ways that have bypassed or overtaken the TJ process at the national level. Is the use of the victim/perpetrator label required here, or might it also be detrimental? Of particular interest in the case of Nepal is how do TJ actors deal with natural disasters that compound and complicate notions of victimhood and suffering and harm. This is an area which requires further research.

The complex identities of individuals in post-conflict environments have implications for the ways external actors engage with TJ. These pertain to who victims are, but also to what they need and want. For some, the term victim (as it is currently conceived) connotes weakness, passivity, negativity, vulnerability and disempowerment. These connotations have opened a space for other terms, particularly 'victim-survivor' or 'survivor' that evoke resistance and recovery (McLeer 1998, 44). While individuals have the right to adopt whatever labels they prefer, perhaps adopting the term 'conflict-affected person' in TJ discussions would reflect the ambiguous and complex reality on the ground. Ultimately, as Bouris argues, a complex victimisation discourse, which 'supplements' simplistic discourses, is required; this will allow for effective recognition of victims as well as more diverse sets of peacebuilding strategies that will increase the chance of achieving long-term peace (2007, 51). This suggestion does not require simplistic discourses to be abandoned but rather being cognisant of the ways labels such as 'victim' and 'perpetrator' can enable and constrain practices that seek to deal with the legacy of the conflict.

Accordingly, I argue that victim-centred context-specific approaches to TJ require TJ experts, implementers and brokers to be willing to conceive of TJ as a process beyond implementing institutions, which are frequently unknown to, or misunderstood by, victims. Also required is consideration of how the role of TJ experts impacts local actors; this consideration includes the time and space provided for these local actors to be the architects of TJ: to imagine, create and adopt TJ mechanisms which are not currently part of the TJ toolkit.

The key is not to impose a pre-determined set of notions and institutions, but rather, through a deep engagement with the affected communities, to let people articulate their needs regarding post-conflict processes. I recognise the dangers of romanticising the local, but it is in such spaces that community-relevant initiatives can be identified. These local initiatives can operate within communities or be scaled up to have a wider impact (see Hayman 2014). Consider, for example, the local initiatives for social reconstruction in Guatemala (the 'houses of memory') that were founded upon community participation; the people who recorded participants' testimonies were trusted and ultimately they were able to document more in their localities than the two national truth commissions (Arriaza and Roht-Arriaza 2010, 212–213; Shaw and Waldorf 2010, 12–13). Reorienting TJ funding to concentrate on locally designed projects such as these could be a better, or complementary method of, distribution of funds earmarked for TJ.

Further, victims seek everyday needs and support for long-term survival but so too do rural, poor Nepalis who were not directly impacted by the conflict. This brings into question the extent to which broader TJ debates engage with issues of marginalisation, social exclusion, development and the shortcomings of the Nepali state. This is another area which requires further research.

I also contend that there is the need for a greater appreciation of the multiple, overlapping and at times competing post-conflict priorities. These priorities can change what TJ implementers and brokers do and how they do it. Finding a way to address the consequences of conflict is not a simple or neat affair. Again, compromises will have to be made about what TJ looks like on the ground, a position that sits in tension with toolkit approaches to post-conflict interventions. Rather than compartmentalising TJ, the challenge is to recognise that it occurs in tandem with other key processes (development, governance and security reform) and TJ can both enable and impede these processes. As Millar asserts:

> The local experience of the performance of truth-telling cannot be excised from the local experience of the supply of aid, the administration of justice, the provision of reparations or the ongoing implementation of development plans, no more than it can be separated from local issues of taxation, corruption or service provision. The ongoing reality is experienced as a whole, not in separate pieces.
>
> (2010, 495)

Sequencing post-conflict priorities, including acknowledging that sooner is perhaps not better, is vital.

Spirituality, religion and language

This book highlights people's religious understandings potentially impacted a range of issues related to victimisation. This included people's attitudes about why harm occurred, who/what was responsible, punishment and peace. This should come as little surprise given that religion has played and continues to play a major role in Nepal, however, given the top-down approach in which the TJ process was shaped in Nepal (Chapter 6), it does not seem likely that these factors were considered.

I reveal that various TJ brokers and implementers stated their concerns that the Christian approach from South Africa was not relevant to the Hindu and Buddhist context of Nepal (Chapter 7). With this in mind there are dangers when TJ experts, brokers and implementers work with assumptions that are rooted in secularity and Christian ideals. It is vital to ensure TJ experts, brokers and implementers pay greater attention to victims' beliefs and, more generally, identities.

I contend that consideration of the role of religion in peacebuilding opens up different possibilities to the dominant TJ approach in Nepal and other post-conflict contexts. In the case of Nepal, Buddhism and Hinduism can contribute to how victims define, experience and express revenge, anger and forgiveness; they can also shape understandings of justice, reconciliation and peace (see Gandhi 2004; Hertog 2010; Omer 2012; Coward and Smith 2004). Exploring these issues and ascertaining the ways that religious actors and faith-based organisations might be able to contribute to TJ require patience and long-term commitment; this elongated time frame is contrary to the typical pressures to enact TJ mechanisms as soon as possible in the wake of conflict. This acknowledgement of the religious context is vital given that 'studies in religious peacebuilding and conflict assessment have shown that an emphasis on understanding the conflict context dramatically enhances the prospects of peacebuilding interventions being effective and sustainable' (Owen 2014, 57). Harnessing the efforts of individuals, international and national faith-based organisations and peacebuilding organisations in Nepal could be one entry point (see King 2014, 358; see also Omer 2014; Appleby 2014).

This book highlights that another key aspect when implementing TJ is the meaning and choice of words used in TJ discussions. Issues of justice and peace are influenced by locality, yet under the auspices of TJ it is the understanding and definitions of TJ experts, and at times those of TJ brokers and implementers, that dominate the process. This practice sidelines local cultures and beliefs (see Weinstein 2007, 2; Robins 2012). Further, for many people in Nepal, TJ and its accompanying language is unfamiliar. As discussed in this book, in a country where there are over 100 languages, the choice of language is also significant. Terms such as 'reconciliation' and 'forgiveness' have been confused and at times appropriated to serve political agendas. This relates to the point raised about the implications for translating 'disqualified' into Nepali during the Disarmament, Demobilisation and Reintegration process. Problems of translation are exacerbated by the fact that many TJ terms already lack conceptual clarity. The different understandings of various concepts reveal the layers of complexity with which TJ must engage; although it should be stressed that such complexities are also points of opportunity to engage with the local. All of this reminds us of the importance of recognising what external actors do not know and ensuring local ownership from the beginning of the TJ process.

I suggest that an area of opportunity is to ensure Nepali terminologies such as justice (*nyaya*), disappeared/missing (*bepatta*), rights (*adhikar*), transition/transformation/change (*paribartan*) (see Sharrock 2013) are incorporated into conversations and research about TJ.[4] Also important is asking questions about locally recognised cultural and religious concepts related to terms such as injustice (*anyai*), conflict (*dwanda*), victim (*pīḍita*), fighter (*yoddha*), enemy (*satru*), anger (*ris*), revenge (*badala*), peace (*shanti*), forgiveness (*kṣamā*), heart (*mutu*), loss (*noksaana*), soul (*aatmaa*), spirit (*preta*), right and wrong (*dharma*) or the notion of bitterness in one's heart (*pida ma hunu* or *pidit*), sin (*pap*), the good or spiritually beneficial (*sreyas*), forbearance (*titiksha*) and non-violence (*ahimsa*) (see Weinstein 2011, 4; Winterbotham 2012, 12). Being attentive to local interpretations of these terms will broaden TJ terminology and enable TJ to address issues that pertain to the locality.[5] Similar measures could be adopted in other post-conflict contexts.

To finish, in this book I contend TJ will benefit from an increased focus on the participation of victims combined with an understanding of the political nature of TJ. This reappraisal of TJ is challenging, but it may be facilitated by a shift in thinking about the timing of TJ. An integrative TJ program infused with a broader notion of justice is paramount. Fundamental to this conceptualisation is a more open approach to what constitutes justice itself and a preparedness to accept that it may not contain pronouncements of forgiveness, reconciliation and healing, and indeed may be driven by the material concerns and basic needs of victims. TJ actors need to be able to recognise and support such notions of justice.

Ultimately, TJ needs to look beyond its existing normative assumptions and have a greater appreciation of victims' everyday realities. To use the words of Veena Das, 'a descent into the ordinary' (2007, 7) is required to illuminate localised conceptions of TJ. We need to appreciate that everyday life is a space of radical social change (and not passivity) and 'pay closer attention to what the everyday renders visible and audible' (Antoniades 2008, 424; Riaño-Alcalá and Baines 2012, 389). Macro-level perspectives and policies should be informed by the micro, including, for example, the 'local environmental knowledge' of a poor female villager which contributes to her household's survival (see Jeong 1995, 345). The multitude of voices at the local level may complicate current TJ approaches, but if they are heeded they will provide greater potential for addressing victims' problems and everyday needs and this will ensure that TJ is closer to becoming more victim-centric and context-specific.

Notes

1 As discussed in Chapter 1, to date there have been two major academic comparative studies by Simon Robins and Tazreena Sajjad, which focus on certain aspects of TJ in Nepal.
2 Until recently, research on TJ in this region has been limited (see Jeffery and Kim 2013, 2–3). A recent collection of essays, *Transitional Justice in the Asia-Pacific*, provides a representative sample of cases in the Asia-Pacific region (Jeffery and Kim 2013, 26–27). These cases were Sri Lanka, Indonesia, Cambodia, East Timor, Solomon Islands and South Korea. While this publication provided an in-depth account of TJ in the region it does not include Nepal.
3 These were: the definitions and understandings of justice; politics versus justice; the timing of TJ interventions; the role of external and local actors; and, the victim/perpetrator binary.
4 I thank an anonymous journal reviewer for suggesting a few of these terminologies.
5 As discussed in Chapter 1, while there is little specific anthropological literature on TJ in Nepal, there is a wide range of anthropological and other literature that addresses issues such as conflict, everyday politics and marginalisation in Nepal and in South Asia more generally. I thank an anonymous journal reviewer for emphasising this point.

References

Antoniades, Andreas. 2008. 'Cave! Hic everyday life: Repetition, hegemony and the social.' *British Journal of Politics and International Relations* 10(3):412–428.

Appleby, R. Scott. 2014. 'The new name for peace? Religion and development as partners in strategic peacebuilding.' In *The Oxford handbook of religion, conflict, and peacebuilding*, edited by Atalia Omer, R. Scott Appleby and David Little, 183–211. New York: Oxford University Press.

Arriaza, Laura J., and Naomi Roht-Arriaza. 2010. 'Weaving a braid of histories: Local post-armed conflict initiatives in Guatemala.' In *Localizing Transitional justice interventions and priorities after mass violence*, edited by Rosalind Shaw, Lars Waldorf and Pierre Hazan, 205–227. Stanford, CA: Stanford University Press.

Bouris, Erica. 2007. *Complex political victims.* Herndon: Kumarian Press.

Coward, Harold, and Gordon Smith, eds. 2004. *Religion and peacebuilding*. Albany, NY: State University of New York Press.

Das, Veena. 2007. *Life and words: Violence and the descent into the ordinary.* Berkeley: University of California Press.

de Greiff, Pablo. 2013. 'Report of the Special Rapporteur on the promotion of truth, justice, reparation and guarantees of non-recurrence.' http://repository.un.org/bitstream/handle/11176/305523/A_HRC_24_42-EN.pdf?sequence=2&isAllowed=yA/HRC/24/42.

Gandhi, Rajmohan. 2004. 'Hinduism and peacebuilding.' In *Religion and peacebuilding*, edited by Harold Coward and Gordon Smith, 45–68. New York: State University of New York Press.

Hayman, Carolyn. 2014. 'Ten lessons from our ten years.' Last modified 2 November 2014. www.peacedirect.org/uk/ten-lessons-ten-years/?utm_source=Main+List&utm_campaign=a8c8558ddd-PD-AidQuarterly-Nov14&utm_medium=email&utm_term=0_72c3c9e100-a8c8558ddd-236126129.

Hertog, Katrien. 2010. *The complex reality of religious peacebuilding: Conceptual contributions and critical analysis.* Plymouth: Lexington Books.

Jeffery, Renee, and Hun Joon Kim. 2013. 'New horizons: Transitional justice in the Asia-Pacific.' In *Transitional justice in the Asia-Pacific*, edited by Renee Jeffery and Hun Joon Kim, 1–31. New York: Cambridge University Press.

Jeong, Ho-Won. 1995. 'Alternative development strategies and regeneration of social space for human development.' *Peace & Change* 20(3):329–347.

King, Anna. 2014. 'Peacebuilding and post-conflict theory recovery in Nepal: A Buddhist case study.' Buddhist perspective towards achieving the UN Millennium Development Goals, Ninh Binh Province, Vietnam, 7–11 May.

Lundy, Patricia, and Mark McGovern. 2008. 'The Role of community in participatory transitional justice.' In *Transitional justice from below: Ggrassroots activism and the struggle for change*, edited by Kieran McEvoy and Lorna McGregor, 99–120. Oxford: Hart Publisher.

McEvoy, Kieran. 2007. 'Beyond legalism: Towards a thicker understanding of transitional justice.' *Journal of Law and Society* 34(4):411–440.

McLeer, Anne. 1998. 'Saving the victim: Recuperating the language of the victim and reassessing global feminism.' *Hypatia* 13(1):41–55.

Menocal, Alina Rocha. 2014. *Getting real about politics: From thinking politically to working differently.* www.odi.org/sites/odi.org.uk/files/odi-assets/publications-opinion-files/8887.pdf.

Merry, Sally Engle. 2006. 'Anthropology and international law.' *Annual Review of Anthropology* 35:99–116.

Millar, Gearoid. 2010. 'Assessing local experiences of truth-telling in Sierra Leone: Getting to 'why' through a qualitative case study analysis.' *International Journal of Transitional Justice* 4:477–496.

Omer, Atalia. 2012. 'Religious peacebuilding: The exotic, the good, and the theatrical.' *Practical Matters* 5:1–31.

Omer, Atalia. 2014. 'Religious peacebuilding: The exotic, the good, and the theatrical.' In *The Oxford handbook of religion, conflict, and peacebuilding*, edited by Atalia Omer, R. Scott Appleby and David Little, 3–32. New York: Oxford University Press.

Owen, Mark. 2014. 'Devising a methodological framework for analysing the potential of buddhist peacebuilding.' Buddhist perspective towards achieving the UN Millennium Development Goals, Ninh Binh Province, Vietnam, 7–11 May.

Riaño-Alcalá, Pilar, and Erin K. Baines. 2012. 'Editorial note: Special issue on transitional justice and the everyday.' *International Journal of Transitional Justice* 6 (3):385–393.

Robins, Simon. 2012. 'Transitional justice as an elite discourse: Human rights practice where the global meets the local in post-conflict Nepal.' *Critical Asian Studies* 44 (1):3–30.

Sanford, Victoria, and Martha Lincoln. 2010. 'Body of evidence: Feminicide, local justice, and rule of law in 'peacetime' in Guatemala.' In *Transitional justice: global mechanisms and local realities after genocide and mass violence*, edited by Alexander Laban Hinton, 67–91. New Brunswick, NJ: Rutgers University Press.

Selim, Yvette. 2012. 'Transitions: creating space to address injustice after conflict or political turmoil.' *openDemocracy*, Last modified 12 February 2012. www.opendemocracy.net/opensecurity/yvette-selim/transitions-creating-space-to-address-injustice-after-conflict-or-politica.

Selim, Yvette. 2014. 'The opportunities and challenges of participation in transitional justice: Examples from Nepal.' *Journal of International Development* 29(8):1123–1148.

Selim, Yvette, and Tim Murithi. 2011. 'Transitional justice and development: Partners for sustainable peace in Africa?' *Journal of Peacebuilding and Development* 6(2):58–72.

Sharrock, James. 2013. 'Stability in transition: Development perspectives and local politics in Nepal.' *European Bulletin of Himalayan Research* 42:9–38.

Shaw, Rosalind, and Lars Waldorf. 2010. 'Introduction: Localizing transitional justice.' In *Localizing transitional justice interventions and priorities after mass violence*, edited by Rosalind Shaw, Lars Waldorf and Pierre Hazan, 3–26. Stanford, CA: Stanford University Press.

Tyynela, John. 2014. *Can truth commissions strengthen peace processes?* ICTJ. www.ictj.org/sites/default/files/ICTJ-Report-KAF-TruthCommPeace-2014.pdf.

van Zyl, Paul. 2005. 'Promoting transitional justice in post-conflict societies.' In *Shaping a security governance agenda in post-conflict peacebuilding*, edited by Alan Bryden, Timothy Donais and Heiner Hänggi, 224–225. Geneva: Geneva Centre for the Democratic Control of Armed Forces.

Weinstein, Harvey M. 2007. 'Editorial note.' *International Journal of Transitional Justice* 1(1):1–5.

Weinstein, Harvey M. 2011. 'Editorial note: The myth of closure, the illusion of reconciliation: Final thoughts on five years as co-Editor-in-Chief.' *International Journal of Transitional Justice* 5:1–10.

White, Sarah. 1996. 'Depoliticising the development: The uses and abuses of participation.' *Development in Practice* 6(1):6–15.

Winterbotham, Emily. 2012. 'Healing the legacies of conflict in Afghanistan: Community voices on justice, peace and reconciliation.' Afghanistan Research and Evaluation Unit Synthesis Paper. https://areu.org.af/wp-content/uploads/2016/02/1201E-Healing-the-Legacies-of-Conflict-in-Afghanistan-SP-2011.pdf.

Index

Page numbers in **bold** refer to tables; page numbers in *italics* refer to figures; 'n' after a page number indicates the endnote number.

For Product Safety Concerns and Information please contact our EU representative GPSR@taylorandfrancis.com
Taylor & Francis Verlag GmbH, Kaufingerstraße 24, 80331 München, Germany

www.ingramcontent.com/pod-product-compliance
Ingram Content Group UK Ltd.
Pitfield, Milton Keynes, MK11 3LW, UK
UKHW022132190926
475702UK00013B/1775
9780367589370